AWS Cloud Projects

Strengthen your AWS skills through practical projects, from websites to advanced AI applications

Ivo Pinto

Pedro Santos

AWS Cloud Projects

Copyright © 2024 Packt Publishing

All rights reserved. No part of this book may be reproduced, stored in a retrieval system, or transmitted in form or by any means, without the prior written permission of the publisher, except in the case of brief quotations embedded in critical articles or reviews.

Every effort has been made in the preparation of this book to ensure the accuracy of the information presented. However, the information contained in this book is sold without warranty, either express or implied. Neither the authors, nor Packt Publishing or its dealers and distributors, will be held liable for any damages caused or alleged to have been caused directly or indirectly by this book.

Packt Publishing has endeavored to provide trademark information about all of the companies and products mentioned in this book by the appropriate use of capitals. However, Packt Publishing cannot guarantee the accuracy of this information.

Group Product Manager: Preet Ahuja

Publishing Product Manager: Prachi Rana

Book Project Manager: Ashwini Gowda

Senior Editor: Sayali Pingale

Technical Editor: Rajat Sharma

Copy Editor: Safis Editing

Indexer: Manju Arasan

Production Designer: Vijay Kamble

DevRel Marketing Coordinator: Rohan Dobhal

First published: October 2024

Production reference: 1130924

Published by Packt Publishing Ltd.
Grosvenor House
11 St Paul's Square
Birmingham
B3 1RB, UK

ISBN 978-1-83588-928-2

www.packtpub.com

To my amazing wife, Celia, your love and support mean the world to me. Thanks for always believing in me and for putting up with my late-night writing sessions. And to our two adorable furballs, Oscar and Tofu, your purrs and playful antics made the writing process so much more fun. Thanks for keeping me company on yet another writing journey.

– Ivo Pinto

This book is dedicated to my wife, Juliana, for her continuous support and motivation that have been a driving force behind this work, and for being a source of strength. To my mother, whose life was an example of perseverance, resilience, and determination, and for all the invaluable lessons of never giving up and always pushing forward, even in the face of adversity. And lastly, to my mentor, with whom I'm lucky enough to have had the opportunity to co-author this book.

– Pedro Santos

Contributors

About the authors

Ivo Pinto, CCIE No. 57162 (R&S, Security, and Data Center), CISSP, is a principal solutions architect with many years of experience in the fields of cloud, automation, and enterprise and data center networking. Ivo has worked at Cisco in different roles and different geographies, and he has led the architecture and deployment of many automated global-scale solutions for Fortune 500 companies that are in production today. In his latest role, he is responsible for the architecture of multiple ISV products at **Amazon Web Services** (**AWS**). Ivo has authored two books, *Network Automation Made Easy* and *Automating and Orchestrating Networking with NetDevOps*.

Pedro Santos is a senior solutions architect with over a decade of experience in the technology industry. With a background in data engineering and cloud computing, he focuses on designing and implementing innovative cloud-based solutions. After experiencing different cloud providers and companies of different sizes, Pedro is now working for AWS where he helps SaaS providers design and improve their products.

About the reviewers

Manuel Pata, at the time of this writing, is a senior technical account manager for AWS based in Portugal. In this role, he helps large ISV customers get the most out of AWS, and he loves doing that. You'll also find him regularly working with Edge services, such as Amazon CloudFront, AWS Global Accelerator, or AWS WAF. He loves a good technical challenge and will happily spend his time prototyping solutions for his customers.

Kuldeep Singh is a seasoned project manager with over 16 years of experience in ICTS, specializing in infrastructure projects, tech upgrades, and service enhancements. He has delivered secure cloud BI platforms for banks and led data center migrations. Kuldeep has collaborated with major telecom providers globally. As a tech reviewer for Packt, he has enriched readers with insights in *Cloud Native Software Security Handbook* and *Architecting Serverless Solutions*. Currently at Birlasoft, he focuses on cloud platforms, cybersecurity, and IT governance. Kuldeep holds AWS and Azure architect certifications, is PMP certified, and is a valuable PMI member.

I extend my heartfelt thanks to my son, Aadvik, and my wife, Ankita—my sunshine on cloudy days—for their unwavering support during the creation of this book. Their patience and encouragement have been invaluable. I also wish to thank my colleagues at Birlasoft for their insights and collaboration, which have greatly contributed to this work.

Roman Ceresnak is an accomplished AWS architect and AWS Community Builder with deep expertise in cloud technologies, holding over 30 AWS certifications. With an HPD title, Roman brings a wealth of knowledge and hands-on experience in designing and implementing scalable, secure, and efficient cloud solutions. Throughout his career, he has worked extensively with a variety of advanced technologies, including AWS Glue, Apache Airflow, Grafana, Prometheus, IAM, and Kubernetes, among many others.

As an AWS Community Builder, Roman actively contributes to the AWS ecosystem, sharing his knowledge and expertise with a broader audience. He is committed to fostering a collaborative environment where professionals can learn and grow together.

I am deeply grateful to the vibrant AWS community and open source contributors who generously share their knowledge and expertise. Their collective efforts have been instrumental in shaping my journey. I owe special thanks to the AWS Community Builders program for fostering a culture of collaboration and learning.

Table of Contents

Preface   xiii

Part 1: Beginner Level Projects

1

Deploying and Interacting with AWS Services   3

Technical requirements	3	Navigating AWS CLI and AWS SDK	13
Architecting on AWS	4	AWS CLI	13
Requirements gathering	4	AWS SDK	17
Choosing an architecture pattern	5	Understanding IaC	17
Selecting a service	6	Using CloudFormation	19
Diagramming	7	Using Terraform	20
Exploring the Well-Architected Framework	9	Summary	22
Getting started with AWS Console	9		
Using the Console	9		

2

Creating a Personal Website   23

Technical requirements	23	Amazon CloudWatch metrics	29
Scenario	24	Coding the solution	29
Requirements	24	Editing the website	30
Architecture patterns	25	Publishing the website	33
Architecture	25	Monitoring the website	36
AWS services	26	Cleaning up	37
Amazon Simple Storage Service (S3)	27	Future work	38

Implementing custom DNS	38	Final architecture	42
Taking security to the next level	39	**Summary**	**43**
Having better observability	41		

Part 2: Intermediate Level Projects

3

Building a Recipe-Sharing Application 47

Technical requirements	**48**	Section 2 – Solution deployment	65
Scenario	**48**	Section 3 – Additional configurations (option 1 only)	69
Requirements	48	Section 4 – Frontend configuration and deployment	70
Architecture patterns	53		
Architecture	54	Section 5 – Testing and exploring your application	73
AWS services	**56**	Section 6 – Cleaning up	77
Amazon S3	56		
Amazon CloudFront	56	**Future work**	**80**
Amazon Virtual Private Cloud (VPC)	56	Using secure protocols	80
Amazon EC2	57	Infrastructure auto-scaling	80
Application Load Balancer (ALB)	57	Managed hosting and CI/CD	81
Amazon DynamoDB	57	Authentication	81
AWS CloudFormation	58	Logging and monitoring	81
Coding the solution	**58**	Caching	82
Cloning the project	59	**Summary**	**84**
Section 1 – DNS configuration and certificate issuing (option 1 only)	60		

4

Building a Serverless Recipe-Sharing Application 85

Technical requirements	**86**	**AWS services**	**93**
Scenario	**86**	Amazon Simple Storage Service (S3)	93
Requirements	87	Amazon CloudFront	93
Architecture patterns	90	Amazon DynamoDB	93
Architecture	91	AWS CloudFormation	93
		Amazon Cognito	93

Amazon Lambda	94	Test and explore your application	104
API Gateway	94	Clean up	113
Coding the solution	**94**	**Future work**	**115**
Cloning the project	95	Enrich your application with media content	115
Solution deployment	95	User profile	115
Frontend configuration and deployment	99	**Summary**	**117**

5

Implementing an Image Analyzer to Detect Photo Friendliness — 119

Technical requirements	**119**	Understanding the image analyzer code	131
Scenario	**120**	Testing your application	132
Requirements	120	Cleaning up	134
Architecture patterns	121	**Future work**	**135**
Architecture	**121**	Implementing authentication and authorization	135
AWS services	**123**	Improving your security posture	135
Amazon Rekognition	123	Implementing custom names	135
Amazon API Gateway and AWS Lambda	126	Improving the image analysis algorithm	136
Coding the solution	**127**	Hosting your own ML model	136
Building the infrastructure	127	**Summary**	**137**

6

Architecting a Content Translation Pipeline — 139

Technical requirements	**139**	Amazon Translate	144
Scenario	**140**	AWS CodePipeline and AWS CodeBuild	145
Requirements	140	**Coding the solution**	**146**
Architecture patterns	141	Building the web application	146
Architecture	**141**	Building the CI/CD pipeline	150
AWS services	**143**	Testing the solution	155
Lambda@Edge	144	Cleaning up	156
		Future work	**157**

Implementing custom names	157	Adopting CI/CD for infrastructure code	157
Expanding your application functionality	157	**Summary**	**158**

Part 3: Advanced Level Projects

7

Implementing a Chatbot Using Machine Learning — 161

Technical requirements	**162**	Cloning the project	170
Scenario	**162**	Solution deployment	170
Requirements	162	Frontend configuration and deployment	174
Architecture patterns	166	Amazon Lex configuration and build	177
Architecture	166	Test and explore your application	179
AWS services	**168**	Clean up	187
Amazon CloudFront and Amazon Simple Storage Service (S3)	168	**Future work**	**188**
Amazon DynamoDB	168	Extend the actions performed by your chatbot	189
Amazon Cognito, Amazon API Gateway, and Amazon Lambda	168	Multilingual support	189
Amazon Lex	168	Maintain user profiles for different sessions	190
Coding the solution	**169**	**Summary**	**190**

8

Building a Business Intelligence Application — 191

Technical requirements	**191**	Amazon QuickSight	197
Scenario	**192**	**Coding the solution**	**197**
Requirements	192	Section 1 – Cloning the project	197
Architecture patterns	193	Section 2 – Solution deployment	198
Architecture	193	Section 3 – Clickstream event generator	201
AWS services	**195**	Section 4 – The Glue ETL job	204
Amazon Simple Storage Service (S3)	195	Section 5 – Data exploration with Athena	205
AWS Glue	196	Section 6 – Data visualization with QuickSight	208
Amazon Athena	196	Section 7 – Clean up	216

Future work	217	Data life cycle management	218
Automate the ETL pipeline	217	Summary	218

9

Exploring Future Work — 219

Technical requirements	219	Pricing the solution from Chapter 6	230
AWS services overview	219	AWS re:Post	232
Containers	220	AWS documentation, Solutions	
Other API types	222	Library and Prescriptive Guidance	232
Generative AI	223	AWS documentation	233
Other communication patterns	225	AWS Solutions Library	233
AWS Pricing Calculator	228	AWS Prescriptive Guidance	234
Pricing the solution from Chapter 2	228	Summary	235

Index — 237

Other Books You May Enjoy — 246

Preface

In the ever-evolving landscape of cloud computing, **Amazon Web Services** (**AWS**) stands as the leader, offering a collection of services that empower businesses and developers. But for you, AWS can be more than a technology platform; it can be a gateway to a thriving job market. So, whether you are an aspiring cloud engineer, a seasoned developer, or an IT professional, if you want to level up your skills on AWS, this book is for you.

This book's approach is project-focused, with each chapter guiding you through the implementation of real-world scenarios using AWS services. From setting up basic infrastructure to host a website to leveraging advanced features such as serverless computing and machine learning to power a chatbot, the projects in this book are tailored to equip you with the skills required to tackle the challenges you will face in the field. But there's more – you will also learn about alternative services and architectures that you can use to accomplish the same business objectives because, in the end, it's all about weighing up the pros and cons.

By the end of this book, you will feel confident in your hands-on AWS capabilities and be able to build your own cloud projects. You will be an eye-catching AWS expert.

Who this book is for

This book was written for students who want to start their career in cloud computing and professionals who have experience in other technical areas such as software development but want to embrace a new professional path or complement their technical skills in cloud computing. If you are either, this book is for you.

Being a practical book, a background in computer science or engineering and basic programming skills are recommended but not mandatory. All the projects come with theoretical explanations of the services used and do not assume any previous AWS knowledge.

What this book covers

Chapter 1, Deploying and Interacting with AWS Services, explains how using the AWS console is a good starting point, but there are more advanced options that will help you manage your resources in a scalable way. In this chapter, you will learn the different ways to create and manage AWS resources. You will also learn about the AWS CLI and SDKs and get familiar with Infrastructure as Code.

Chapter 2, *Creating a Personal Website*, as the first practical chapter, introduces what you are going to build: a personal website to use as your CV. This is followed by an architectural diagram of the solution, accompanied by step-by-step instructions on how to build it on your own AWS account. This chapter ends with suggestions to improve the application you have built.

Chapter 3, *Building a Recipe-Sharing Application*, covers how to build a recipe-sharing application. You will learn about how dynamic applications are built, and how to interact with databases. It's structured in the same way as the previous chapter, starting with a description of the new functionality followed by the technical architecture, and step-by-step instructions on how to build and test it.

Chapter 4, *Building a Serverless Recipe-Sharing Application*, rebuilds the recipe-sharing application, but with a twist. Much like in the previous chapter, this is a dynamic web application. However, this time, you are going to only use serverless services. Because of the confidentiality nature of the project, you are also going to add an authentication mechanism.

Chapter 5, *Implementing an Image Analyzer to Detect Photo Friendliness*, covers how, before choosing your CV photo, you ask for feedback from your peers to see how friendly it looks, so what if you could do it automatically? Let's say that every time you upload a new photo, your application automatically rates it in terms of friendliness and suggests whether it is a good fit for a professional CV. In this chapter, you will build this functionality using AWS-native AI services.

Chapter 6, *Architecting a Content Translation Pipeline*, covers accessibility. Have you accessed a website that automatically translated itself into your language? Accessibility is important to reach wider audiences. In this chapter, you will learn how to automatically have your content translated to multiple languages using a CI/CD pipeline and then dynamically served using your users' browser preferences.

Chapter 7, *Implementing a Chatbot Using Machine Learning*, explores the use of chatbots. Everyone has heard of ChatGPT. In this chapter, you will build a virtual assistant that answers queries related to web development. This virtual assistant is powered by the newest machine learning advancements: large language models.

Chapter 8, *Building a Business Intelligence Application*, explains how, more than building web applications, you can also build business intelligence solutions to analyze data and identify trends. In this chapter, you will use AWS-native services to analyze clickstream data. Clickstream data is collected when users access websites and applications. Understanding it allows application owners to better tailor their content to their audience. At the end of this chapter, you will be ready to query, transform, and visualize several formats with ease.

Chapter 9, *Exploring Future Work*, explains how, in AWS, there are more than 200 services that you can use to power your applications. Unlike the previous chapters, which had step-by-step instructions to build applications, this chapter has an overview of what AWS has to offer and strategies to accelerate and support your project ideas. This chapter is not a practical one, it is inspirational; use it to brainstorm your next big project.

To get the most out of this book

You will need an AWS account to follow along. If you don't yet have an AWS account, you can create one following these instructions: `https://docs.aws.amazon.com/accounts/latest/reference/manage-acct-creating.html`.

You will also need the following software installed on your local machine.

Software/hardware covered in the book	Operating system requirements
AWS CLI version 2	Windows, macOS, or Linux
Terraform 1.9.1	
Node.js v18.12.0	
npm 1.9.1	

Although the examples were tested in these versions, they should work in any newer version, too.

If you are using the digital version of this book, we advise you to type the code yourself or access the code from the book's GitHub repository (a link is available in each section). Doing so will help you avoid any potential errors related to the copying and pasting of code.

Download the example code files

You can download the example code files for this book from GitHub at `https://github.com/PacktPublishing/AWS-Cloud-Projects`. If there's an update to the code, it will be updated in the GitHub repository.

We also have other code bundles from our rich catalog of books and videos available at `https://github.com/PacktPublishing/`. Check them out!

Conventions used

There are a number of text conventions used throughout this book.

`Code in text`: Indicates code words in text, database table names, folder names, filenames, file extensions, pathnames, dummy URLs, user input, and Twitter handles. Here is an example: "If you are using React with i18n, you will need to create `translation.json` files"

A block of code is set as follows:

```
def lambda_handler(event, context):
...
response = bot.recognize_text(
botId = '${MeetyBot}',
botAliasId='TSTALIASID',
localeId='en_US',
sessionId='your_session_id',
text = user_input
)
...
```

Any command-line input or output is written as follows:

```
$ npm install && npm run build
```

Bold: Indicates a new term, an important word, or words that you see onscreen. For instance, words in menus or dialog boxes appear in **bold**. Here is an example: "In the **Prerequisite – Prepare Template** section, select **Choose an existing template**."

> Tips or important notes
> Appear like this.

Get in touch

Feedback from our readers is always welcome.

General feedback: If you have questions about any aspect of this book, email us at customercare@packtpub.com and mention the book title in the subject of your message.

Errata: Although we have taken every care to ensure the accuracy of our content, mistakes do happen. If you have found a mistake in this book, we would be grateful if you would report this to us. Please visit www.packtpub.com/support/errata and fill in the form.

Piracy: If you come across any illegal copies of our works in any form on the internet, we would be grateful if you would provide us with the location address or website name. Please contact us at copyright@packt.com with a link to the material.

If you are interested in becoming an author: If there is a topic that you have expertise in and you are interested in either writing or contributing to a book, please visit authors.packtpub.com.

Share Your Thoughts

Once you've read *AWS Cloud Projects*, we'd love to hear your thoughts! Scan the QR code below to go straight to the Amazon review page for this book and share your feedback.

https://packt.link/r/1835889298

Your review is important to us and the tech community and will help us make sure we're delivering excellent quality content.

Download a free PDF copy of this book

Thanks for purchasing this book!

Do you like to read on the go but are unable to carry your print books everywhere?

Is your eBook purchase not compatible with the device of your choice?

Don't worry, now with every Packt book you get a DRM-free PDF version of that book at no cost.

Read anywhere, any place, on any device. Search, copy, and paste code from your favorite technical books directly into your application.

The perks don't stop there, you can get exclusive access to discounts, newsletters, and great free content in your inbox daily

Follow these simple steps to get the benefits:

1. Scan the QR code or visit the link below

`https://packt.link/free-ebook/9781835889282`

2. Submit your proof of purchase
3. That's it! We'll send your free PDF and other benefits to your email directly

Part 1: Beginner Level Projects

In *Part 1* of this book, you are going to learn how to interact with AWS services using the AWS Console, AWS CLI, and Terraform. Then, you will build a simple web application powered by S3 and CloudFront following a step-by-step approach. These are beginner-level projects, but they will get you started on the path to autonomously building your own web applications.

This part has the following chapters:

- *Chapter 1, Deploying and Interacting with AWS Services*
- *Chapter 2, Creating a Personal Website*

1
Deploying and Interacting with AWS Services

Embarking on the journey to build solutions on the **Amazon Web Services** (**AWS**) platform requires a comprehensive understanding of the available tools and approaches. This chapter introduces various methodologies for architecting on AWS, beginning with preparatory activities such as requirements gathering, service selection, and diagramming.

You will then explore the various methods and tools available for deploying and interacting with AWS services, including the AWS Console, AWS **Command Line Interface** (**CLI**), AWS **Software Development Kits** (**SDKs**), and **Infrastructure as Code** (**IaC**).

This is a theoretical chapter, structured around the following main topics:

- Architecting on AWS
- Getting started with AWS Console
- Navigating AWS CLI and SDK
- Understanding IaC

By the end of this chapter, you will possess the knowledge and skills necessary to create, operate, and monitor AWS services using the approach that best aligns with your requirements and preferences, whether it be through the user-friendly AWS Console, the CLI, programmatic access via SDKs, or the powerful IaC tools.

Technical requirements

Although this is a theoretical chapter, you will find code snippets in the GitHub repository of this chapter at https://github.com/PacktPublishing/AWS-Cloud-Projects/tree/main/chapter1/code.

To follow along, you will need an AWS account.

Architecting on AWS

Architecting on AWS refers to the process of designing and planning cloud-based solutions using AWS. It involves understanding the various AWS services, their capabilities, and how they can be combined to build scalable, secure, and cost-effective architectures.

When architecting on AWS, the following four aspects should be considered, each detailed later in this chapter:

- **Requirements gathering**: This is a crucial step in the process of architecting solutions on AWS. It involves understanding the business needs, functional requirements, non-functional requirements, and constraints that will shape the design and implementation of the AWS architecture.
- **Architecture patterns**: AWS provides various architecture patterns and reference architectures that serve as starting points for common use cases, such as web applications, data processing pipelines, or serverless architectures. You can leverage these patterns and customize them to meet their specific requirements.
- **Service selection**: AWS offers a broad range of services, including compute, storage, databases, networking, analytics, machine learning, and more. You must carefully evaluate the requirements of the applications and select the appropriate AWS services that best fit those needs.
- **Diagramming**: Creating visual representations of the proposed architecture is a crucial step in the architecting process. There are no AWS official tools, but **draw.io** or simply Microsoft PowerPoint can be used to create architecture diagrams, which helps communicate the design and facilitate collaboration and implementation.

Let's look at these aspects in detail.

Requirements gathering

Clear and well-defined requirements are crucial for architects to design AWS solutions that meet the specific needs of the organization and provide the desired outcomes. Gathering requirements can involve collaborating with stakeholders, conducting workshops, analyzing existing systems and data, and understanding the business context.

However, if your project has a smaller scope, not all these steps may apply. Nonetheless, it is important to understand what type of requirements can be gathered before a project starts:

- **Business requirements**: The first step is to understand the business objectives, goals, and drivers behind the solution being architected. This includes factors such as the target market, expected growth, revenue models, and any specific business constraints or regulations that need to be considered.

- **Functional requirements**: These requirements define the specific features, functionalities, and capabilities that the solution must provide. This could include requirements related to user interfaces, data processing, integration with existing systems, or specific business logic.
- **Non-functional requirements**: Non-functional requirements define the qualitative attributes that the solution must possess, such as performance, scalability, availability, security, and compliance. These requirements are often critical in determining the appropriate AWS services and architectural patterns to be used.
- **Technical requirements**: Technical requirements encompass the specific technologies, programming languages, frameworks, and tools that need to be used or integrated with the AWS solution. This could include requirements for specific databases, messaging systems, or third-party services.
- **Data requirements**: Understanding the data requirements is essential when architecting on AWS. This includes the types of data (structured, unstructured, or semi-structured), data volumes, data sources, data processing needs, and any specific data governance or compliance requirements.
- **Integration requirements**: If the AWS solution needs to integrate with existing on-premises systems, third-party services, or other cloud environments, the integration requirements must be clearly defined. This includes identifying the integration points, data formats, protocols, and security considerations.
- **Security and compliance requirements**: Depending on the industry and the nature of the data being handled, there may be specific security and compliance requirements that need to be addressed in the AWS architecture. These could include regulatory standards, data protection laws, or industry-specific certifications.
- **Financial requirements**: AWS offers a pay-as-you-go pricing model. Understanding the budget constraints and cost requirements is essential for selecting the appropriate AWS services and implementing cost-effective architectures.

Bear in mind that some folks consider costs or security requirements part of the umbrella of functional and non-functional requirements. Don't be pedantic about naming; just gather all your requirements.

Choosing an architecture pattern

Architecture patterns and reference architectures serve as starting points for designing and implementing cloud-based solutions. These patterns encapsulate best practices, proven designs, and architectural principles tailored to specific use cases and requirements. You can find many of these in the AWS Architecture Center: `https://aws.amazon.com/architecture`.

By leveraging AWS architecture patterns and reference architectures, you can build upon proven designs, accelerate the development process, and ensure that your solutions align with AWS best practices and industry standards.

Architecture patterns address common scenarios and requirements. These include patterns for web applications, data processing pipelines, serverless architectures, microservices, event-driven architectures, and more. You can leverage these patterns as a foundation and customize them to meet specific needs.

In addition to general patterns, AWS provides reference architectures for specific domains and industries, such as e-commerce, media and entertainment, healthcare, financial services, and more. These reference architectures offer detailed guidance on how to design and implement solutions using AWS services and best practices specific to those domains.

To select a pattern or architecture, you must carefully evaluate the requirements, constraints, and use cases of their solutions to select the most appropriate one. This selection process involves understanding the strengths, weaknesses, and trade-offs of each pattern, as well as their alignment with the rest of the technical stack. This is often detailed in their description.

While architecture patterns provide a solid starting point, they are rarely implemented as-is. You must customize and adapt the patterns to fit your specific requirements, integrating additional AWS services, adjusting configurations, and incorporating security, monitoring, and operational considerations.

It can also happen that what you need is a hybrid or multi-pattern architecture. Some solutions require a combination of multiple architecture patterns or a hybrid approach that combines components of different patterns. There is an extra challenge in determining how to effectively integrate and orchestrate the different patterns into a cohesive and scalable architecture. This is an advanced topic, which you will learn more about in later chapters of this book.

Selecting a service

By now, you have a well-defined problem and a generic architectural pattern. The next step is service selection. This is a critical aspect of architecting solutions in AWS. With over 200 services available, AWS provides a vast array of building blocks that can be combined to create scalable, secure, and cost-effective architectures.

Service selection is an iterative process that involves balancing architectural best practices and all kinds of requirements: non-functional, functional, cost, security, and so on. You must continuously evaluate and refine service selections as the solution evolves and new requirements or constraints emerge.

The first step in service selection is to map the gathered requirements to the available AWS services. This involves understanding the capabilities and use cases of each service and identifying the ones that can address the specific functional, non-functional, and technical requirements of the solution. To make this mapping, you will need to first understand what category of service you should look at. Services are organized into different categories, such as compute, storage, databases, networking, security, analytics, and more. You will see different services in each of these categories in the following chapters of this book.

After you have identified the service category that maps to your requirements, you will need to evaluate the different service capabilities. Each AWS service offers a unique set of capabilities and features. For example, if the solution requires a highly available and scalable database, services such as Amazon RDS or Amazon Aurora might be suitable choices. This will become clearer as you advance through the chapters of this book.

Some interesting non-functional capabilities that you should consider are as follows:

- **Service integrations**: AWS services are designed to work together seamlessly. You should consider the integration points between different services and ensure that the selected services can be integrated effectively to deliver the desired functionality.
- **Managed versus self-managed services**: AWS offers both managed services, where AWS handles the underlying infrastructure and maintenance, and self-managed services, where the customer has more control but also more responsibility. You must evaluate the trade-offs between these service types based on factors such as operational overhead, cost, and compliance requirements.
- **Pricing and cost optimization**: AWS services have different pricing models, and you must consider the cost implications of their service selections. Cost optimization strategies, such as leveraging reserved instances, spot instances, or auto-scaling, should be evaluated and incorporated into the architecture.
- **Roadmap**: AWS services are constantly evolving, with new features and services being released regularly. You should consider the future roadmap of the services they select and ensure that the architecture can accommodate potential changes or new service offerings.

> **Important note**
> Did you know that not every AWS service is available in all regions? That's right. AWS services are not uniformly available across all AWS regions. You must therefore also consider the regional availability of the services you plan to use.

Sometimes, you will not find a suitable AWS service for your requirements and that is okay. This is where third-party services come in. Don't be scared to leverage third-party tooling if it fits your needs. However, consider all the previously mentioned dimensions such as cost or service integrations.

Diagramming

Visual representations of the proposed architecture help communicate the design, facilitate collaboration among team members, and ensure a shared understanding of the solution's components and their interactions. It also provides a map of the implementation.

There is no standard tool to diagram AWS solutions. The most well-accepted tools are PowerPoint using AWS Architecture Icons (`https://aws.amazon.com/architecture/icons/`) or draw.io (`https://app.diagrams.net`). These tools include icons and shapes that represent the different AWS services.

Figure 1.1 shows a high-level diagram, using PowerPoint, of the communication flow between two EC2 instances in different regions.

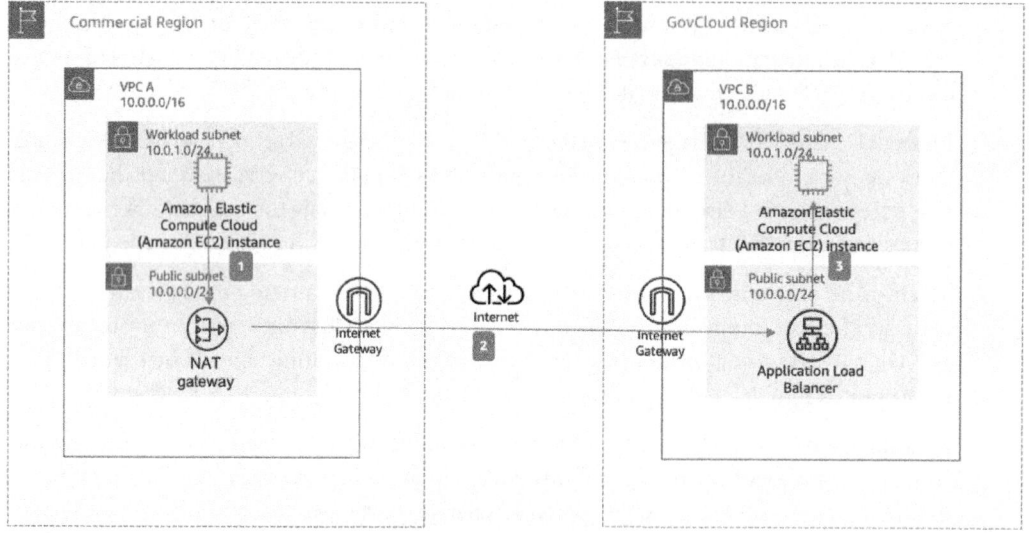

Figure 1.1 – Cross-region EC2 communication flow

Diagrams serve as a universal language for communicating the architecture design to stakeholders, developers, operations teams, and other involved parties. You should not only represent the various AWS services, but also their relationships, as well as the overall flow of data and processes within the solution. You can create several diagrams for the same solution, each with a different level of detail.

> **Important note**
> Diagramming is not over in the design phase. Rather, it is an ongoing process throughout the architecture life cycle. Regularly updating and reviewing diagrams ensures that they accurately reflect the current state of the architecture.

Diagrams are an essential part of the architecture documentation process. They serve as a reference for the design decisions, component interactions, and rationale behind the chosen architecture. However, documentation is not limited to diagrams. Creating thorough documentation is invaluable for future maintenance, troubleshooting, and knowledge transfer within the team or organization. This book will not cover in-depth documentation because it is a practical book focused on hands-on building.

Exploring the Well-Architected Framework

AWS provides a set of best practices and design principles known as the **Well-Architected Framework** (**WAR**), (https://aws.amazon.com/architecture/well-architected/). This framework covers six pillars: operational excellence, security, reliability, performance efficiency, cost optimization, and sustainability.

Cloud architects use this framework to ensure that their solutions align with AWS best practices, usually after they are built, but it can also be used during the design phase. Although the WAR could be a chapter of its own, we just want you to be aware of it for now, and see how we later refer to it while building the projects throughout this book.

Now that we've covered the designing and planning phase, let's delve into the implementation phase. You will explore multiple tools while getting some hands-on experience.

Getting started with AWS Console

The AWS Console is a web-based user interface provided by AWS that allows users to access and manage various AWS services and resources through a **Graphical User Interface** (**GUI**).

The AWS Console is designed to be user-friendly and accessible from any web browser, allowing users to manage their AWS resources from anywhere with an internet connection. It provides a visual representation of AWS services and resources, making it easier for users to understand and interact with the AWS ecosystem.

Using the Console

During this section, you will deploy an EC2 instance, which is an AWS virtual machine.

To use the Console, you must have an AWS account. The creation process of an AWS account is outside the scope of this book, but you can find all the necessary information on the AWS website at https://aws.amazon.com/free.

> **Important note**
> Every example in this book assumes that you have a standalone AWS account that is not part of AWS Organizations.

Let's get started:

1. The first step to access the AWS Console is to navigate to `https://console.aws.amazon.com/`.

    You will be greeted by a login screen like the one shown in *Figure 1.2*.

    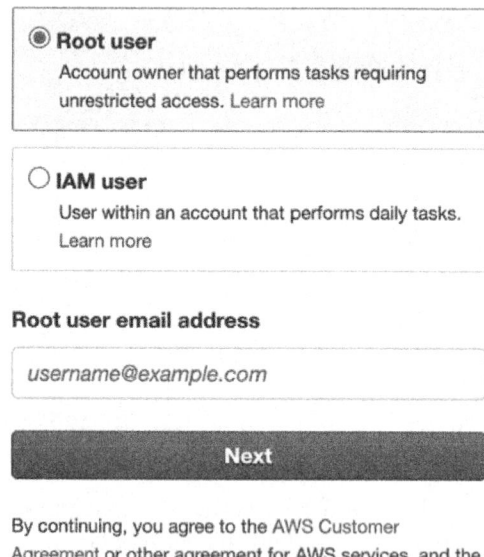

    Figure 1.2 – AWS Console login screen

2. If you are using a root user, insert the email of your user followed by the password. If you are using an IAM user, you will also need to input the 12-digit account ID.

3. Upon successful login, you will see the AWS Console home page, as shown in *Figure 1.3*.

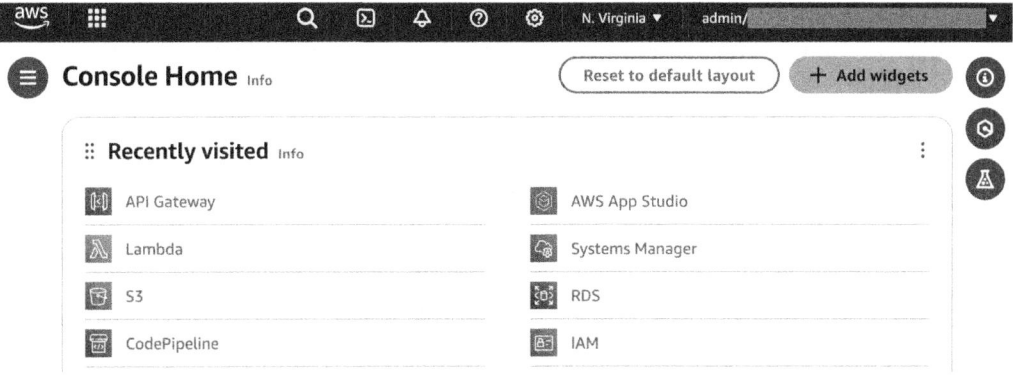

Figure 1.3 – Console Home

Sections worth highlighting for this figure are as follows:

- The **Search** bar at the top, which you can use to search for a specific service.

- The AWS Region you are currently managing shows at the top-right corner; it's **N. Virginia** in this case.

- The user or role you are currently logged in as, which is also in the top-right corner, hidden under the red square.

- The recently visited section, which will be empty if you haven't opened the AWS Console before.

> **Important note**
> Why are the role and account ID hidden under a red square in *Figure 1.3*? Although AWS account IDs, users, and roles are not considered sensitive, it's an AWS best practice not to publicly disclose them.

4. Navigate to the EC2 service console. To do this, enter `ec2` in the search bar and select **EC2**, as shown in *Figure 1.4*.

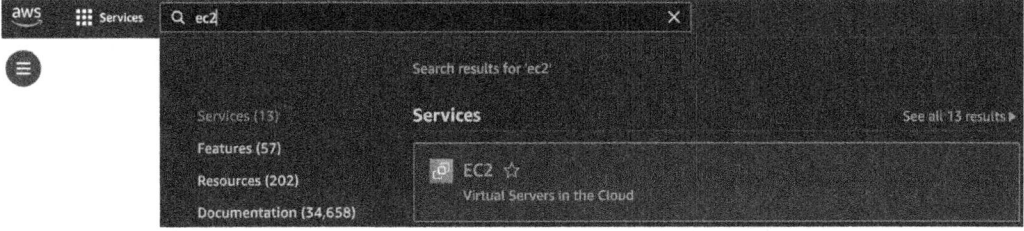

Figure 1.4 – Search for the EC2 service using the AWS Console

5. To launch the simplest possible virtual machine, without any customization, select **Launch instance**, as shown in *Figure 1.5*.

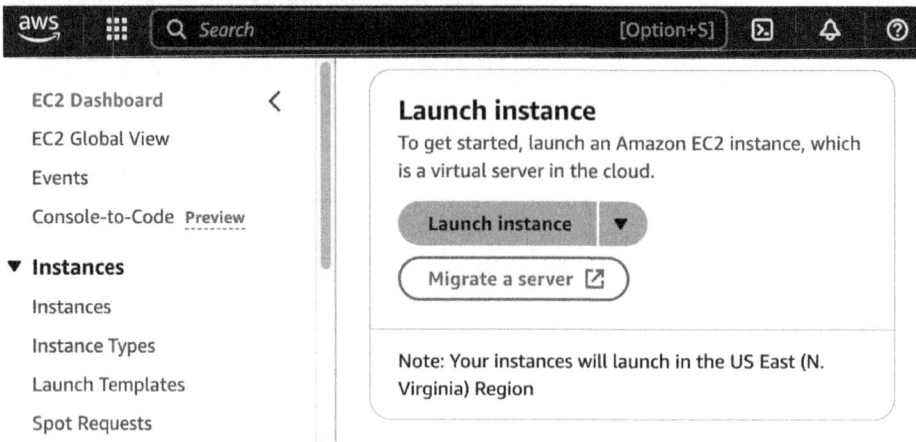

Figure 1.5 – EC2 dashboard

6. In the following menu, **Launch an instance**, select **Proceed without a key pair (Not recommended)**, from the **Key pair name** drop-down menu. Lastly, select **Launch instance** again, this time on the right menu.

7. Navigate to your running instances. You can do this by selecting Instances on the EC2 left menu or by navigating to https://console.aws.amazon.com/ec2/#Instances. You should see something similar to *Figure 1.6*: a running EC2 instance with a funny-looking instance ID and some other attributes.

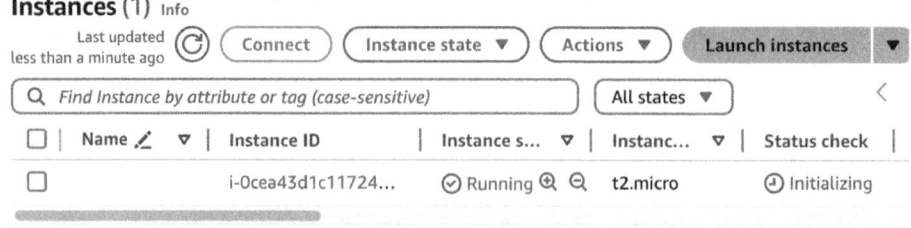

Figure 1.6 – EC2 instance status

This is not a very useful instance because you cannot connect to it. The reason for that is you that did not select a key pair. This was just a simple demo to show you how the AWS Console works.

8. You can terminate the instance by selecting **Terminate (delete) instance**, as shown in *Figure 1.7*.

Figure 1.7 – Terminate EC2 instance using the AWS Console

While the AWS Console is a convenient way to manage and troubleshoot AWS resources, you can probably guess some of its drawbacks. Imagine you had to create one hundred of these EC2 instances, or a thousand. It would take you a very long time, especially if you had to configure specific parameters, such as the ones you skipped during the previous guide.

AWS provides command-line tools and SDKs for programmatic access and automation of AWS services that address these drawbacks.

> Important note
>
> It is not recommended to perform actions in your AWS account using the root credentials. We strongly recommend that you don't use the root user for your everyday tasks and that you follow the root user best practices for your AWS account, which can be found at https://docs.aws.amazon.com/IAM/latest/UserGuide/root-user-best-practices.html.

It's recommended that before you advance into the next section, you navigate through the AWS Console a little more to get accustomed to it.

Navigating AWS CLI and AWS SDK

The AWS CLI and AWS SDK are programmatic tools to access and manage AWS services. In this section, you will dive deeper into each of these, and execute them in your own environment.

AWS CLI

The AWS CLI is a unified tool by AWS that allows you to interact with and manage AWS services from a command line such as macOS terminal or Windows Command Prompt. It provides a convenient and scriptable way to automate and control various AWS resources and operations.

It's a CLI tool, so it requires an installation process. This differs per operating system but it is well-documented by AWS (`https://docs.aws.amazon.com/cli/latest/userguide/getting-started-install.html`). Besides standalone actions, it can be integrated with other CLI scripts or automation tools you already have. For example, a larger workflow that touches on various components such as local and remote processes.

Using the AWS CLI

In this section, you will create an EC2 instance like in the previous section, this time using the AWS CLI.

Authentication works differently from the AWS Console. AWS CLI supports various authentication methods, including AWS access keys, IAM roles, and external credential providers. You can read all the details about the different types of security credentials on the AWS website: `https://docs.aws.amazon.com/IAM/latest/UserGuide/security-creds.html`.

In this section, we will focus on AWS access keys.

If you are using the root user or an IAM user, by default, your user does not have access keys enabled. Using the root user is not recommended. However, you can create access keys for it. The process is described on the AWS website: `https://docs.aws.amazon.com/IAM/latest/UserGuide/id_root-user_manage_add-key.html`.

Follow these steps to create a new IAM user:

1. Navigate to IAM using the console (`https://us-east-1.console.aws.amazon.com/iam/home?region=us-east-1#/users`).
2. Select **Create User**, and give it a username.
3. From the **Set permissions** menu, select **Attach policies directly**, then find and select **PowerUserAccess**. Finally, click **Next**.
4. Click **Create user**.

Your user should now show in the list of users. To create access keys for this user, follow these steps:

1. Select your newly created user.
2. Navigate to the **Security credentials** tab, and select **Create access key**.
3. On the **Use case** menu, select **Command Line Interface (CLI)**, accept the confirmation message, and select **Next**.
4. On the following menu, click **Create access key**.
5. Before navigating away from this page, note your access and secret access keys.

AWS also has these processes For all possible permutations well documented on their website:

- Creating an IAM user: `https://docs.aws.amazon.com/IAM/latest/UserGuide/id_users_create.html#id_users_create_console`
- Managing access keys for IAM users: `https://docs.aws.amazon.com/IAM/latest/UserGuide/id_credentials_access-keys.html`

Open your preferred local CLI tool and set the following variables with your own keys. This allows your terminal to interact with your AWS account:

```
$ export AWS_ACCESS_KEY_ID=XXXXXXXXX
$ export AWS_SECRET_ACCESS_KEY=xxxxxxxxxx
$ export AWS_DEFAULT_REGION=us-east-1
```

With these variables set, you are now able to execute AWS CLI commands on your own account. Notice how we are hardcoding the region to `us-east-1`. We recommend that you run all the following examples in this region. If you are using a different region, some parameters, such as the **Amazon Machine Image** (**AMI**), require modifications.

Try the following command; it returns your running instances. If you don't have any, it will be empty:

```
$ aws ec2 describe-instances
```

To create the simplest possible instance, run the following command. This command creates an EC2 of the smallest instance type, `t2.micro`, using that AMI ID, which effectively means Amazon Linux 2023. There will be more on AMIs in *Chapter 3*:

```
$ aws ec2 run-instances --image-id ami-0c101f26f147fa7fd
--instance-type t2.micro
```

Your command output should be similar to the following. Bear in mind that part of the output was omitted, but check whether your `ImageId` and `InstanceType` match:

```
{
    "Groups": [],
    "Instances": [
        {
            "AmiLaunchIndex": 0,
            "ImageId": "ami-0c101f26f147fa7fd",
            "InstanceId": "i-0a65cf3ecaec728a8",
            "InstanceType": "t2.micro",
            "LaunchTime": "2024-03-24T10:47:25+00:00",
            "Monitoring": {
                "State": "disabled"
            },
```

```
            "Placement": {
                "AvailabilityZone": "us-east-1a",
                "GroupName": "",
                "Tenancy": "default"
            },
            "PrivateDnsName": "ip-172-31-38-84.ec2.internal",
            ###OUTPUT OMMITED###
```

If you run the previous `describe` command again, this time, the output will show your running instance. Try it with the following filter, which only shows `t2.micro`-sized instances:

```
$ aws ec2 describe-instances --filters "Name=instance-type,
Values=t2.micro" --query "Reservations[].Instances[].InstanceId"
[
    "i-0a65cf3ecaec728a8"
]
```

To terminate the instance, run the following command. Replace the instance ID with your own:

```
$ aws ec2 terminate-instances --instance-ids i-0a65cf3ecaec728a8
```

You can use the `describe` command again to make sure the instance is no longer running.

Exploring the AWS CLI

Explore the AWS CLI further on your own. The syntax is the same for every service:

```
$ aws <command> <subcommand> [options and parameters]
```

Here's what each of these commands mean:

- The base call to the `aws` program.
- The top-level `command` typically corresponds to an AWS service supported by the AWS CLI.
- The `subcommand` specifies which operation to perform.

> **Important note**
> You created an IAM user with `PowerUserAccess` permissions. This grants full access to AWS services and resources, but does not allow the management of users or groups. In production scenarios, you can scope down your user access to a narrower set of permissions.

A handy feature of AWS CLI is the `help` feature. You can get help with any command using this. To do so, simply type `help` at the end of a command name. Execute the following commands. The result will be a very verbose description of everything available with those commands:

```
$ aws ec2 help
$ aws ec2 describe-instances help
```

If navigating command by command is not your thing, you can also find the specific syntax for each service in AWS CLI Command Reference (https://docs.aws.amazon.com/cli/latest/), but you will see and use more of it in the following chapters.

AWS SDK

The AWS SDKs are a collection of open-source libraries that provide programmatic access to AWS services from various programming languages including Java, Python, Node.js, .NET, Ruby, Go, PHP, and others. These SDKs allow developers to build applications that interact with AWS resources and services directly, without the need for low-level AWS service APIs.

The AWS SDKs abstract away the complexities of making authenticated HTTP/HTTPS requests to AWS services, handling retries and error handling, and parsing the responses from AWS services. They provide a higher-level, language-specific interface that makes it easier for developers to integrate AWS services into their applications.

This are considered an advanced concept and you won't see much of it in this book. It is more often used by application developers. If you are interested in understanding the syntax to create an EC2 instance using the SDK for Python, it's available under the *Learn the basics* section at https://docs.aws.amazon.com/code-library/latest/ug/python_3_ec2_code_examples.html.

From manual actions using the console to semi-automated ones such as the AWS CLI, you've not yet witnessed the full potential of automation. In the next section, you will learn how to scale your deployments with IaC.

Understanding IaC

IaC is an approach to provision and manage resources such as cloud infrastructure. It allows you to define and deploy your resources using human-readable definition files or code.

Instead of manually configuring resources through the AWS Console or CLI tools as you saw in previous sections, IaC allows a declarative specification of the desired infrastructure state. In our context, that's the AWS cloud. This means compute instances, storage, networking, security groups, and other AWS services.

By treating your IaC, you will get multiple benefits:

- **Configuration consistency**: IaC promotes the concept of immutable infrastructure, whereby infrastructure components are treated as disposable and replaceable rather than being manually modified. This approach ensures consistency, reduces configuration drift, and simplifies the process of scaling or updating infrastructure.
- **Version control and collaboration**: IaC templates and code can be stored in version control systems such as Git, enabling collaboration, code reviews, and tracking of changes to the infrastructure definitions. This promotes best practices in infrastructure management and facilitates knowledge sharing among teams.
- **Automated deployments**: IaC templates and code can be integrated with **Continuous Integration and Continuous Deployment (CI/CD)** pipelines, enabling automated deployments and updates. This reduces manual effort, minimizes human errors, and ensures consistent and repeatable deployments across different environments (e.g., development, staging, and production).
- **Infrastructure testing and validation**: IaC templates and code can be tested and validated before deployment, ensuring that the defined infrastructure meets the desired specifications and adheres to organizational policies and best practices.
- **Cost optimization and resource management**: By treating infrastructure as code, organizations can more easily track and manage their AWS resources, enabling better cost optimization and resource utilization strategies. You will no longer forget that one virtual machine running somewhere.

There are multiple IaC tools. AWS provides its own native IaC tools such as AWS CloudFormation, which allows users to define their infrastructure resources using JSON or YAML templates. It also provides the AWS **Cloud Development Kit (CDK)**. This is not to be confused with AWS SDK, which offers a higher-level abstraction over CloudFormation, enabling developers to define AWS constructs using familiar programming languages such as TypeScript, Python, Java, and C#.

Beyond AWS-native tools, there are also plenty of third-party IaC solutions such as **Terraform**. Terraform is cloud-agnostic; it supports a wide range of cloud providers, including AWS, and provides a consistent workflow for managing infrastructure across multiple platforms. It is one of the most well-known IaC tools.

Choosing an IaC tool boils down to personal preference, existing skills, and specific features each tool can offer. In this book, you will get hands-on experience with CloudFormation and Terraform. However, if you are interested in this topic, AWS offers prescriptive guidance on how to choose an IaC tool at `https://docs.aws.amazon.com/prescriptive-guidance/latest/choose-iac-tool/introduction.html`.

Using CloudFormation

In this section, you will create an EC2 instance using CloudFormation. This is an introductory section; it won't dive deep into all CloudFormation syntax and features.

To get started, follow these steps:

1. Create the following file in your local environment; it is a YAML template to create one EC2 instance of the specified AMI and `t2.micro` size:

    ```
    Resources:
      NewEC2Instance:
        Type: AWS::EC2::Instance
        Properties:
          ImageId: "ami-0c101f26f147fa7fd"
          InstanceType: "t2.micro"
    ```

    Notice how human-readable CloudFormation is in YAML format. This is one of its advantages.

2. Navigate to CloudFormation using the AWS Console at `https://us-east-1.console.aws.amazon.com/cloudformation` and select **Create stack**.
3. Select **Upload a template file** and choose your previously created `ec2.yml`, and select **Next**.
4. Give the stack a name.
5. Skip through all the options and deploy the stack.

At the end of the deployment process, the status of your stack should show **CREATE_COMPLETE**. If the deployment isn't created successfully, verify that you are using the `us-east-1` region.

You can verify the EC2 you just created by navigating to the EC2 service. Confirm that it has the correct size and AMI.

Don't worry if you don't fully understand the whole process. CloudFormation is a world of its own with specific syntax and features. Navigate through your stack details; you will be able to find many characteristics, such as when was it created, by whom it was created, and which resources were created and in what order, as well as more advanced concepts such as parameters and outputs.

To learn more about CloudFormation, you can use official AWS documentation: `https://docs.aws.amazon.com/AWSCloudFormation/latest/UserGuide/Welcome.html`.

Before moving on, to stop you from incurring extra costs, don't forget to delete your EC2. To delete all stack's resources, select your stack and click **Delete**.

Using Terraform

You will now create another EC2 instance, this time using Terraform. This section assumes that you already have your terminal configured with your AWS credentials the exercise in the previous *AWS CLI* section.

Here's how to do it:

1. Create a file in your local workstation, in any directory, and name it `ec2.tf`.
2. Populate it with the following code that creates an EC2 of the smallest instance type, `t2.micro`, in `us-east-1`, using the AMI ID. This effectively means using Amazon Linux 2023:

   ```
   provider "aws"{
       region = "us-east-1"
   }
   resource "aws_instance" "ec2" {
     ami           = "ami-0c101f26f147fa7fd"
     instance_type = "t2.micro"
   }
   ```

   Notice that the **HashiCorp Configuration Language** (HCL) code is still human-readable, albeit perhaps a bit less so than the CloudFormation YAML.

   > **Important note**
   > AMI IDs are different in each region. If you are using a different region than `us-east-1`, and you want to use Amazon Linux 2023, you will need to find the corresponding AMI ID.

3. To execute Terraform code, you need to have it installed. The installation is beyond the scope of this book. It differs per operating system but it's a straightforward process that you can find good documentation about on the HashiCorp website (`https://developer.hashicorp.com/terraform/tutorials/aws-get-started/install-cli`).

4. When you have it installed, execute the following commands in the same directory where you created your `ec2.tf` file. They initiate Terraform in your environment and apply your previously created template to your AWS account, effectively creating the resources:

   ```
   $ terraform init
   $ terraform apply
   ```

   You will be prompted to confirm. If your execution is successful, it will look like the following shortened output:

   ```
   Terraform used the selected providers to generate the following
   execution plan. Resource actions are indicated with the
   following symbols:
   ```

```
        + create

    Terraform will perform the following actions:
      # aws_instance.ec2 will be created
      + resource "aws_instance" "ec2" {
          + ami                          = "ami-0c101f26f147fa7fd"
          + instance_type                = "t2.micro"
          ###OUTPUT OMMITED###
          + root_block_device {
              + delete_on_termination = (known after apply)
              + device_name           = (known after apply)
              + encrypted             = (known after apply)
              + iops                  = (known after apply)
              + kms_key_id            = (known after apply)
              + tags                  = (known after apply)
              + tags_all              = (known after apply)
              + throughput            = (known after apply)
              + volume_id             = (known after apply)
              + volume_size           = (known after apply)
              + volume_type           = (known after apply)
            }
        }

    Plan: 1 to add, 0 to change, 0 to destroy.
    Do you want to perform these actions?
      Terraform will perform the actions described above.
      Only 'yes' will be accepted to approve.
      Enter a value: yes

    aws_instance.ec2: Creating...
    aws_instance.ec2: Still creating... [10s elapsed]
    aws_instance.ec2: Still creating... [20s elapsed]
    aws_instance.ec2: Still creating... [30s elapsed]
    aws_instance.ec2: Creation complete after 34s [id=i-0de732fda772c16cf]
    Apply complete! Resources: 1 added, 0 changed, 0 destroyed.
```

5. You can use your AWS Console to navigate through the EC2 that was created. Make sure you verify in the correct region. To delete all the resources, execute the following Terraform command:

```
$ terraform destroy
```

Terraform offers many more functionalities, such as dry-runs using `terraform plan`, or visualizations of the deployed resources through `terraform state list`. You can read more about these in the Terraform official documentation at https://developer.hashicorp.com/terraform/cli/commands.

Take a look at a practical example of why IaC is useful. Let's say you needed to create 100 of these machines. You could alter the previous code to the following:

```
provider "aws"{
    region = "us-east-1"
}
resource "aws_instance" "ec2" {
  ami           = "ami-0c101f26f147fa7fd"
  instance_type = "t2.micro"
  count         = 100
}
```

Do not run this example because it can incur high costs. However, notice how easy it is compared to doing the same task using the AWS Console.

Summary

In this chapter, you learned what it means to architect on AWS. It's not only about deploying AWS services but also about gathering different types of requirements, contrasting those to known patterns and reference architectures, choosing different services, and documenting it all.

You also explored the various methods and tools available for deploying and interacting with AWS services after you have your design. The AWS Console provides a user-friendly graphical interface, while the AWS CLI and SDKs enable programmatic access and automation. Additionally, you were exposed to various IaC techniques such as Terraform, CloudFormation, and AWS CDK, which allow you to define and manage your AWS infrastructure using code.

By understanding these different approaches, you can choose the most appropriate method based on your requirements and skill level, as well as the complexity of your AWS deployments. Whether you prefer a visual interface, command-line tools, programmatic access, or IaC, AWS offers a range of options to meet your needs and streamline your cloud operations.

In the next chapter, you will build a personal website using the AWS Console.

2
Creating a Personal Website

This is the beginning of your hands-on experience. Over the next chapters, you'll immerse yourself in various scenarios. In this first practical chapter, you are going to navigate through a scenario of building a personal website for your CV from a list of requirements. With those requirements in mind, you are going to be guided through the methodology presented in *Chapter 1* and architect a solution using AWS services such as S3 for storage and CloudFront for serving.

After that, you are going to build this architecture using the AWS Console.

In summary, this chapter covers the following main topics in order:

- What you are going to build – a personal website
- How you are going to build it – using S3 and CloudFront
- Actually building it – using the AWS Console
- How to improve the solution – security and DNS

By the end of this chapter, you will be able to confidently create and host your own static websites in AWS. This is a precursor to more advanced web applications that you will see in the following chapters.

Technical requirements

In order to create your own personal website, you will need access to an AWS account.

This chapter has a dedicated folder in the GitHub repository of this book. There, you will find the code snippets required to follow along: `https://github.com/PacktPublishing/AWS-Cloud-Projects/tree/main/chapter2/code`.

Scenario

Imagine you're a recent graduate or a professional looking to showcase your skills, experience, and accomplishments to potential employers or clients. You want to create an online presence that is easily accessible and professional-looking, where you can share your CV or resume.

What better way to do this than to host your own personal website?

Requirements

Recall that in *Chapter 1*, gathering requirements was the first step to architect in AWS. No matter how simple or complicated your scenario is, it's good practice to lay down the requirements on paper. It may sound silly, but spending time describing what you need, and how you will build it, will help you in the long run.

In this specific case, you want to build something simple. You want a website that provides a good user experience. You don't want a recruiter to see the page loading slowly, making them just move on to the next candidate. Likewise, you don't want a recruiter to try to access your website while it's down. To avoid this, you need to know what kind of experience your users are having.

CVs change often. You might pick up a new skill, change jobs, or otherwise affect your CV. Due to this, you'll want to have an easy mechanism to update the website. Lastly, as this is a personal project, you must keep costs as low as possible.

All of these factors can be translated into functional and non-functional requirements.

Functional requirements

Functional requirements define the specific features, functionalities, and capabilities that the solution must provide. In this case, those are as follows:

- Ability to create, edit, and update the content of the CV, including sections for personal information, education, work experience, skills, and projects
- Support for non-text content such as images
- Accessible on any browser over the internet
- Ability to generate insights based on website data

Non-functional requirements

Non-functional requirements define the qualitative attributes that the solution must provide. In this case, those are as follows:

- Low latency – fast page load times
- High availability – available when accessed

- Ease of maintainability – easy process to update, and patch the website
- Low cost – cheap pay-as-you-go services

Now, you have the requirements for the personal website. In keeping with the *Chapter 1* methodology, you must now check for known well-accepted patterns.

Architecture patterns

A simple search in AWS Architecture Center (https://aws.amazon.com/architecture/) does not yield any reference architecture diagrams or sample code. However, it returns a YouTube series with an episode named *Back to Basics: Hosting a Static Website on AWS* (https://www.youtube.com/watch?v=N0nhkyhaqyw&ab_channel=AmazonWebServices).

Watch it; this is a good starting point.

Outside the context of the AWS cloud, it is important to understand what a static website is. A **static website** is a type of website where the content is pre-built and served to users as static files, typically HTML, CSS, and JavaScript files. Static websites do not require server-side processing.

Dynamic websites, on the other hand, generate content on the server side based on user requests and other data. You will see and build these in the coming chapters.

The simplest example of a static website is having a single HTML file on your local desktop and opening it in your browser. This works; however, nobody other than yourself will be able to access it. This is why you need a hosting platform for your static websites.

After having the static files built, you upload your files and other people will be able to access them through this hosting platform. This is where AWS and solution architecture play a role.

Architecture

By now, you understand what a static website is, have your requirements set, and are ready to create an architecture diagram of the solution.

There are two possible options:

- Diagram without specific services
- Diagram with specific services

Following a formal process, you create a diagram without specific services. After that, during service selection, you can match the unspecific services with the requirements and replace them with specific services.

For example, you know you want a **Content Delivery Network** (**CDN**), so you should represent that. After that, if Amazon CloudFront matches your requirements, replace the agnostic CDN icon with CloudFront's icon in your architecture diagram.

However, for this simple scenario and after learning about the architecture pattern, you can jump straight into a diagram populated with AWS services.

Remember, you need a place to store your static files and a mechanism to make those available.

Your diagram should look like the one in *Figure 2.1*: a three-component diagram, with Amazon S3, Amazon CloudFront, and Amazon CloudWatch. Clients connect through CloudFront, which fetches your website static files from S3. Both of these services emit metrics to CloudWatch.

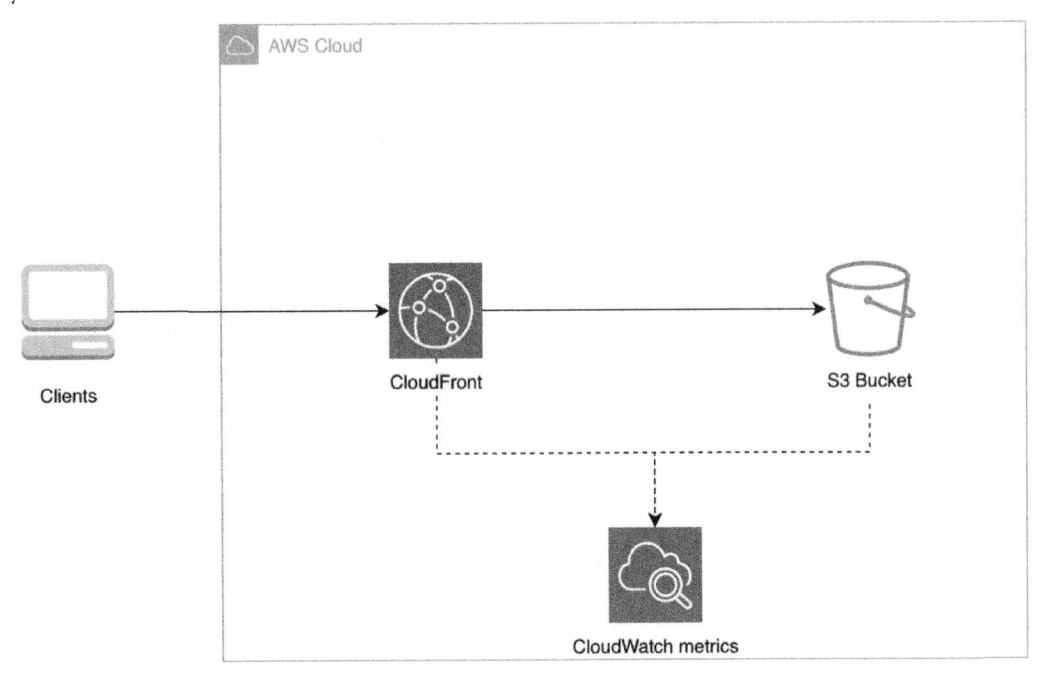

Figure 2.1 – Static website architecture on AWS

Although clients are represented with a computer icon, they can also be other types of devices such as phones or tablets.

AWS services

This architecture only uses three services. In this section, you will learn what these services do and why they address your requirements.

Amazon Simple Storage Service (S3)

Amazon S3 is a highly scalable and durable object storage service. S3 has many characteristics. The ones relevant to our use case are as follows:

- S3 is an object storage service, meaning that it stores data as objects (files) in buckets (directories).
- Designed for high availability, with data automatically replicated across multiple AWS availability zones within a region, ensuring that your data remains accessible even in the event of an outage or component failure.
- Fully managed service; you don't have to worry about the operational overhead of managing storage infrastructure, as all is handled for you.
- Supports versioning, as a means of keeping multiple variants of an object in the same bucket allowing you to preserve, retrieve, and restore every version of every object stored in your buckets.
- Highly cost-effective storage solution, with pay-as-you-go pricing and tiered storage classes.

Relate these statements to your requirements:

- You want to store files (e.g. HTML, CSS, and images), and you want to store them in a place where they will be available for the recruiters to access at any time. S3 is highly available.
- You want the solution to be easily maintained, without having to do operating system patches and all those boring activities. S3 is a fully-managed service.
- Likewise, you want to be able to update your CV in an easy manner, and if you make a mistake, you want to be able to roll back to a previous version. S3 supports file versioning.
- Lastly, you need this at the lowest possible cost. S3 has a free tier, it only charges for what you consume, and it is considered a cost-effective service.

It checks all the boxes as the service to store your static files.

Did you know that S3 has a native functionality to function as a static website? You can read all about it on the AWS website at https://docs.aws.amazon.com/AmazonS3/latest/userguide/WebsiteHosting.html.

However, it presents two key limitations:

- S3 is a regional service, and therefore, the website is available at the AWS region-specific website endpoint of the bucket.
- It does not support HTTPS.

This leads us to the next service: CloudFront. If you want to learn more about S3, including what is included in the free tier, you can read about it at https://aws.amazon.com/pm/serv-s3.

Amazon CloudFront

Amazon CloudFront is a service that speeds up the distribution of your static and dynamic web content, such as `.html`, `.css`, `.js`, and image files, to your users. It is Amazon's CDN.

A CDN is a geographically distributed group of servers that caches content close to end users. In short, the way it works is that your users terminate their connections at CloudFront locations closer to them, and travel the rest of the way using Amazon's high-speed backbone network. If your content is already cached in the location, it returns it without traveling all the way to the origin.

Some of its key characteristics are as follows:

- **Globally distributed**: By caching static content at edge locations closer to users, CloudFront can serve the website's files more quickly, resulting in faster load times and an enhanced user experience. This is particularly beneficial for users with slower internet connections or those located in regions far from the origin S3 bucket.

- **Highly available and fault tolerant**: CloudFront is built on top of AWS's highly available and fault-tolerant infrastructure. The edge locations and underlying services are designed with redundancy and fault tolerance in mind, minimizing the impact of individual component failures.

- **Increased resiliency**: CloudFront supports multiple origin servers (e.g., Amazon S3 buckets or web servers) for a single distribution. If the primary origin server becomes unavailable, CloudFront automatically fails over to a secondary or tertiary origin server, ensuring continuous content delivery.

- **Content delivery optimization**: CloudFront optimizes the delivery of static content by automatically compressing files, minimizing the amount of data transferred, and supporting advanced caching mechanisms such as cache control headers and query string forwarding.

Again, relate these characteristics to your requirements:

- You want a distribution mechanism that is available through the internet on any device. You don't know where your users will be or what types of devices and bandwidth constraints they might have. You benefit from CloudFront's globally distributed nature with out-of-the-box caching.

- S3 is highly available, but you also need the CDN to be highly available. When you chain components together, a failure in any one affects the whole system. CloudFront also helps to increase your availability further by bypassing S3 failures using a secondary origin or bucket.

- Lastly, cost is important. CloudFront's pricing model is based on data transferred out and the number of requests with a pay-as-you-go model. CloudFront automatically compresses your files, if supported by the client's browser, minimizing data transfers.

If you want to learn more about CloudFront including what is included in the free tier, you can read about it in the AWS documentation: `https://aws.amazon.com/cloudfront`.

Amazon CloudWatch metrics

Amazon CloudWatch monitors resources and the applications you run on AWS in real time. You can use CloudWatch to collect and track metrics, logs, events, and traces.

CloudWatch has many features, but in this project, we will only focus on CloudWatch metrics. Some key characteristics of CW metrics are as follows:

- **Comprehensive coverage**: It collects metrics from a wide range of AWS services, including Amazon S3 and Amazon CloudFront, alongside many others. This comprehensive coverage allows you to monitor and analyze the performance and health of your entire AWS infrastructure and applications from a single centralized location.
- **Alarms and notifications**: It supports the creation of alarms based on metric thresholds or patterns. These alarms can trigger notifications (e.g., email, SMS, or AWS Lambda functions) when specific conditions are met, allowing you to proactively respond to potential issues or take automated actions.
- **Cost-effectiveness**: With pricing based on the number of metrics ingested and the data retention period and a pay-as-you-go model, it allows you to scale your monitoring efforts as your AWS infrastructure and applications grow, without incurring significant upfront costs.

For any solution you deploy, you need to monitor it. This means that you need to know whether it's working, and if it isn't, you need to know why not. In this case, even though this is a simple website with your CV, you want to know whether anyone is accessing it, and what type of experience they are having. This will satisfy the *ability to generate insights based on website data* requirement.

CloudWatch is deeply integrated into the AWS ecosystem. It will natively show you both CloudFront and S3 metrics, for example: the number of requests, error rates, and latency. You will have access to these metrics while minimizing your costs. If you have no visits, you will have no costs.

If you want to learn more about CloudWatch metrics, including what is included in the free tier, you can read about it in the AWS documentation: `https://docs.aws.amazon.com/AmazonCloudWatch/latest/monitoring/working_with_metrics.html`.

Coding the solution

Congratulations, you have designed an architecture that fulfills all your requirements. It's time to build it. During this chapter, you are going to do it using the AWS console in the **N. Virginia** region.

Editing the website

Start by downloading the assets in the Git repository of this book at `https://github.com/PacktPublishing/AWS-Cloud-Projects`. You can do it from your workstation terminal using the Git tool, or by downloading the repository as a ZIP file. A detailed step-by-step guide on how to use Git and GitHub is beyond the scope of this book, but if you want to deep dive into the topic, the book *Mastering Git*, available at `https://www.packtpub.com/product/mastering-git/9781783553754`, covers it holistically.

You will find three files in the `chapter2/code` folder. Open `index.html` in your favorite code editor. There, you will find a standard HTML that references some styles in the header, along with an HTML body with multiple divisions, highlighted with the tags `div`, populated with CV information:

```html
<!DOCTYPE html>
<html>
<head>
  <link href="https://maxcdn.bootstrapcdn.com/font-awesome/4.2.0/css/font-awesome.min.css" rel="stylesheet">
  <link rel="preconnect" href="https://fonts.googleapis.com">
  <link rel="preconnect" href="https://fonts.gstatic.com" crossorigin>
  <link href="https://fonts.googleapis.com/css2?family=Archivo+Narrow&family=Julius+Sans+One&family=Open+Sans&family=Source+Sans+Pro&display=swap" rel="stylesheet">
  <link rel="stylesheet" href="index.css">
</head>
<body>
  <page size="A4">
    <div class="container">
      <div class="leftPanel">
        <img src="avatar.png"/>
        <div class="details">
          <div class="item bottomLineSeparator">
            <h2>
              CONTACT
            </h2>
  ### OUTPUT OMMITED ###
```

If you are not familiar with HTML, this is the 1,000-foot overview: HTML files are what browsers read to render web pages. They are represented by the .html or .htm extensions. HTML documents have a series of elements, represented in between tags. Tags are represented with a word between < > symbols. There are opening and closing tags; the content is between them. There are well-defined tags, for example, <p>, which means paragraph. To represent a paragraph, you would do the following:

```html
<p>This is a paragraph in HTML</p>
```

You can find documentation about many other tags on the w3school website at `https://www.w3schools.com/tags/`.

However, if you just use plain HTML, your website will not have a good aesthetic. To visualize this, open the `index.html` file in your browser. If you haven't modified it yet, it will look like *Figure 2.2*.

Figure 2.2 – index.html browser visualization

Now, open it in a text editor and remove these link tags in the header:

```
<link href="https://maxcdn.bootstrapcdn.com/font-awesome/4.2.0/css/font-awesome.min.css" rel="stylesheet">
<link rel="preconnect" href="https://fonts.googleapis.com">
<link rel="preconnect" href="https://fonts.gstatic.com" crossorigin>
<link href="https://fonts.googleapis.com/css2?family=Archivo+Narrow&family=Julius+Sans+One&family=Open+Sans&family=Source+Sans+Pro&display=swap" rel="stylesheet">
<link rel="stylesheet" href="index.css">
```

Refresh your browser page. Now, it will look like *Figure 2.3*:

CONTACT

(+351) 123 456 789

lorem@ipsum.com

Lisbon, Portugal

in/ivopinto01

SKILLS

AWS Services
10 years
System Design
3 years
Architecture
3 years
Python
2 years
Javascript
2 years
Terraform
2 years
CloudFormation
2 years
AWS CDK
1 year

EDUCATION

Bachelor of Cloud

University of Lisbon

2009 - 2012

Ivo Pinto

Figure 2.3 – index.html browser visualization without styles

Hopefully, you see the value. Styles in HTML add style to an element, such as color, font, size, and more. Everything in HTML can be styled, even `div` elements. Re-add the five link tags you have removed.

Now, open the file named `index.css` in a text editor. In this code, you can find specific font sizes and colors for each type of tag used in your HTML file. Likewise, you can find positioning attributes:

```
h1 {
  font-family: 'Julius Sans One', sans-serif;
}

h2 { /* Contact, Skills, Education, About me, Work Experience */
  font-family: 'Archivo Narrow', sans-serif;
}

h3 { /* Accountant */
  font-family: 'Open Sans', sans-serif;
}
.container {
  display: flex;
  flex-direction: row;
  width: 100%;
  height: 100%;
}

.leftPanel {
  width: 27%;
  background-color: #484444;
  padding: 0.7cm;
  display: flex;
  flex-direction: column;
  align-items: center;
}
## OUTPUT OMMITED ###
```

Contrast the names found here, such as `leftPanel` or `container`, with the `div class` attributes of your `index.html` file.

The third file, `avatar.png`, is just a photo. To insert an image in an HTML, use the `<img>` tag.

Now that you understand the three files and how they relate to each other, replace the content with your own CV information and photo. If you feel confident, alter some of the styles as well.

Publishing the website

So far, all you have done is use your local workstation. In this section, we are going to make your website globally available.

Access your AWS account using the Console like in *Chapter 1*. Navigate to S3: `https://s3.console.aws.amazon.com/s3/home?region=us-east-1#`.

Create a bucket. In its configuration settings, give it a unique name, and leave **Block all public access** checked.

Navigate inside the newly created S3 bucket and upload the three files that you downloaded earlier from the book's GitHub repository: `index.html`, `index.css`, and `avatar.png`. These, as mentioned, were example files, and you can and should replace them with your own. If you have not done this by the end of this chapter, you will have a website of one of the book's authors' CVs.

Navigate to the CloudFront console (`https://us-east-1.console.aws.amazon.com/cloudfront/v4/home?region=us-east-1#/distributions`) and create a new distribution:

1. Select your bucket as **Origin domain**.
2. Change **Origin access** from **Public** to **Origin access control settings**.
3. Create a new OAC with the default options, and select it under **Origin access control**.
4. Under the **Web Application Firewall (WAF)** section, do not enable the security protections.
5. Before creating your distribution, read through all the options. Notice some interesting ones, such as the cache policy, the ability to compress objects automatically, and the different types of pricing.

When you create the distribution, a yellow popup will appear at the top of your screen, like the one shown in *Figure 2.4*. Select **Copy policy**, followed by **Go to S3 bucket permissions to update policy**.

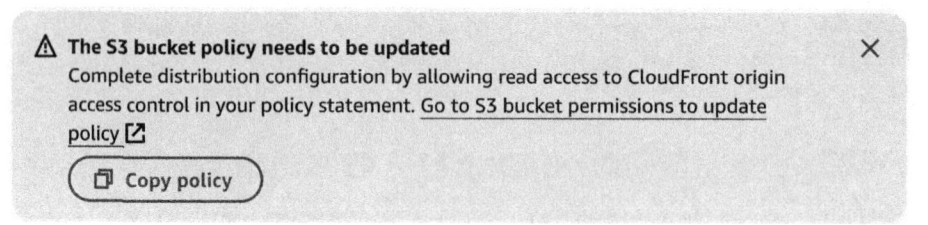

Figure 2.4 – CloudFront OAC popup

You will be presented with your S3 bucket settings. Select **Edit** under the **Bucket policy** section, paste the policy you copied, and save it.

The policy should look like the following one. It allows the CloudFront service to access the resources inside your bucket. In this case, that's the `cloudprojectwebsitebucket` bucket:

```
{
    "Version": "2008-10-17",
    "Id": "PolicyForCloudFrontPrivateContent",
    "Statement": [
```

```
        {
            "Sid": "AllowCloudFrontServicePrincipal",
            "Effect": "Allow",
            "Principal": {
                "Service": "cloudfront.amazonaws.com"
            },
            "Action": "s3:GetObject",
            "Resource": "arn:aws:s3:::cloudprojectwebsitebucket/*",
            "Condition": {
                "StringEquals": {
                    "AWS:SourceArn":
 "arn:aws:cloudfront::111111111111:distribution/E33NUQ32Z0XQZB"
                }
            }
        }
    ]
}
```

Navigate back to your CloudFront distribution and note the distribution name. Note that the CloudFront distribution might take a minute or two to become available.

Append index.html at the end, and after your distribution status shows **Enabled**, open it in your browser. The URL should have the following format; the highlighted part should be different in your case:

https://**d1hjtv5xjv873g**.cloudfront.net/index.html

However, nobody likes to have to write index.html at the end of the URL, right?

Navigate to your CloudFront distribution and select **Edit** under **Settings**. In the **Default root object** field, insert index.html and save your changes.

Your distribution state will change to **Deploying** momentarily, as shown in *Figure 2.5*, under the **Last modified** column.

ID	Domai...	Origins	Status	Last modified
E3M96EE...	d1sdxelk...	tf-test-bucket-9	⊘ Enabled	⊙ Deploying

Figure 2.5 – CloudFront distribution status during an update

When the distribution finishes propagating your changes, the status column shows the **Enabled** status, and the **Last modified** column shows a date as shown in *Figure 2.6*.

	ID	Domai...	Origins	Status	Last modified
☐	E3M96EE...	d1sdxelk...	tf-test-bucket-9	✓ Enabled	May 30, 2024 at 12:31:31 PM UTC

Figure 2.6 – CloudFront distribution status after an update

Refresh your CV page, this time without the path, as shown in the following line. Remember to replace the highlighted string with your own domain:

```
https://d1hjtv5xjv873g.cloudfront.net/
```

Et voilà! Your CV is now online and available for recruiters to visit it.

Monitoring the website

Your website is online, you can share the URL with other people and they will always have access to your latest CV. However, how do you know whether they actually accessed it, or whether they are having a good experience?

You already know the answer; it's CloudWatch metrics:

1. Navigate to the CloudWatch metrics console (`https://us-east-1.console.aws.amazon.com/cloudwatch/home?region=us-east-1#metricsV2`).

2. In the **Browse** tab, you will find all kinds of AWS services. Select CloudFront, followed by **Per-Distribution Metrics**.

3. If you have more than one distribution, you will need to identify the relevant one by ID. If you just have one, select **BytesDownloaded**, **Requests**, **5xxErrorRate**, and **4xxErrorRate**.

CloudWatch will plot a graphic for you on the top of your screen, like the one shown in *Figure 2.7*. At 16h25, 18K bytes were downloaded and some users were facing HTTP 400 errors. These metrics were calculated as five-minute averages.

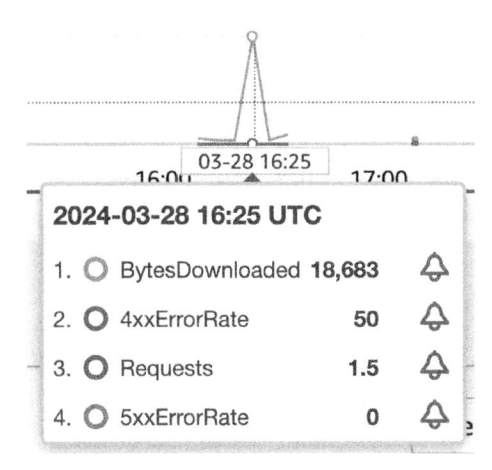

Figure 2.7 – CW metrics graph for CloudFront

These metrics are free and were automatically populated without you having to do anything other than just configuring CloudFront. However, if you want more detailed metrics such as **4xx** and **5xx** error rates by the specific HTTP status code, or cache hits as a percentage of total cacheable requests, you can enable that in your CloudFront distribution at a cost.

Explore CloudWatch metrics further and see what other metrics were automatically populated. Here's a hint: consider your file storage service.

Cleaning up

AWS resources incur costs. Although most services initially fall under the free tier, eventually that runs out, and you will incur costs. We recommend that you delete every application after you are done playing with it.

Start by deleting your CloudFront distribution:

1. Navigate to CloudFront console (`https://us-east-1.console.aws.amazon.com/cloudfront/v4/home?region=us-east-1#/distributions`).
2. Select and disable your CloudFront distribution.
3. After it's disabled, delete the distribution.

Next, delete your S3 bucket:

1. Navigate to S3 console (`https://s3.console.aws.amazon.com/s3/home?region=us-east-1`).
2. Select your bucket. Inside, delete all three files. Buckets can only be deleted if they are empty.
3. Delete your bucket.

Future work

Congratulations, you now have a working static website hosted on AWS. There are multiple features you can complement it with. This section details a few ideas, but it doesn't guide you through their implementation.

Implementing custom DNS

Right now, your CV is at a non-memorable URL. It would be easier for you and others to remember if your URL was something such as `bestcandidatecv.com`.

When you access a URL, in the backend, your workstation does a lookup of this URL to retrieve the IP address. Then it connects to that address.

To verify this behavior, open your favorite terminal and execute the following command; it returns a series of IP addresses. Make sure you replace the URL with your own:

```
$ nslookup d1hjtv5xjv873g.cloudfront.net
```

CloudFront supports having custom domain names.

To achieve it, first, you will need to register a new domain. Domains are unique. Within the AWS ecosystem, you can register a new domain using **Route 53**. However, you can also register your domain with other providers. Domains have a yearly cost.

Secondly, you will need to create a DNS record inside your domain. If you are managing your domain in Route 53, this will be done under hosted zones. This DNS record points your new name to your CloudFront distribution DNS name.

In simple terms, if someone looks up `bestcandidatecv.com`, the server will return `d1hjtv5xjv873g.cloudfront.net`, and then recursively, the IP.

Lastly, you will need a new certificate. Navigate to your current CV website and check the certificate details. They should look like *Figure 2.8*. This certificate is only valid for common names that end with `cloudfront.net`.

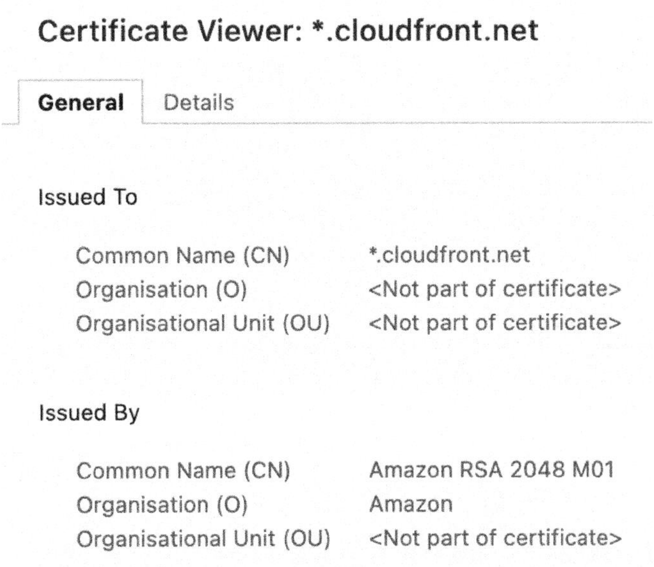

Certificate Viewer: *.cloudfront.net

General | Details

Issued To

Common Name (CN)   *.cloudfront.net
Organisation (O)   <Not part of certificate>
Organisational Unit (OU)   <Not part of certificate>

Issued By

Common Name (CN)   Amazon RSA 2048 M01
Organisation (O)   Amazon
Organisational Unit (OU)   <Not part of certificate>

Figure 2.8 – CloudFront default certificate

Since you will access your CV with a custom name, you will need a certificate that supports that naming. Within the AWS ecosystem, you can use the **AWS Certificate Manager** (**ACM**) to issue a new certificate.

If you are interested in implementing this feature, the AWS documentation details the whole process: `https://docs.aws.amazon.com/AmazonCloudFront/latest/DeveloperGuide/CNAMEs.html`.

Taking security to the next level

Your website is simple, and while static websites are generally considered less vulnerable to certain types of web attacks due to their lack of dynamic content and server-side processing, they can still be targeted by various attacks, such as **Distributed Denial-of-Service** (**DDoS**) attacks, or content injection.

For example, a malicious person can launch a DDoS attack on your website right before an interview. Then during the interview, when you mention it, the website is not available, making you look bad.

Security is a huge topic, but some quick wins that you can implement are AWS **Web Application Firewall** (**WAF**) and AWS Shield.

Web Application Firewall

AWS WAF is a web application firewall (not all AWS services are what the name implies) that helps to protect from common web exploits that could affect application availability, compromise security, or consume excessive resources.

WAF is a managed service, and it offers managed rules called **rulesets**. They are groups of security rules that protect you against common attacks and are automatically updated as new threats emerge. This is especially useful if you are not a security expert, or if you don't want to spend your time managing security rules.

WAF is neatly integrated with CloudFront, and you can enable it by editing your CloudFront distribution. It's a one-click action. Doing so creates a WAF web ACL for you with 3 Amazon-managed rulesets. You can view them in your WAF console.

You can add more rules to the created Web ACL, or if you want to, you can configure a custom web ACL and attach it to your CloudFront distribution.

Your static website does not interact with user inputs. In later chapters, as your application attack surface increases, you will see more benefits of WAF.

If you are interested in implementing this feature, the AWS documentation details the whole process: `https://docs.aws.amazon.com/AmazonCloudFront/latest/DeveloperGuide/distribution-web-awswaf.html`.

Shield

AWS Shield is a managed DDoS protection service. It is designed to safeguard applications running on AWS against DDoS attacks, which are attempts to make a website or application unavailable by overwhelming it with malicious traffic.

Shield uses techniques such as traffic flow monitoring, network anomaly detection, and traffic scrubbing to identify and filter out malicious traffic.

It has two offerings: **Standard** and **Advanced**.

You are already using Shield Standard. This tier is automatically enabled for all AWS customers at no additional cost. It shields you from the most common and frequently occurring DDoS attacks targeting web applications.

Shield Advanced is an optional paid subscription that you can enable on a resource basis. It provides additional detection and mitigation capabilities against more sophisticated and larger DDoS attacks, including those targeting higher layers (HTTP/HTTPS) and specific applications. Shield Advanced integrates with services such as AWS WAF for more advanced security controls.

We do *not* recommend that you enable Shield Advanced for this project. It has a long subscription commitment, one year, and a big price tag for a personal project at $3,000/month.

If you are interested in knowing more about AWS Shield, visit the AWS documentation at https://aws.amazon.com/shield/.

Having better observability

Logging refers to the process of recording events, messages, and other information generated by an application during its execution. It is an essential practice in software development and operations as it provides insights into the behavior, performance, and potential issues of an application.

You configured and verified metrics for your static website, but not logs. S3, CloudFront, WAF, and other AWS services have the ability to generate logs.

Consider enabling CloudFront access logs. They are log files that contain detailed information about every user request that CloudFront receives. You can enable access logs by editing your CloudFront distribution.

CloudFront logs contain 33 fields. Since that's too many to list, some important ones to have in mind are as follows:

- `date`
- `time`
- `c-ip` – the IP address of the viewer
- `cs(UserAgent)` – the browser identifier
- `x-edge-location` – the physical location the request entered from

> **Important note**
> Although this feature might not seem very useful for this specific project, having an observable solution is considered an industry best practice. You will regret not having logs at the time of troubleshooting issues.

Logs can be written to various destinations, such as files, databases, or centralized logging services such as CloudWatch, Elasticsearch, or Splunk. CloudFront logs are written to an S3 bucket of your choice. If, later, you decide that you want to centralize your logs in CloudWatch, you can move them from S3. AWS designed this architecture in a blog post: https://aws.amazon.com/blogs/mt/sending-cloudfront-standard-logs-to-cloudwatch-logs-for-analysis/.

After you have access to your CloudFront log files, you can correlate them with your CloudWatch metrics and have a complete picture of your user experience. For example, you will be able to tell, for the users having 4xx errors in *Figure 2.7*, which countries are they from, which browser versions are they running, and which SSL security ciphers they tried to negotiate.

As mentioned, it's also possible to enable logs for the other components of your architecture, such as S3. Investigate the benefits of that on your own.

If you are interested in implementing CloudFront access logs, the AWS documentation details the whole process: `https://docs.aws.amazon.com/AmazonCloudFront/latest/DeveloperGuide/AccessLogs.html`.

Final architecture

The final architecture, after enhancements, should look like the one in *Figure 2.9*. Notice the addition of WAF, Route 53, and Certificate Manager. Your final architecture might look slightly different if you did not implement all the enhancements.

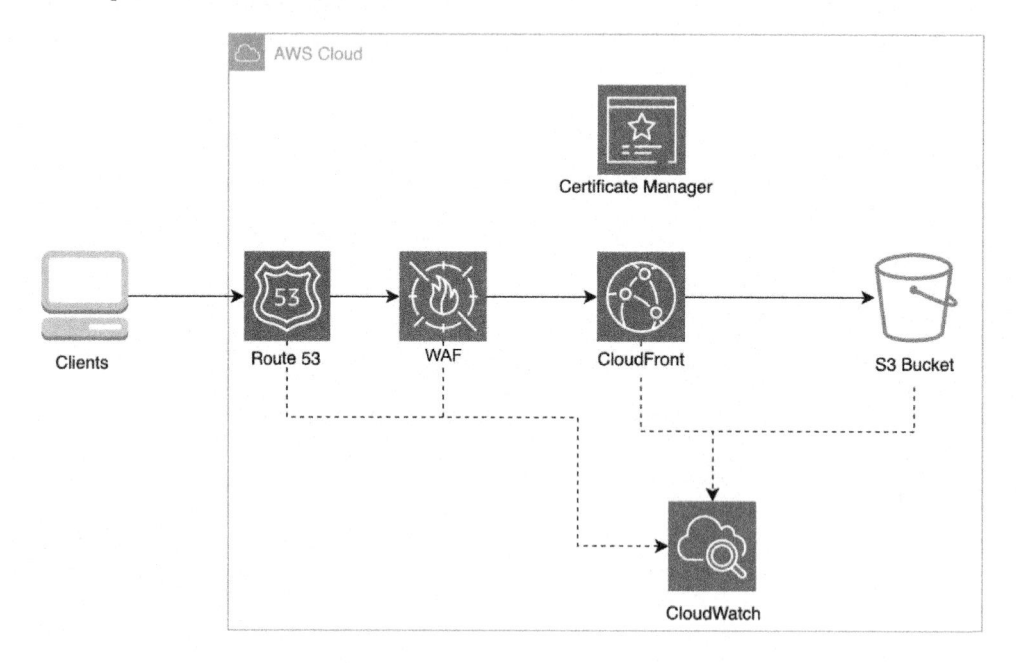

Figure 2.9 – Final static website architecture with improvements

The final simplified traffic flow is as follows:

1. The client enters your custom URL in its browser.
2. Route 53 responds to the DNS query.
3. The client's browser sends the HTTP request to CloudFront IPs.
4. The request is inspected by WAF.
5. CloudFront replies to the request, and returns the static assets.
6. The client's browser renders the website locally.

All the components send metrics and logs to CW as configured.

Summary

In this chapter, you learned what static websites are. You also learned about the common files that compose them, such as HTML, CSS, and JavaScript. You followed *Chapter 1*'s methodology of requirements gathering, architecture patterns, service selection, and diagraming to draw the architecture of your own static website, a personal page.

Then, using the AWS console, you built it.

Lastly, you learned about multiple possible enhancements that can take your static website to a production-level website. By now, you are capable of building globally distributed, highly available, highly resilient, secure static websites.

In the next chapter, you are going to go beyond static websites and create a dynamic web application to share recipes. You will put all your knowledge in static websites to use, but take it one step further.

Part 2: Intermediate Level Projects

In *Part 2* of this book, you are going to continue with what you have learned and built in *Part 1*. However, this part has an increased level of difficulty. You will build four applications in a step-by-step manner powered by many different AWS services, including EC2, Lambda, API Gateway, Rekognition, and DynamoDB. By the end of this chapter, you will be able to autonomously build your own distributed web applications.

This part has the following chapters:

- *Chapter 3, Building a Recipe-Sharing Application*
- *Chapter 4, Building a Serverless Recipe-Sharing Application*
- *Chapter 5, Implementing an Image Analyzer to Detect Photo Friendliness*
- *Chapter 6, Architecting a Content Translation Pipeline*

3
Building a Recipe-Sharing Application

A **web application** is a software program that is accessible from a web browser, such as Google Chrome or Mozilla Firefox, through the internet and can be as simple and informative as the example in *Chapter 2*, where you made your CV available to end users, up to including complex business logic and critical data management capabilities.

A web application can be decomposed into two parts: the **frontend** and the **backend**. The frontend, visible to users, is commonly built using HTML, CSS, JavaScript, and modern frameworks such as React.js or Vue.js. The backend will handle business logic, authentication, data processing, and communication with external services and databases, and is normally developed using programming languages such as Python, Java, or C#. The communication between the frontend and the backend is done typically through an **application programming interface** (**API**), allowing developers to abstract the complexity and efficiently reuse functionality across different applications.

In this chapter, you will work on an application for sharing recipes, where a user can create, delete, or read their recipes. Moreover, you will implement both a backend and a frontend to develop a fully functional web application.

In summary, this chapter covers the following topics in order:

- What you are going to build – an application to share recipes
- How you are going to build it – using S3 and CloudFront for the frontend, EC2 to host your API and DynamoDB as the data store for your recipes
- Building it – through CloudFormation and using the AWS console
- How to improve the solution – improve the monitoring and application logging, enforce secure protocols to access your application, and implement authentication

By the end of this chapter, you will have hands-on experience in building a dynamic web application on AWS, leveraging different services for specific purposes, and understanding the basics of frontend and backend development.

Technical requirements

To build and deploy your own recipe-sharing application, you need to have access to an AWS account, and optionally a domain if you want to implement secure communication through HTTPS. It is important to recall that, as you will see from the chapter, we offer a second option configured with HTTP that does not require the ownership of a domain.

Also, this book has a dedicated folder within its GitHub repository, where you can find the necessary code snippets to follow along: `https://github.com/PacktPublishing/AWS-Cloud-Projects/tree/main/chapter3/code`.

Scenario

In the last chapter, you worked on a personal website to share your CV, which is already becoming popular among recruiters, and other peers are looking for similar ways to share their resumes. That is great for your professional life, and you start thinking about how cloud technologies could help you in your side projects and hobbies; one of those has to do with your cooking skills.

You spend a lot of your free time creating recipes and reinventing desserts, and you usually write them down in a notebook. In parallel, you have started your own profile on social media, and you already have 800,000 followers that react to the photos of your dishes and ask you for the recipes. Because you are getting so popular, friends and family have started calling you "the chef," and often ask you for some suggestions for specific recipes that they have tried in the past.

Up till now, you have had to go search in your recipe notebook, take a photo, and share it, but with time and the number of recipes you have authored, it is becoming unmanageable, and you need to think of an alternative.

While getting familiar with cloud technologies, you start looking for alternatives to your current method of sharing recipes for your second cloud project, a project called Recipe Sharing Application.

Requirements

Before we start answering *how* we are going to solve this problem, it is important to clarify *what* we are going to build and structure it in a clear and concise list of requirements, as we introduced in *Chapter 1* and exemplified in *Chapter 2*.

In this project, you want to develop a recipe-sharing application to provide a convenient platform for people to discover, share, and access different recipes. Unlike the previous chapter, this application will need to handle dynamic content inherent to recipe management. There are different key personas that will access your application:

- **Platform admin**: The platform owner, who may want to create a new recipe, maintain it, or even delete it.
- **End users/consumers**: The end user, who uses the platform for accessing a specific recipe, and should not be able to create, change, or delete any record.

Actual implementation should be the last step of application development, and an accurate and detailed requirement-gathering exercise is key to defining a clear development plan.

The technologies you use, the services you adopt, and the architecture you design should be the consequence of the requirements, technical and non-technical, that you list to achieve your objective.

Business requirements

After the market study you perform, and the amount of likes and comments you get during the week, you conclude that people tend to spend more time cooking on Fridays and Saturdays, especially for dinnertime. You also analyze the geo-distribution of your users, and 85% are located in the US, 12% in Europe, and the remaining 3% are spread across the globe.

You are approached by a food delivery service that wants to sign an ads contract with you, but they only agree if you reach a total of 100,000 active users in your application. Until then, you will have no revenue stream for your application.

Based on these findings and the potential revenue opportunity, you have identified the following key business requirements:

- Reach 100,000 users globally before the end of the year
- Increase presence in Europe
- Become cost-effectiveness to support growth without significant cost

Functional requirements

Your application should serve two different profiles: *admins* and *end users*. For the initial project, you will start with two different pages, `/user` for the end users and `/admin` for admins, to support the two different personas.

You also aim to create a seamless experience through a simple UI. Additionally, you want your application to be responsive and support different devices, such as tablets, mobile phones, and laptops.

One crucial step for describing the functional requirements is creating a mockup of the interface, as shown in *Figures 3.1*, *3.2*, and *3.3*.

Figure 3.1 – UI mockup home page

Let us break down the different functionalities and interfaces:

- `/user`:

    - Access the list of recipe titles
    - Ability to choose a specific recipe and access all the details
    - Responsive

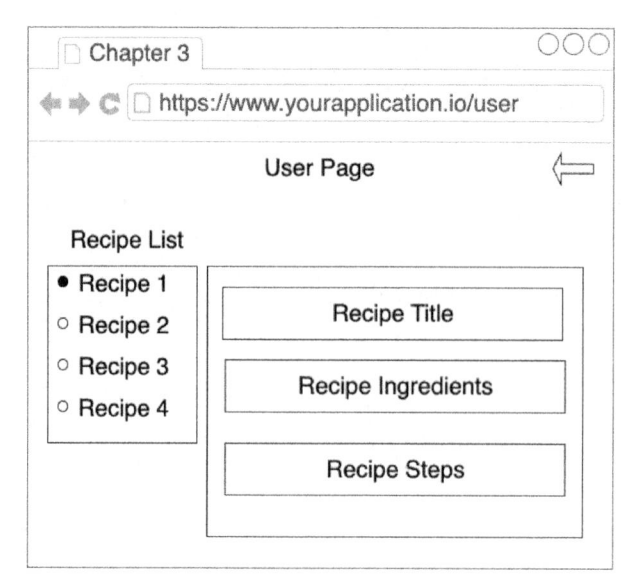

Figure 3.2 – The User Page UI mockup

- `/admin`:
  - Access the list of recipe titles
  - Ability to delete recipes
  - Support recipe creation
  - Control the maximum amount of ingredients, steps, and recipes supported
  - Responsive

Figure 3.3 – The Admin Page UI mockup

Non-functional requirements

Your application needs to handle spiky access patterns since expected utilization should only increase close to meal times. Also, you plan to increase your user base in Europe in the upcoming months, so you need to prepare your application to serve users globally. Also, cost-effectiveness is crucial since you do not have an income stream from your application. To summarize, here is what you need:

- Global distribution to serve users spread across the globe
- Auto-scaling to handle the spiky usage pattern
- Cost-effectiveness

Technical requirements

As stated in the *Functional requirements* section, you want to support multiple devices, so your application needs to be responsive to keep a consistent and good user experience. So, for the frontend, you want a framework that simplifies responsiveness and accelerates the development process. For the backend, you want to adopt Python as the programming language due to its simplicity, versatility, and large ecosystem of libraries and frameworks as well as the support for the AWS SDK. Besides all the interaction with AWS services, you will need to develop your API and for that, you choose FastAPI, a modern web framework built in Python and designed to be highly performant, user friendly, and lightweight. Here's what we will use:

- Modern frontend framework – React.js
- Backend programming language – Python
- FastAPI as the framework for API development

Data requirements

In your application, you are dealing with recipes, and there are several ways to store them. Recipes can be stored as single documents, and there is no relationship between records or items. You do not expect to run any complex queries over your data, and instead, you want to implement simple operations to do the following:

- **List the recipes**: Present a list of the recipes created.
- **Delete a recipe**: If an admin no longer wants a specific recipe to be part of the portfolio, it should be possible to delete the item.
- **Create a recipe**: Create a new recipe to share with the users.

Also, you are aiming for a highly scalable data store that requires minimum to no maintenance effort, ideally a management service. As the structure of your recipe document, you designed `recipe_example.json`:

```
{    "ID":"GUID",
  "Title":"recipe title",
  "Ingredients":[…],
  "Steps":[…]  }
```

Considering the average size of a recipe containing 10 steps and 10 ingredients, you reach a value of 1 KB per recipe. In terms of read operations, assuming that for 20,000 concurrent users during peak time, you have 20,000 concurrent read operations, and you want to ensure performance consistency even during peak hours.

Architecture patterns

The AWS Architecture Center offers a comprehensive collection of resources crafted by cloud architecture experts from AWS Partners, with solutions that are tested and recommended and can be used as a starting point. For this project, AWS presents an architecture pattern that fully applies to your scenario: *Deploy a React-based single-page application to Amazon S3 and CloudFront* (`https://docs.aws.amazon.com/prescriptive-guidance/latest/patterns/deploy-a-react-based-single-page-application-to-amazon-s3-and-cloudfront.html`). Reading this prescriptive guidance will give you an overview of the process you will follow.

To dive deep into each AWS service, the AWS documentation is probably the best source of information. Each service has its own documentation, and it is highly recommended to have a look and go through it to grasp both basic to more advanced concepts. Moreover, it is important to understand the role of AWS in your projects. AWS will support, host, and help you with your requirements, but generic web development knowledge is essential. Before proceeding with the implementation, it's crucial to understand some key concepts related to your application architecture. For example, you should be able to answer the following questions:

- What is a **single-page application** (**SPA**) and how does it differ from traditional web applications?
- What is the role of an API in your application? Why do you need one?

For the first question, a **SPA** is a web application that loads a single HTML page and dynamically updates that page as the user interacts with the app. In contrast to traditional multi-page applications, where each user action requires loading a new page from the server, SPAs load all the necessary HTML, CSS, and JavaScript files initially, and subsequent interactions occur seamlessly through JavaScript and requests to the server.

Ensure that you can answer the remaining ones to build solid knowledge before jumping into AWS.

Architecture

By now, you should be familiar with the technologies you are going to use, and you may already have a small proof of concept working locally. The next step is to create your diagram with the architecture that will support your project. *Figure 3.4* is an abstract diagram referencing the main layers that compose your full architecture and is a good starting point for architecture design.

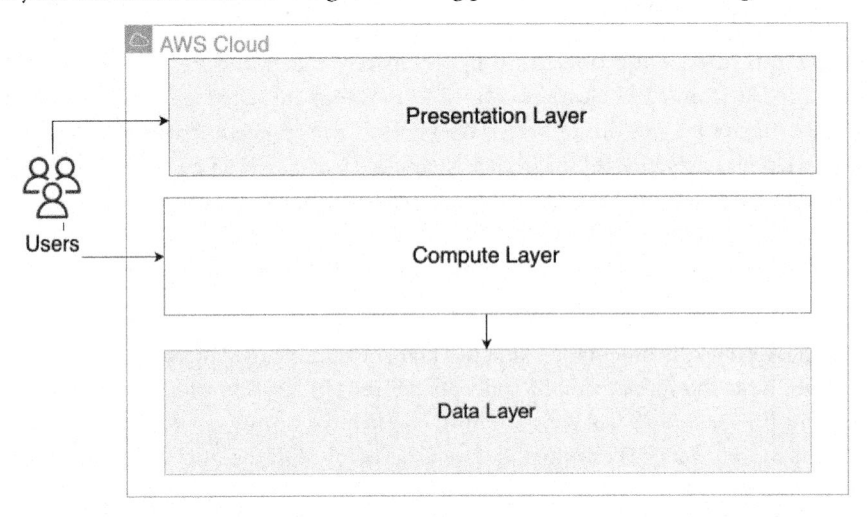

Figure 3.4 – Abstract architecture

End users interact with the presentation layer to get the frontend application, and perform requests to the compute layer, but never access the data layer directly. Instead, the compute layer is responsible for performing the data operations through an API.

Designing your API is crucial to ensure you use the right model to perform all the data operations you will need, and both data and functional requirements should be taken into consideration. *Figure 3.5* represents your initial API structure based on the analysis performed.

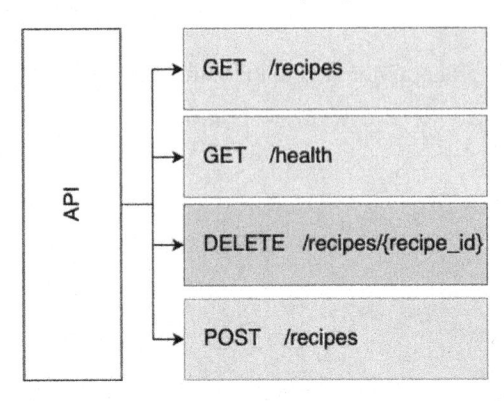

Figure 3.5 – API structure

Here's the breakdown:

- `GET /recipes`: This gets the list of recipes.
- `GET /health`: This is a simple health check endpoint.
- `DELETE /recipes/{recipe_id}`: This deletes a specific recipe with a defined ID.
- `POST /recipes`: This creates a new recipe record.

With all this in mind, you should be able to proceed with the complete architecture with the respective AWS services. For your frontend, like the solution used in the previous chapter, you will use Amazon S3 and Amazon CloudFront to serve your application. The compute layer is implemented in Amazon EC2, and that's where you plan to deploy your API. For the data layer, after considering all the requirements, you end up choosing Amazon DynamoDB as your data store. For simplicity, you will group both the compute and data layers in a single layer called the backend, and by the end, your architecture diagram should look like *Figure 3.6*.

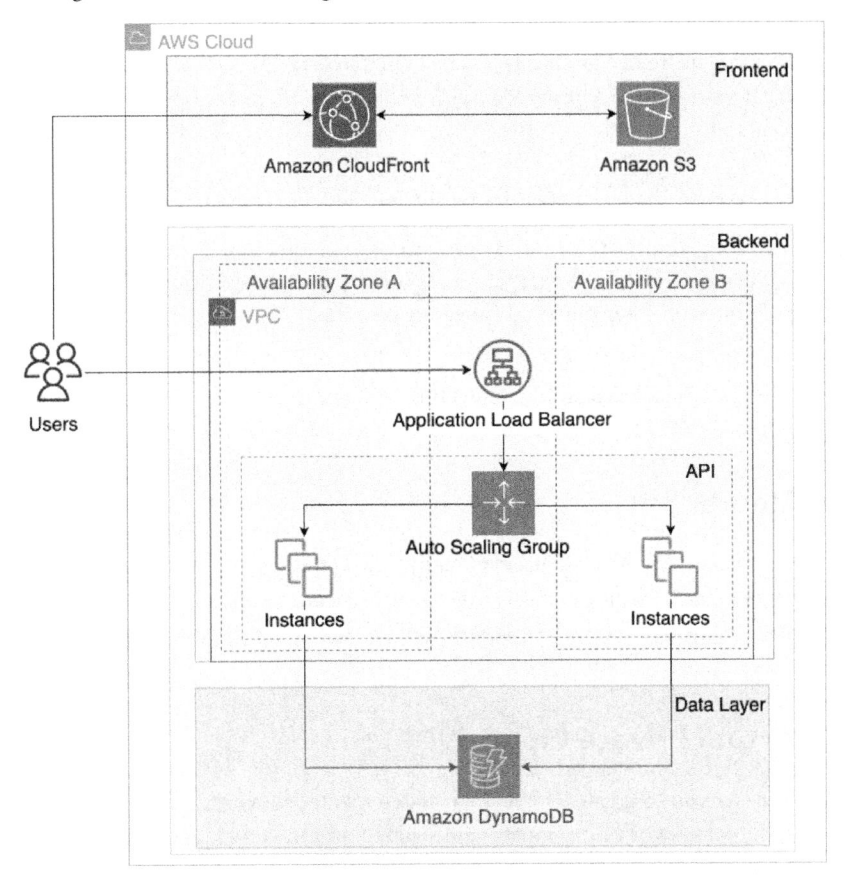

Figure 3.6 – AWS architecture for your recipe-sharing application

With the high-level architecture in place, let's dive deeper into the specific AWS services you've chosen to build this solution and understand how they align with the requirements defined earlier.

AWS services

AWS has available, at the time of this writing, more than 200 services to support different purposes and with different levels of management. Choosing AWS services is an important exercise, and the choices should be driven by the pre-defined requirements and not the opposite. In this section, you will explore the services adopted in your solution, and understand how they align with the requirements defined. Parts of the services have already been covered in the previous chapters. So, to avoid content duplication, we will briefly mention the advantages of the current use case and reference the chapter where you can find a detailed explanation.

Amazon S3

Your frontend is a SPA built in React.js, and it translates into static files, such as HTML, CSS, and JavaScript, that should be treated as objects. As explained in *Chapter 2*, S3 is a scalable, highly available, and durable object storage service provided by AWS, and overall, a cost-effective solution for hosting static websites, including SPAs.

> **Important note**
> S3 is designed to guarantee the 11 9s of data durability. This means that, if you store 10,000 objects in S3, you could expect to lose at most one of those objects every 10 million years due to hardware failures or other potential causes of data loss.

If you want to dive deep into Amazon S3 architecture, we recommend watching the *AWS re:Invent 2023 - Dive deep on Amazon S3* session: https://www.youtube.com/watch?v=sYDJYqvNeXU.

Amazon CloudFront

You plan for your application to serve users globally and want to ensure a secure access protocol with HTTPS not supported in S3. These are just two of many reasons to include CloudFront as part of your architecture, and for a more detailed explanation of the service and its advantages, we recommend checking the *AWS services* section in *Chapter 2*.

Amazon Virtual Private Cloud (VPC)

Amazon VPC allows you to create a logically isolated virtual network in the AWS cloud. It enables you to define a virtual networking environment where you can launch and manage AWS resources, such as **Amazon Elastic Compute Cloud (EC2)** instances, in a secure and controlled manner. As part of the VPC configuration, you can define your network topology with multiple subnets, which can be public or private, meaning with or without internet access, respectively, to segregate your traffic and increase the security posture.

Amazon EC2

From the technical requirements, you decide to develop your own API, and now you need a service to deploy and host it. Amazon EC2 allows you to provision virtual machines (instances) inside your VPC to run your applications, or, in this case, your API. EC2 offers a wide range of instance types with different configurations of CPU, memory, storage, and networking capacity, allowing you to choose the right instance type for your specific application requirements, ensuring optimal performance and cost-effectiveness.

EC2 offers different pricing models that bring additional cost-effectiveness if you have a clear view of your requirements, as well as an on-demand option with a pure pay-as-you-go model, which is what you will choose for this project.

If you want to learn more about EC2 pricing models and how they work, you can read about it in the AWS documentation: `https://docs.aws.amazon.com/whitepapers/latest/how-aws-pricing-works/amazon-ec2.html`.

Application Load Balancer (ALB)

An ALB is a fully managed load-balancing solution designed to distribute traffic across multiple targets, namely EC2 instances. Being a managed solution, it is highly scalable by design and automatically scales according to the traffic load. Moreover, and considering your requirements, ALB brings two main advantages:

- **Health checking**: Every load balancer needs to have at least one target group, and you can configure health checks to your targets to ensure traffic is only sent to healthy targets, avoiding a bad user experience and increasing the resilience and fault-tolerance levels of your application.
- **SSL termination**: ALBs support SSL termination, offloading the computational burden of encryption and decryption from your EC2 instances.

ALBs also integrate with AWS Web Application Firewall out of the box, and this would bring additional security against common attacks, such as SQL injection, **cross-site scripting** (**XSS**), and other web application vulnerabilities.

Amazon DynamoDB

Choosing your database solution should be driven by your data and requirements. For this project, you need to store recipes as single documents. Also, you have defined requirements around query consistency and high performance, even with many concurrent query operations.

Amazon DynamoDB is a fully managed NoSQL database service, more specifically a key-value and document store that delivers single-digit millisecond performance at any scale. By choosing DynamoDB, you will leverage the native high availability due to data replication performed under the hood with a pay-as-you-go model and automatic scaling to handle spiky workloads, like the case of your application.

> Important note
>
> DynamoDB is by nature a distributed service, but this should not be a blocker even if you need high consistency. DynamoDB offers two types of consistency models: eventually consistent (default) and strongly consistent. With the last option, you can ensure high consistency and data integrity by ensuring the data returned is always up to date.

If you want to know more about the story of DynamoDB, the lessons learned after the 10th anniversary, and the future plans, check out this article from Amazon Science: `https://www.amazon.science/latest-news/amazons-dynamodb-10-years-later`.

AWS CloudFormation

In *Chapter 1*, we briefly touched on AWS CloudFormation as a tool to provision infrastructure, but considering this is the first chapter where it will be extensively used, we will dive a bit deeper into it and explain it in more detail.

CloudFormation is an **Infrastructure as Code** (**IaC**) service that allows you to define and provision AWS resources in a declarative way, described as template documents that can be written either in YAML or JSON. Like any IaC tool, CloudFormation enables infrastructure automation in its life cycle, from creation and update to deletion. It supports drift detection to identify any changes that may be performed outside the template, which can cause inconsistencies. Making manual changes to resources managed by CloudFormation is not recommended because it can result in configuration drift, where the actual state of the resources differs from what is defined in the template.

One of the key benefits of CloudFormation is its ability to manage and provision resources as a single unit, known as a stack. This stack can include resources from various AWS services, such as EC2 instances, VPCs, S3 buckets, and more. CloudFormation takes care of creating and configuring these resources in the correct order, based on the dependencies defined in the template.

Coding the solution

By now, you should have a solid understanding of the core services used, the reasons behind the services chosen, and most importantly, how everything aligns with your requirements. You are finally able to proceed with the actual implementation.

Cloning the project

If you are following along with the previous chapters, you should have already cloned the repository associated with this book, but if you just arrived, start by cloning the repo, or optionally download the repository as a ZIP file. The repository is structured with folders for each chapter, and all the code for this chapter is located in `chapter3/code`.

Inside the `chapter3/code` folder, you will find three subfolders, as shown in *Figure 3.7*:

- `frontend`: This contains the code for your frontend
- `backend`: This contains the code for your API
- `platform`: This contains two different CloudFormation templates to deploy the main infrastructure for your application

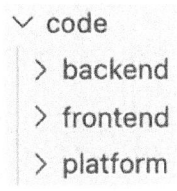

```
∨ code
  > backend
  > frontend
  > platform
```

Figure 3.7 – The Chapter 3 folder structure

Why do you have two different templates available?

A SPA has two types of connections: one to retrieve the frontend resources from CloudFront, and another to communicate with the backend through JavaScript API requests from the browser, as represented in *Figure 3.6*.

While CloudFront automatically provides HTTPS for delivering your frontend resources, your API requires additional configuration. To secure the API with HTTPS, you'll need to own a domain and issue a certificate to prove ownership.

We understand that you may not own one domain right now nor want to purchase one, and that should not be a blocker to deploy your application, so we've got you covered!

We've worked on two different options for this section, and thus the two different templates in the `platform` folder. The following table maps the options with the templates, and will help you choose the right path:

	Description	**CloudFormation Template**	**Recommended**
Option 1	You either own a domain or are willing to purchase one to configure HTTPS communication to your API	`ch3-https-complete.yaml`	Yes
Option 2	You want to test the application without owning or purchasing a domain	`ch3-http.yaml`	No

Table 3.1 – Mapping between the CloudFormation template and the option you want to follow

A detailed explanation of the differences between HTTP and HTTPS is beyond the scope of this book, but if you want to know more, you can read the following article: `https://aws.amazon.com/compare/the-difference-between-https-and-http/`.

The steps you follow depend on the option you choose. To simplify the process, steps specific to option 1 will be marked as *(Option 1 Only)*, and steps for option 2 will be marked as *(Option 2 Only)*. Steps without any marking apply to both options. Consider that, even if you choose option 2, it's recommended to read the HTTPS configuration steps for option 1 to gain more knowledge.

> **Important note**
> While this application and CloudFormation templates are designed to work in any AWS region, if you choose option 1, you must use the same region for creating the certificate and deploying the solution. This is because option 1 requires creating a certificate using AWS Certificate Manager, which is a regional service.

Section 1 – DNS configuration and certificate issuing (option 1 only)

To configure HTTPS, you need to own a domain and prove ownership by obtaining a certificate, and this section covers configuring your DNS service and issuing a certificate for your domain.

Domains are purchased from domain registrars, which manage the reservation and registration of internet domain names. In AWS, Route 53 can serve as both your domain registrar for purchasing domains as well as a DNS service for managing them. Alternatively, you can choose popular third-party registrars, such as GoDaddy or Namecheap, among others, to purchase your domain.

DNS configuration in Route 53

For this example, we just bought a domain from a third-party provider, and we will demonstrate how to set up DNS management in Route 53 for a domain bought outside Route 53.

From the console, go to the Route 53 service by typing `route 53` in the search bar, as shown in *Figure 3.8*, or you can access it directly through the following link: https://console.aws.amazon.com/route53.

Figure 3.8 – Console access to Route 53 service

On the left pane of the Route 53 console, do the following:

1. Click on **Hosted Zones**.
2. Then, select **Create Hosted Zone**.
3. Fill the **Domain name** field with the domain you own (in our case, it's `awscloudprojects.site`).
4. Select **Public Hosted Zone** as the type.
5. Press **Create Hosted Zone**.

Your configuration window should look like *Figure 3.9*, except for the **Domain name** field.

Figure 3.9 – Route 53 hosted zone creation form

If you return to the **Hosted Zones** menu, you should be able to see your domain listed. To access the nameservers associated with your hosted zone, follow these steps:.

1. Click on the domain you created.
2. Take note of the associated nameservers as you will need them to configure the DNS next.

You should have four nameserver values as part of your hosted zone details as shown in *Figure 3.10*:

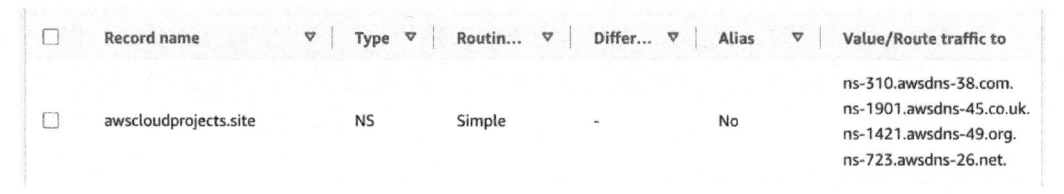

Record name	Type	Routin...	Differ...	Alias	Value/Route traffic to
awscloudprojects.site	NS	Simple	-	No	ns-310.awsdns-38.com. ns-1901.awsdns-45.co.uk. ns-1421.awsdns-49.org. ns-723.awsdns-26.net.

Figure 3.10 – Hosted zone details

The following steps involve updating the nameservers for your domain, which may vary depending on your domain registrar. Regardless of your registrar, AWS provides step-by-step guides for configuring nameservers with popular registrars: `https://docs.aws.amazon.com/Route53/latest/DeveloperGuide/migrate-dns-domain-in-use.html`.

> **Important note**
> A **hosted zone** in Amazon Route 53 is a container that holds all the DNS records and routing configurations for a specific domain name and its subdomains. It allows you to manage and route traffic to your AWS resources or external resources based on your defined routing policies.

Certificate issuing

You will now proceed with the certificate-issuing process with the **AWS Certificate Manager (ACM)** service. From the console, go to the ACM service at `https://console.aws.amazon.com/acm`.

Figure 3.11 – Console access to the ACM service

To issue a certificate for your domain, you need to follow these steps:

1. Click on the **Request a certificate** button.
2. On the **Certificate Type** screen, select the **Request a public certificate** option and click **Next**.
3. Fill out the required information on the form. Most fields can be left with their default values, but for the **Fully qualified domain name** field, you have two options:

   - **Option A**: Generate separate certificates for each subdomain (e.g., `app.example.com`, `api.example.com`).
   - **Option B**: Use a wildcard certificate that will be valid for all subdomains (e.g., `*.example.com`).

4. Ensure that **Validation method** is set to **DNS validation**, as recommended by AWS.
5. Click **Request**.

Figure 3.12 depicts the final state of the form, containing all the necessary fields.

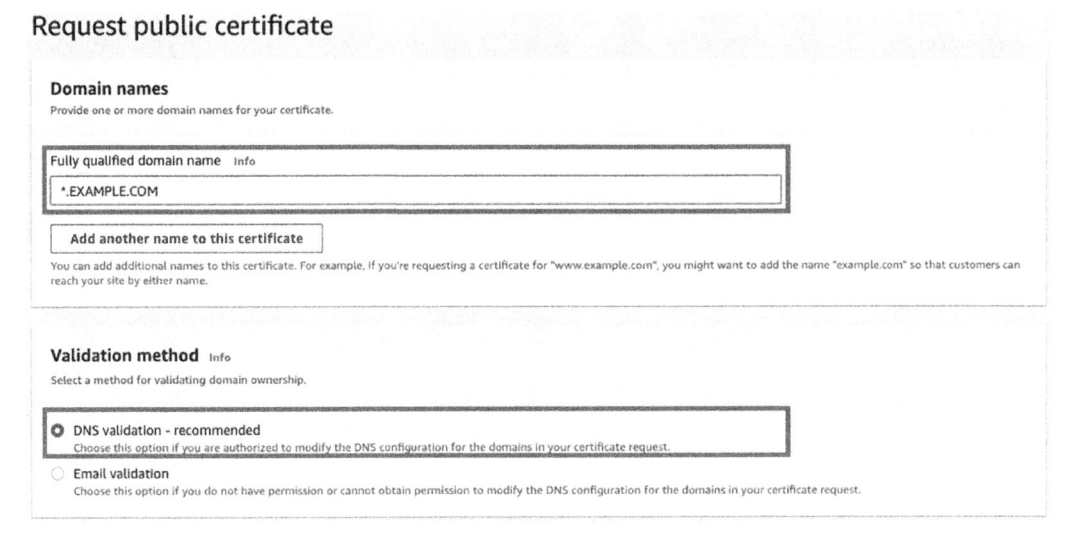

Figure 3.12 – Certificate request form

After requesting the certificate, you will see it listed with the **pending validation** status. To validate the certificate and prove domain ownership, you need to create a DNS record in your hosted zone.

If your domain is managed by Route 53, you can click **Create Records in Route 53** for an easier setup, as you can see in *Figure 3.13*.

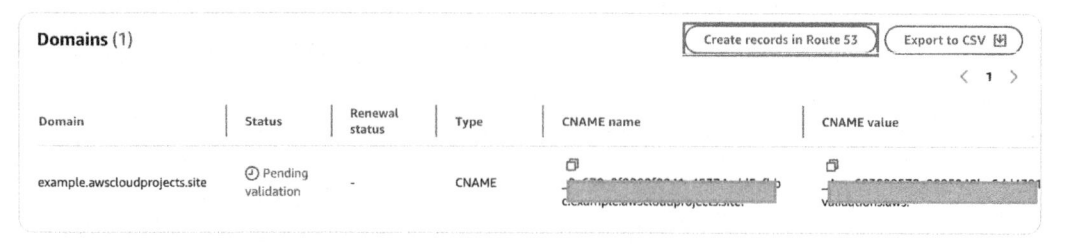

Figure 3.13 – Certificate validation with a DNS record

Before proceeding, you need to wait until the status changes to **Issued** as in *Figure 3.14*. If everything is well configured, it should not take more than 10 minutes, but it can take up to a couple of hours, as per the AWS documentation (https://aws.amazon.com/certificate-manager/faqs/).

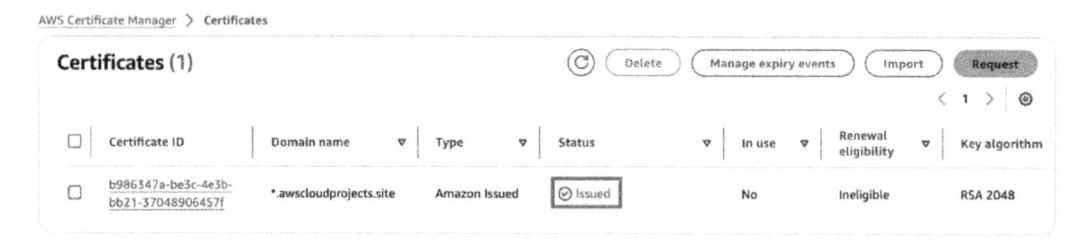

Figure 3.14 – ACM certificates list

The final step is to note down `certificateARN`, which you'll need to input as a parameter in the CloudFormation template:

1. Navigate to the ACM console in the region where you created the certificate.
2. Select **List Certificates** from the left pane.
3. Locate your "Issued" certificate, as shown in *Figure 3.14*.
4. Click on the certificate, and under **Certificate status**, you'll find **ARN**.

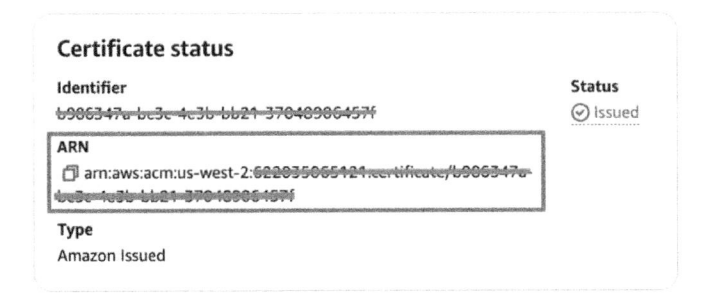

Figure 3.15 – Certificate ARN access

> **Important note**
> In AWS, an ARN is a unique identifier for an AWS service. It follows this format: `arn:part
ition:service:region:account-id:resource-type/resource-id`.

Section 2 – Solution deployment

Now, you will deploy the infrastructure to support your application, both the frontend and backend, with the CloudFormation templates available in your `chapter3/code` folder. Depending on the option you choose, you pick a different template, and it will also create different components, as you can see in the next table.

	Option 1 (HTTPS configured)	**Option 2** (HTTP configured)
Template	`ch3-https-complete.yaml`	`ch3-http.yaml`
Frontend	CloudFront and S3	CloudFront and S3
Backend	<ul><li>1 VPC</li><li>2 public subnets</li><li>2 private subnets</li><li>1 private EC2 instance</li><li>1 ALB</li><li>1 NAT gateway</li><li>EC2 instance role with minimum permissions to interact with DynamoDB recipes table</li></ul>	<ul><li>1 VPC</li><li>1 public subnets</li><li>1 public EC2 instance</li><li>EC2 instance role with minimum permissions to interact with DynamoDB recipes table</li></ul>
Data store	DynamoDB	DynamoDB

Table 3.2 – Resource creation for each CloudFormation template

From the console, go to the CloudFormation service at https://console.aws.amazon.com/cloudformation/. If you are following option 1, ensure you choose the same region you did for the certificate in the drop-down region list located in the upper-right corner of the console, as shown in *Figure 3.16*.

Figure 3.16 – Console access to CloudFormation

To proceed with stack creation, follow these steps:

1. Click on **Create Stack**.
2. In the **Prerequisite – Prepare Template** section, select **Choose an existing template**.
3. In the **Specify Template** section, choose **Upload a template file**.
4. Click on **Choose file**.
5. Select the template from the chapter3/code/platform folder according to the option you are following.
6. Click **Next**.

Your **Create Stack** window should look like *Figure 3.17*.

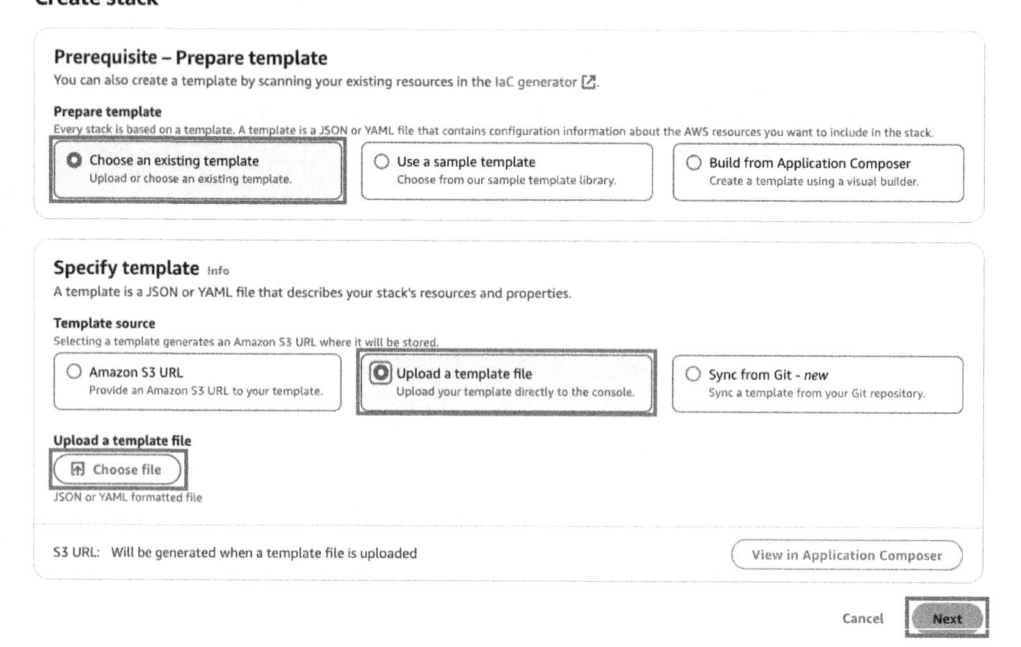

Figure 3.17 – The CloudFormation Create stack form

The next step is to configure the parameters in your CloudFormation stack. Parameters allow you to create dynamic and environment-specific resource configurations, promoting better security and maintainability of your infrastructure as code. In *Table 3.3*, we explain the purpose of each parameter and which ones apply to your chosen option.

Parameter	Description	Option 1 (HTTPS configured)	Option 2 (HTTP configured)
InstanceType	Choose the EC2 instance type from the four available options; the default is the free tier, t3.micro.	Yes	Yes
LatestAmiId	The **Amazon Machine Image (AMI)** to be used in your EC2 instance. By default, it will use the most recent AMI.	Yes	Yes
GitRepoURL	The code repo URL (e.g., https://github.com/packtpublishing/aws-cloud-projects).	Yes	Yes
ALBCertificateArn	The ARN of your recently created certificate.	Yes	No

Table 3.3 – CloudFormation template parameters

In *Figure 3.18*, you can see an example of the expected state of the **Parameters** window, if you followed option 1. For option 2, the only difference is that `ALBCertificateArn` does not exist.

Figure 3.18 – Stack parameters in CloudFormation

Proceed further, acknowledge the creation of `IAMPolicy` for controlling API access to the DynamoDB table, and click **Submit**.

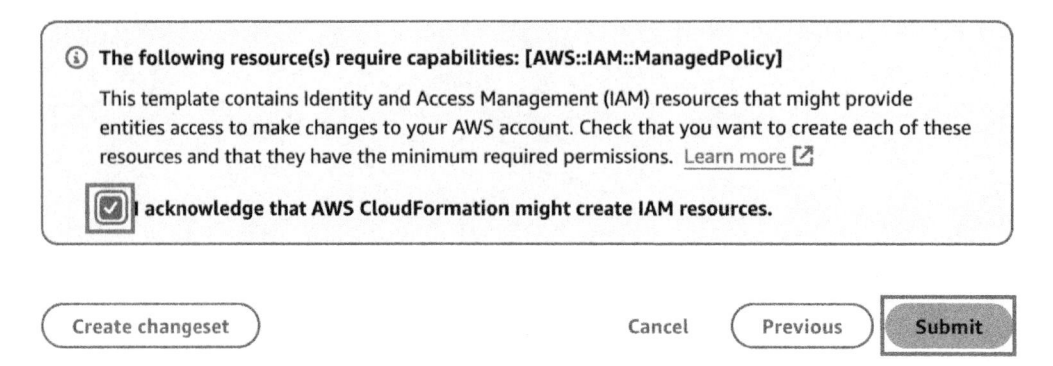

Figure 3.19 – CloudFormation stack submission

The resources for your application are now being provisioned. You need to wait until the stack status changes to **CREATE_COMPLETE**. You should be able to see a status like *Figure 3.20*.

Stacks

chapter-3
2024-08-29 18:33:43 UTC+0100
✓ CREATE_COMPLETE

Figure 3.20 – CloudFormation stack created status

In our case, it took around 10 minutes for the stack to be deployed, but take into consideration that this may vary.

Section 3 – Additional configurations (option 1 only)

You are almost there! You just need one additional configuration to have your application up and running, which is the creation of a subdomain record in your hosted zone pointing to the ALB. This will also enable a friendly API name such as `api.<your_domain>`. Follow these steps:

1. Go to the **Route 53** console.
2. Select your domain's hosted zone.
3. Click on **Create record**.
4. In the **Create record** form, fill in the desired subdomain in the **Record name** field (e.g., `api`).
5. For **Record type**, select **A - IPv4 address**.
6. Click on the toggle under **Record name** to enable **Alias**.
7. In the **Route traffic to** dropdown, select **Alias to Application and Classic Load Balancer**.
8. Choose the AWS region where your application is deployed.
9. In the **Choose Load Balancer** section, select the ALB associated with your CloudFormation stack.
10. If you have multiple load balancers in the selected region, you can find the correct load balancer DNS name by checking the **Outputs** section of your CloudFormation stack in the CloudFormation console.
11. Click the **Create records** button to save the new record.

Your record creation form should look like *Figure 3.21*.

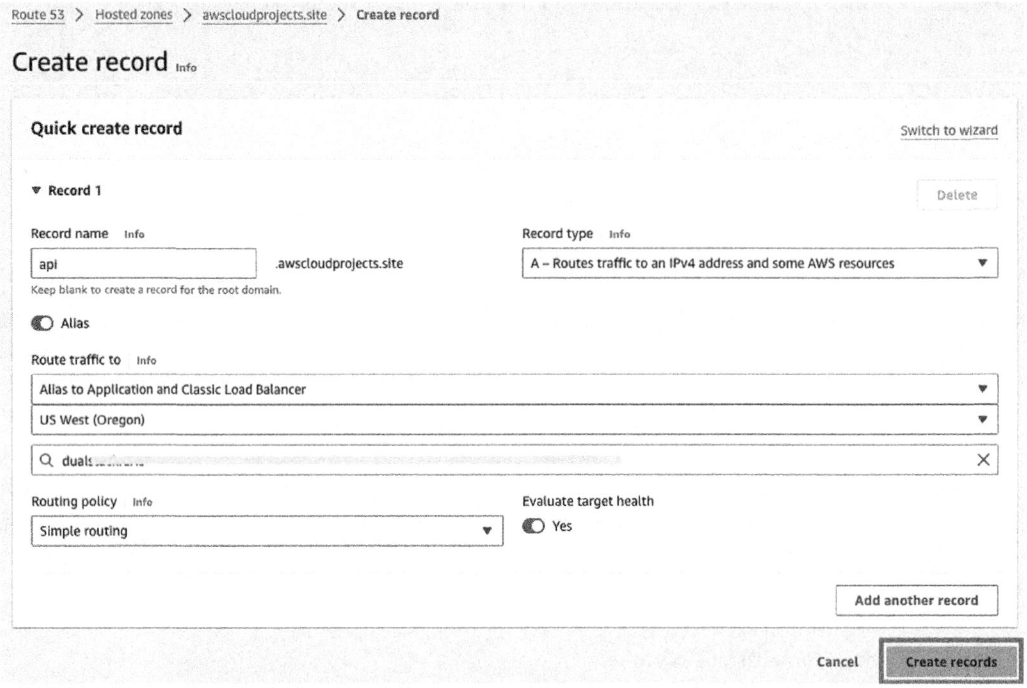

Figure 3.21 – The Route 53 alias record for your ALB

Before you move to the next section, take note of the DNS record you created, as you will need to use it in the next section.

Section 4 – Frontend configuration and deployment

The CloudFormation stack has already deployed the required services for the frontend, and the only pending step is to copy the application files to S3. But prior to that, you will need to modify some configurations in your application. Since React development is not the primary focus of this book, we've created the config file with parameters to customize your application.

Navigate to the .../`frontend/src/configs/configs.tsx` file within the project folder, where the configuration file is located.

The config file is composed of seven configuration variables:

- `CONFIG_MAX_INGREDIENTS`: Max ingredients in a recipe
- `CONFIG_MAX_STEPS`: Max steps in a recipe
- `CONFIG_MAX_RECIPES`: Max recipes supported

- `CONFIG_USER_PAGE_TITLE`: Title for user page
- `CONFIG_ADMIN_PAGE_TITLE`: Title for admin page
- `CONFIG_appConfig`: Object with page title and icon (icons in `/frontend/public/`)
- `API_URL`: API endpoint

```
code > frontend > src > configs > ⊛ configs.tsx > ...
 1   export const CONFIG_MAX_INGREDIENTS = 20;
 2   export const CONFIG_MAX_STEPS = 10;
 3   export const CONFIG_MAX_RECIPES = 4;
 4   export const CONFIG_ADMIN_PAGE_TITLE = "Admin";
 5   export const CONFIG_USER_PAGE_TITLE = "User Page";
 6   export const appConfig = {
 7     title: "My Recipe Sharing App",
 8     iconFileName: "ch3_link.png",
 9   };
10   export const API_URL = "https://api.awscloudprojects.site";
```

Figure 3.22 – Example of a configuration file (config.tsx)

All the configs besides `API_URL` are optional and serve solely to apply small application customizations, so we will focus now on the API endpoint configuration. `API_URL`, as the name suggests, is the endpoint used to send requests, and depending on the option you are following, you need to get this value from different places.

Solution for option 1

In this option, you should have by now created the Route 53 record with an alias record for your ALB, and that's the value you should use for the `API_URL` parameter.

For example, in our case, as per *Figure 3.22*, we created an `api.awscloudprojects.site` record, so `API_URL` should be set to `https://api.awscloudprojects.site` (don't forget to include the protocol).

Solution for option 2

If you are following this option, it means you don't have a DNS record created for your API, nor an ALB provisioned. Moreover, because you didn't set up HTTPS, the protocol used to access your API is HTTP. So, in this case, you need to provide the EC2 public DNS.

You can access the EC2 running instances through `https://console.aws.amazon.com/ec2/home?-Instances:instanceState=running`, but optionally, you can access the DNS of the newly deployed instance in the CloudFormation **Outputs** tab for your stack, with the `APIDNSName` output.

After setting the `API_URL` config, you can save the file and proceed to the build process, which involves several steps to convert the code into a production-ready bundle that can be served to web browsers. In our example, we used `npm` as the package manager, so you need to run the following command:

```
$ npm install && npm run build
```

The result is a folder with the files needed to be copied to our S3 buckets. The folder name may vary but it is typically `build/` or `dist/` and is created at the frontend root, as you can see in *Figure 3.23*.

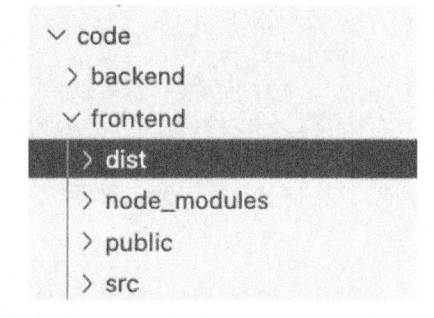

```
v code
  > backend
  v frontend
    > dist
    > node_modules
    > public
    > src
```

Figure 3.23 – Folder structure after build command

Now, the last step is to copy the build folder to S3, with the following instructions:

1. **Locate the S3 bucket**:

    I. First, you need to find the S3 bucket that you created earlier using the CloudFormation template. The name of the bucket should start with `frontend-chapter-3-` followed by a random string of characters (e.g., `frontend-chapter-3-XXXXX`). Click on its name to open it.

    II. Add files from the `dist` folder.

    III. Inside the S3 bucket, click on the **Upload** button. This will allow you to upload files from your local machine to the S3 bucket.

2. **Add the necessary content to the bucket**:

    First click on **Add Files**, locate the `dist` folder on your local machine, select all the files inside the folder, and confirm. Next, on the S3 console, click on **Add folder**, locate the `dist` folder on your local machine, select the `assets` folder, and confirm.

Optionally, you can just drag the content to the S3 window, but despite the method you use, your S3 upload window should look like *Figure 3.24*.

Name	Folder	Type	Size
index-d1565e7a.css	assets/	text/css	19.0 B
index-6fa06235.js	assets/	text/javascript	429.5 KB
ch3_link.png	-	image/png	223.6 KB
ch3_link2.png	-	image/png	220.3 KB
index.html	-	text/html	466.0 B

Figure 3.24 – Frontend files uploaded to S3

> **Note**
> The filenames are auto-generated by the build process, so probably, your names are different than the ones in the preceding figure.

Just make sure that you have the following files:

- `index.html`
- `index-XXXXXX.css`
- `index-XXXXXX.js`
- Static files you may have included in your application, for example, images

After that, at the bottom, click on **Upload**.

You've just finalized all the deployment and configuration of your application, and now is the time to test it.

Section 5 – Testing and exploring your application

This last section is all about testing and exploring your application, and we divided it into two parts: the backend and the frontend. Let's start with the backend!

Testing and exploring the backend

By now, you should have an API running in an EC2 instance, and once again, depending on the option you've chosen, you need to use different URLs for testing and the value you've used for the API_URL parameter in the config.tsx file you updated in the previous section. To test your API, you can send a request to one of the endpoints, and if everything is working properly, you should get a response and a success status code.

To perform the tests, you can define your endpoint as {API_URL}/{ROUTE}, where API_URL is the URL you used in the config.tsx file in the previous section. Here, ROUTE is the specific route you want to reach.

There are different tools to perform the requests, and it is up to you to choose the tool you want to use, but if you prefer a visual tool, you can use, for example, Postman, or instead go with a programmatic approach by running a curl command.

In the following code, you can see an example of a curl command issued to our API endpoint at the /recipes route to get the list of recipes created:

```
$ curl -i 'https://api.awscloudprojects.site/recipes'
HTTP/2 200
date: Wed, 03 Apr 2024 16:06:15 GMT
contente-type: application/json
contente-length: 2
server: nginx/1.18.0 (Ubuntu)
[]
```

Regardless of the method you use, if you try to do a GET request to the /recipes endpoint, you should get an empty object because you haven't created any recipe yet, and a 200 status code of success, which proves the functioning of your API.

Testing and exploring the frontend

For the final test, you will explore the frontend application and ensure all the functionalities you defined in the requirements section work as intended.

To access your frontend, you need to do the following:

1. Go to the **CloudFront** console.
2. Select the distribution you created with the CloudFormation stack. (If you have more than one distribution and you are not sure which one is the one created by the stack, open the CloudFormation service, go to the stack you created earlier, and check the output value for CloudFrontDistributionId.)
3. Copy the URL of the distribution (it should follow the structure https://XXXXXX.cloudfront.net/).

4. If you prefer, you can also get this value from the **Outputs** tab of your CloudFormation stack, with the value of `CloudFrontDistributionUrl`.
5. If you copy and paste the URL into the browser, you should be able to access your newly created application and navigate between the **Users** and **Admin** pages. If you try to access the **Admin** page, you should get the same experience as *Figure 3.25*.

Figure 3.25 – The Recipe Sharing Application Admin page

Because you have not created any recipes yet, the list should be empty, so try creating some recipes, and try to see the difference experience between the **Admin** and **User** pages to ensure the right functional requirements were fulfilled.

If you followed option 1, you should be able to see the recipes being added, deleted, and listed as expected, but for option 2, there are some additional steps to perform.

Enabling HTTP communication in your browser (option 2 only)

Despite security being a constant concern, modern browsers already bring protections to make it easier to maintain a secure posture on the internet. In this example, we are using Google Chrome, but this also applies to other browsers, such as Mozilla Firefox.

If you look closer, on the left of our URL there is an alert saying **Not Secure**, as in *Figure 3.26*.

Figure 3.26 – Recipe Sharing Application Not Secure warning

This happens because HTTP is not a secure protocol, and your application is trying to make HTTP requests to your API. Moreover, your application running in a CloudFront domain is making requests to a different domain over HTTP (an EC2 instance domain), which commonly looks suspicious.

For deeper troubleshooting, you can open the console inside the developer tools, and see that we are getting the following error:

```
Mixed Content: The page at '      ajaxRequestInterceptor.ps.js:1
https://d1phaw0kijgh3n.cloudfront.net/admin' was loaded over
HTTPS, but requested an insecure XMLHttpRequest endpoint '
http://ec2-34-219-18-218.us-west-2.compute.amazonaws.com/recipes'.
This request has been blocked; the content must be served over
HTTPS.
```

Figure 3.27 – Console error example

Only for demo purposes, you can instruct your browser to overpass its default behaviors and accept HTTP connections, but it is very important to highlight that while it may serve for this exercise, it is not a best practice and should not be done regularly.

If you want to skip this blocker, you can do the following:

1. Click on the red **Not Secure** notice/**View site information** button on the left of the URL bar.
2. Go to the site's **Settings**.
3. Scroll down to **Insecure content**.
4. Change from **Block (Default)** to **Allow**.

These instructions apply to Google Chrome and may vary depending on the version or the browser used. After that, your application should work properly and requests will be authorized.

Testing and exploring your DynamoDB table

The last part to test is the integration between your API and your data layer in DynamoDB, where your recipe data is stored. If you want to explore resource creation and deletion, follow these steps:

1. Go to the **DynamoDB** page in your AWS account.
2. Click on **Explore items** on the left menu.
3. Select your recipes table.
4. List the items in your table while you test the operations on your application for creating and deleting recipes. These operations should be reflected in your DynamoDB **Explore items** console.

Figure 3.28 shows how recipes are stored in DynamoDB after recipe creation. As an exercise, compare the structure of your DynamoDB items with the requirements defined at the beginning of the chapter.

Figure 3.28 – Exploring DynamoDB recipes table

Section 6 – Cleaning up

Although we tried to adopt services that are included in the AWS Free Tier, and the majority of the services adopted are serverless and auto-scale based on demand, if you leave your application running, you may incur costs in the future, so this section explains how to delete all the resources in your AWS account associated with this project.

One of the main advantages of using IaC, especially in this CloudFormation example, is the streamlining of infrastructure provision and deletion.

To delete all the resources created, you just need to perform two steps:

1. **Empty bucket**:

    I.   Go to the S3 console in your AWS account.

    II. Select your frontend S3 bucket (the name of the bucket should start with `frontend-chapter-3-` followed by a random string of characters (e.g., `frontend-chapter-3-XXXXX`)).

    III. Click on **Empty** – this will delete all the content inside your bucket.

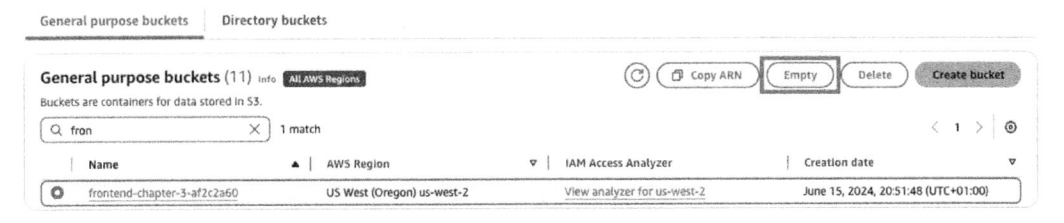

Figure 3.29 – The process of emptying an S3 bucket

2. **Delete the CloudFormation stack**:

    I.   Go to the CloudFormation console in your AWS account.

    II. Select the stack you created.

    III. Click on **Delete**.

> **Note**
>
> If you don't see your CloudFormation stack on the list, try to change the region in the upper-right corner and select the region where you deployed your application. After that, you should proceed with the deletion process described and represented in *Figure 3.30*.

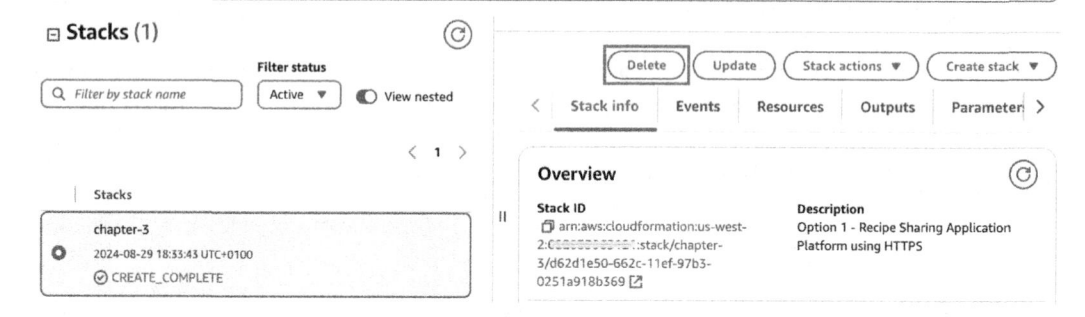

Figure 3.30 – CloudFormation stack deletion

Cleaning up the certificate and DNS management configuration (option 1)

If you followed the first option and created the certificate as well as configured the DNS, you need to perform these additional steps:

1. **Delete the certificate**:

    I.   Go to the **Certificate Manager** console in your AWS account.

    II. Select the certificate you created.

    III. Click on **Delete**.

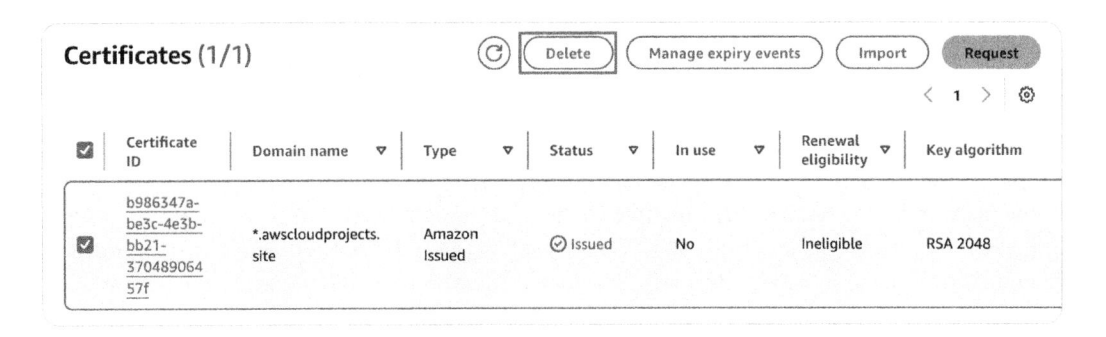

Figure 3.31 – Certificate deletion

> **Note**
> If you don't see your certificate on the list, try to change the region in the upper-right corner and select the region where you deployed your application. After that, you should proceed with the deletion process described and represented in *Figure 3.31*

2. **Clean up the DNS**: If you want to keep managing the DNS in Route 53, you can just delete the record you created for your API:

    I.   Go to the **Route 53** console in your AWS account.
    II. Select **Hosted Zones** on the left pane.
    III. Select the hosted zone you created for your domain.
    IV. Select the record for the API.
    V.   Click on **Delete record**.

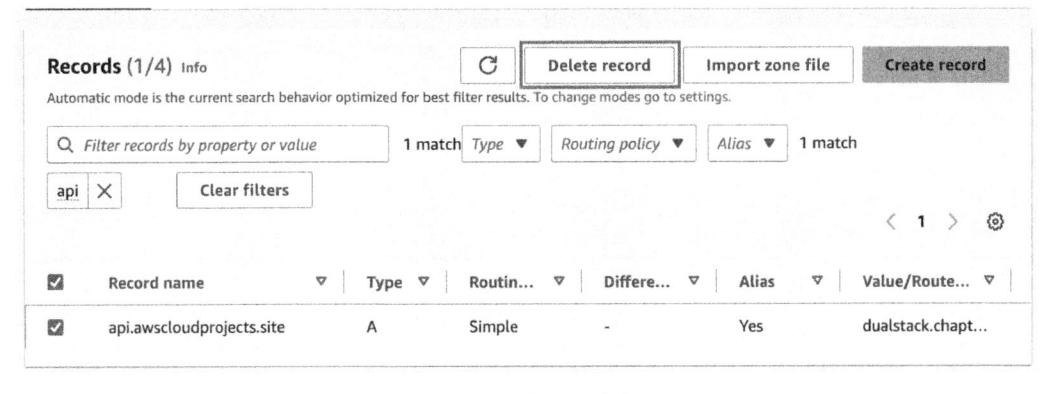

Figure 3.32 – DNS record cleanup

Additionally, if you want to stop using Route 53 for your domain, delete the hosted zone in Route 53 and update the nameservers with your domain registrar to point to your new DNS service.

Future work

Congratulations, you have a fully functional web application to store and share recipes! But for all the projects you develop, it is crucial to keep in mind that there are always points of improvement for your architectures, and you should always conduct a regular review to understand the improvement points. That's what you are going to do now.

Using secure protocols

It's clear why HTTP is not a good option. So, if you followed option 2, the first improvement you could focus on is to migrate to option 1 and configure HTTPS for API communication.

Infrastructure auto-scaling

By now, regardless of the option you followed, you have one EC2 instance supporting your backend, but what happens if the load increases? A lack of compute resources brings a bad user experience and can lead to instance failure, so how can you cope with a failed instance?

Architecting with failure in mind is the path for resilient applications. So, it is always a good practice to ask ourselves, what happens if this component fails? In our case, what happens if our EC2 instance with the API fails, for example, due to extra load? To ensure resilience and scalability, you should automate API provisioning using, for example, AWS **Auto Scaling groups** (**ASGs**).

An ASG automatically provisions and terminates EC2 instances based on defined metrics, such as average CPU usage. You can create an AMI, which is a pre-configured virtual machine image that includes all the necessary configurations and code to run your backend, and associate it with the ASG. To have some boundaries on the number of instances to provision, you could set a minimum and maximum instance count, say four instances as the upper limit, and be sure you will never pass that limit. By monitoring the instance state, the ASG will launch new instances from the AMI when the metric exceeds a threshold and terminate instances when the metric falls below another threshold.

This approach provides auto-healing by replacing unhealthy instances and automatic scaling based on the defined metric, making the API resilient and scalable.

Managed hosting and CI/CD

During this chapter, you experienced the building process that involves changing the application locally, building it and copying the files to the S3 bucket, which is very error prone. Also, while, by now, you are the only developer working on the application, it is common to have a team of developers working together, and the current deployment method is challenging for collaboration.

AWS offers a service that already manages both hosting and **continuous integration and continuous deployment** (**CI/CD**) pipelines that simplifies the process of building, deploying, and hosting modern SPAs like your recipe-sharing application. With Amplify, you can connect your code repository (e.g., GitHub, AWS CodeCommit) and configure a CI/CD pipeline that builds, tests, and deploys your application whenever changes are pushed to the repository. For hosting, Amplify leverages S3 and CloudFront, similar to the setup you have now, so you would keep benefiting from all the advantages mentioned in the *AWS services* section earlier in this chapter.

Authentication

When you made the requests to your API, you did not need to use any authentication mechanism. It means that anyone in the world, just with the endpoint URL, could perform requests, create recipes, and delete them, which is not ideal. Implementing authentication into your application is crucial for ensuring the security and privacy of your data, especially when dealing with sensitive data.

Amazon Cognito is an AWS service that simplifies the process of adding user authentication and authorization to your web and mobile applications. It acts as a user identity provider, allowing you to manage user sign-up, sign-in, and access control, among other features. There will be more on this in the next chapter.

Logging and monitoring

You can only act on something that you measure, and with the current architecture, you do not have any visibility on what is happening in your application. How many accesses are you getting? Where are your users located? Were there any errors in the last 24 hours?

Although sometimes used interchangeably, monitoring and logging are two different, but complementary, concepts. **Logging** involves recording historical events, errors, and activities that occur within your application, while **monitoring** focuses on collecting and analyzing data about the performance, health, and operational state.

As a part of the AWS services portfolio, you can find CloudWatch, a comprehensive monitoring and logging solution that breaks down into two services: CloudWatch Logs for logging and CloudWatch Metrics for monitoring. By leveraging these services, we could get insights into our application's behavior, performance, and health.

So, as an improvement, you could ship your application logs to CloudWatch Logs, as well as create a monitoring dashboard with metrics from all your application components, including CloudFront, S3, EC2, and DynamoDB. This would provide you with a holistic view of your application and give you the tools to analyze it.

Caching

Recipes are created once, accessed many times, and are not supposed to change often, being a great candidate for data caching. If you analyze your current setup, every time a user refreshes the page or selects a recipe, there is a request being sent and a read operation being performed in your database, and this could be improved both from a performance as well as a cost perspective.

DynamoDB Accelerator (DAX) is a fully managed, clustered in-memory cache for DynamoDB. It is designed to improve the read performance of DynamoDB by caching frequent queries and responses. DAX is compatible with the DynamoDB API, which means you can integrate it with your existing applications without making significant code changes. But this is not the only option.

For the cache layer, you could use any caching technology, such as Redis or Memcached, which are available as a managed solution with Amazon ElastiCache.

These are just six of many examples you could find for future work in your application, so our challenge to you is to try to find other options and always ask yourself: what can I improve in my current architecture?

We will leave with an example of an improved version of our application considering the future work mentioned before, depicted in *Figure 3.33*.

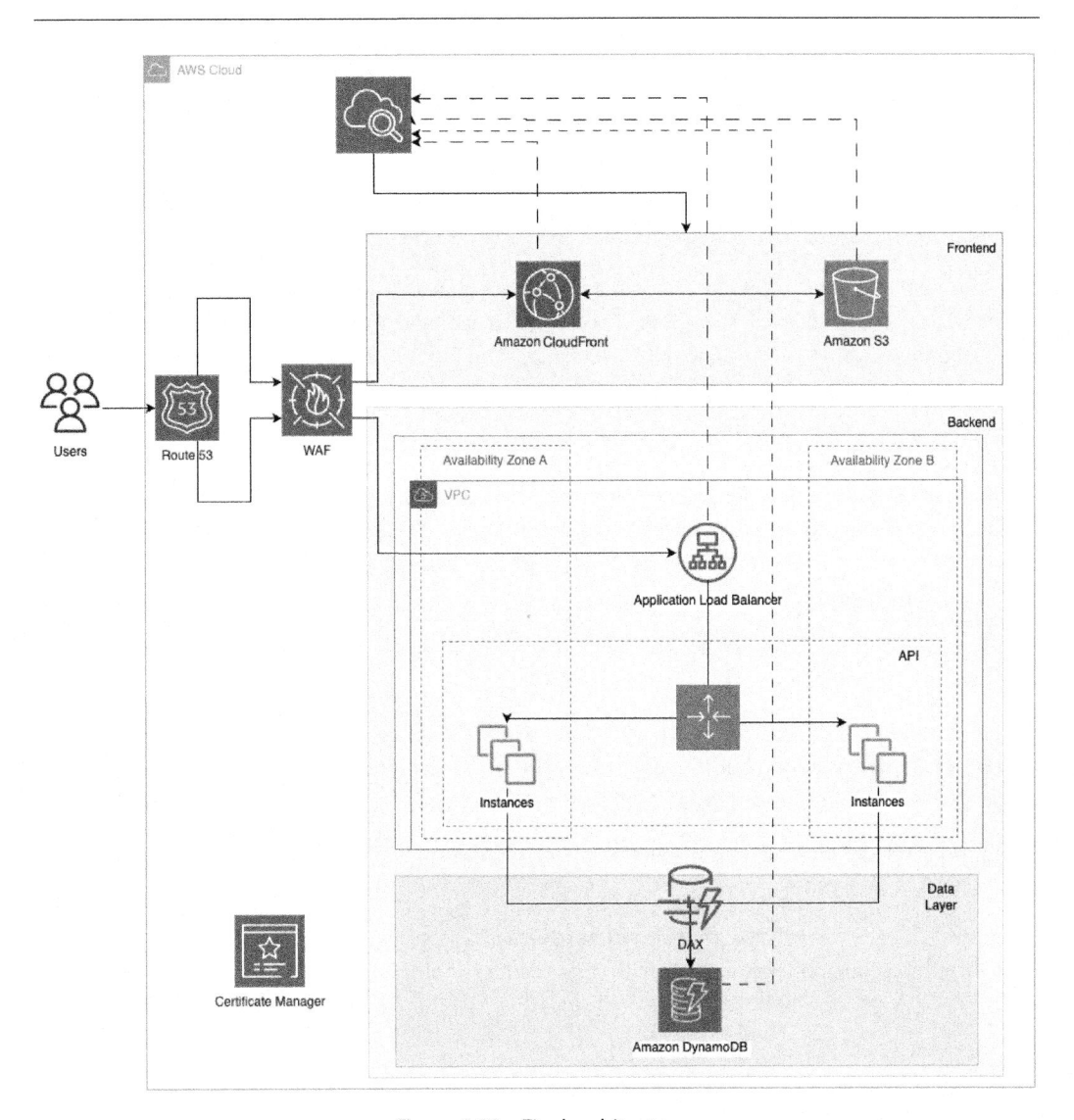

Figure 3.33 – Final architecture

Compared to the initial architecture shown in *Figure 3.6*, this new version already includes part of the future work proposed. On the top, CloudWatch will bring monitoring capabilities and give you more visibility of your application, help you understand the errors that occurred in the past, and, most importantly, act in a timely manner during an event. As explained in the chapter, this architecture follows the security best practices and allows only HTTPS as the access protocol for your application. For that, you configure your domain in Route 53 and issue a certificate to prove your ownership of it.

For your data layer, and taking into consideration that recipes are usually stable and do not get many changes after being published, you adopted DAX as the caching layer to improve the user experience by getting up to a 10 times performance improvement – from milliseconds to microseconds to get an item.

Summary

In this chapter, you practiced the framework introduced in *Chapter 1* for architecture design. Compared to the previous chapter, you now have a more robust application that handles dynamic content, and you ended up with a fully functional recipe-sharing application, which can be used as a starting point and applied to any project you think of.

You had the opportunity to experience the build and deployment process of a SPA to AWS using S3 and CloudFront, which can serve thousands of users.

You explored new AWS services, such as DynamoDB, EC2, and ALB. You also learned the power of IaC with CloudFormation. Additionally, you saw how to configure HTTPS with a custom domain associated with an ALB, and why HTTP is not recommended.

Lastly, you explored possible improvements to your application to make it more scalable, cost-effective, and secure.

In the next chapter, you will take your current recipe-sharing application to the next level and understand how to architect an application solely with serverless technologies.

4
Building a Serverless Recipe-Sharing Application

In the previous chapter, you developed a recipe sharing application with a frontend hosted on Amazon S3 and CloudFront, and a backend using Amazon EC2 instances and DynamoDB. For the end user, only the functionalities and the overall user experience are visible, but it is up to the provider to define how to architect the application and which technologies to use.

Traditional application deployment involves provisioning and managing servers, configuring environments, scaling resources, applying security patches, and monitoring system health. This approach requires significant operational overhead and often leads to inefficient resource utilization as resources are provisioned for peak demand.

In contrast, serverless computing abstracts away the underlying infrastructure, allowing developers to focus solely on writing code. With serverless, the provisioning, scaling, and server management are handled by the cloud provider, enabling a more agile, event-driven approach with a pay-as-you-go model.

Event-driven architectures consist of separate services that interact with each other through events. When a user requests to create a new recipe, for example, that request becomes an event. This event then triggers the necessary code to handle the business logic related to creating the recipe. By using this approach, the system doesn't need to have all the resources prepared and allocated in advance. Instead, it responds to events as they occur, making the architecture more efficient and adaptable.

In this chapter, you will experiment with the adoption of serverless technologies by rearchitecting your recipe-sharing application with solely serverless technologies.

In summary, this chapter covers the following topics in order:

- What you are going to build – the latest version of the recipe sharing application solely supported by serverless technologies
- How you are going to build it – Amazon API Gateway and Lambda for the backend and Amazon Cognito for authentication

- Building it – through CloudFormation and using the AWS console
- How to improve the solution – support media content for your recipes and extend authentication to the end users for a more customized experience

By the end of this chapter, you will gain hands-on experience in rearchitecting a dynamic web application using AWS serverless technologies such as Lambda, API Gateway, Cognito, S3, and DynamoDB. You will also understand the benefits of serverless computing, such as scalability and cost-effectiveness, in modern application development.

Technical requirements

To follow along and implement your serverless version of the recipe-sharing application, you will need to have access to your own AWS account.

Also, this book has a dedicated folder within its GitHub repository, where you can find the necessary code snippets to follow along: https://github.com/PacktPublishing/AWS-Cloud-Projects/tree/main/chapter4/code.

Scenario

After successfully deploying your personal website for your CV as part of *Chapter 2*, you have had your first experience with cloud technologies and started gaining confidence in this area. In the previous chapter, with your recipe-sharing application, you evolved to a more complex application with a backend to handle recipe operations such as creation, deletion, and retrieval, and your user base grew more than expected.

Your application is now considered one of the most popular apps for recipes and cooking. You are spending more time scaling and managing infrastructure than investing in improving your application based on valuable user feedback, not to mention the impact in terms of cost as the application's popularity continues to grow.

Last month, you attended a conference about serverless technologies, and you learned that they really fit your needs. The more you explore, the more you realize that they can provide a more efficient, scalable, and cost-effective solution for your recipe-sharing application. With serverless architectures, you can focus on writing code and building features without worrying about provisioning and managing servers or infrastructure, which is exactly what you are looking for.

After some research, you decide to rearchitect your application to leverage AWS serverless services to benefit from automatic scaling, pay-per-use pricing, and reduced operational overhead.

Requirements

As you have done in the previous chapter, you will start by gathering the requirements for this project. This will serve as the baseline for all the technical choices you will make next, so it is important to have a clear view of the objectives and restrictions.

Overall, you still want to serve two different profiles:

- **Admin**: Platform owner responsible for creating and managing recipes
- **End users or consumers**: Access the shared recipes and put likes on the preferred ones

Considering that this project is an evolution from the previous one, let us focus on the changes and break down the new requirements.

Business requirements

With your previous recipe-sharing application, you exceeded all the expectations. As of now, when people think about cooking and are looking for inspiration, they go directly to your application and your market is not restricted to the US. Instead, you are evenly distributed between the US, Europe, and Asia with 41%, 35%, and 20% geo-distribution respectively, with the remaining 4% spread across the globe, and you reached a total of 150 thousand users in the last year.

Due to your success, you were able to sign more than one contract with companies from different segments (ads, food delivery, and food producers), but your growth plans continue. As you move forward, you have identified the following key objectives to focus on:

- Achieve 10% yearly user growth
- Improve your cost-effectiveness

Functional requirements

Regarding functional requirements, you do not expect major changes compared to the previous chapter, so to summarize, these are as follows:

- Two different profiles (admin and user)
- Simple user interface
- Responsiveness

With the time you've been spending managing the infrastructure, you did not have much time to invest in creating new functionalities for your application. However, based on the feedback received from the users, you want to include two new features:

- Authentication and authorization
- Ability to add likes to recipes, and sort by it

Mockups are a good strategy to create a visual representation of the expected behavior of your application, as you saw in the previous chapter. Therefore, for this section, you will do a similar exercise, focusing only on the new features planned, as shown in *Figures 4.1*, *4.2*, and *4.3*. For the home page you will keep the same layout, as shown in *Chapter 3*, *Figure 3.1*.

You do not expect different profiles to access your application, so the same division applies: users and admins.

> **Note**
> We will not list the features that are maintained, such as the access to the list of recipe titles, since it was covered in the previous chapter and we want to avoid duplication. Assuming you are following along, you should be familiar with the initial requirements, and if that is not the case, we recommend reviewing them in the *Requirements* section from the previous chapter.

Let us explore each profile and the changes expected in terms of interface and behavior:

- `/user`: Like a specific recipe.

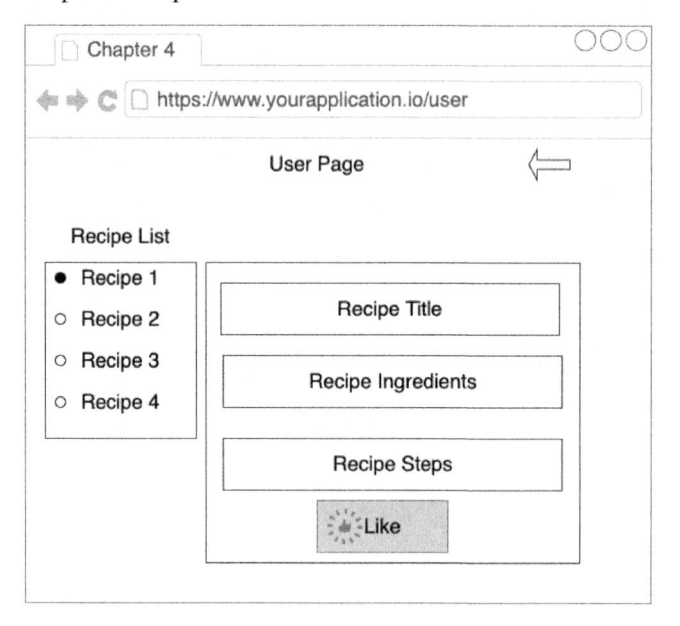

Figure 4.1 – UI Mockup User Page

- `/admin`: Restrict access to the admin portal with an authentication mechanism, with a simple form if a user tries to access the admin page, as depicted in *Figure 4.2*.

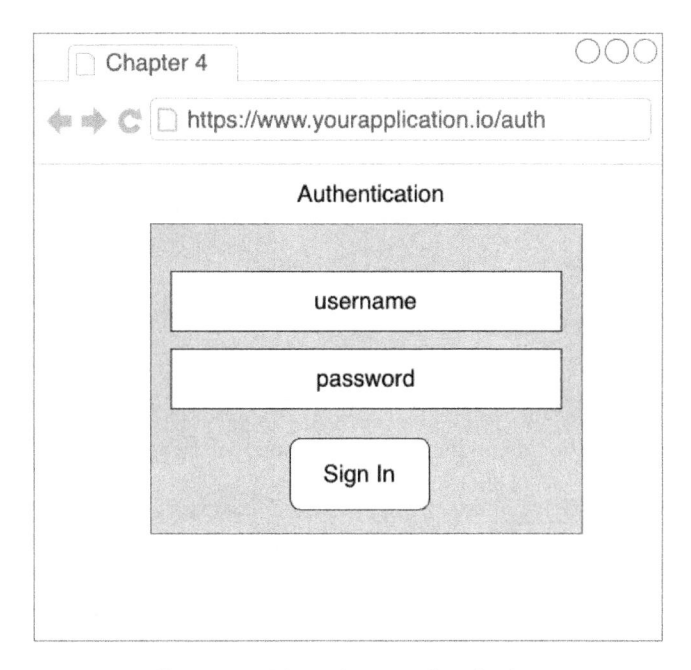

Figure 4.2 – UI mockup – authentication

Non-functional requirements

With the popularity increase of your application, cost and scalability are the new goals. Also, you want to accelerate feature rollout by shifting the time you spend managing infrastructure to application innovation. To summarize, here is what we need:

- Cost-effectiveness
- Event-driven architecture
- Low infrastructure management

Technical requirements

Compared to the previous chapter and considering the overall feedback of your users, you want this re-architecture to be as smooth as possible with no impact on the current users in terms of the interface and user experience. You want to keep the previous technical choices and project from a programming language and frameworks standpoint, as much as possible.

As part of your latest research, you want to base your new platform architecture to use solely serverless technologies.

Data requirements

This latest version is an extension of your previous one, and all the data requirements still apply. Your application is all about storing and managing recipes, which are composed of a set of steps and ingredients, but one of the features you want to implement is adding likes to a recipe. For the operations you perform over a recipe, you must do the following:

- **List the recipes**: Present a list of the recipes created.
- **Delete a recipe**: If an admin no longer wants a specific recipe to be part of their portfolio, it should be possible to delete the item.
- **Create a recipe**: Create a new recipe to share with the users.
- **Like a recipe**: Increase the number of likes in a specific recipe.

Based on the operations listed, the only change you need to support is to store the number of likes per recipe, so you define a recent version for your recipe document as seen in the `recipe_example_2.json` recipe example:

```
{   "ID":"GUID",
    "Title":"recipe title",
    "Ingredients":[…],
    "Steps":[…],
    "Likes":X  }
```

Architecture patterns

Each project is different, but there are some commonalities that can and should be leveraged when designing your applications. AWS has a dedicated portal for serverless architectures and patterns called **Serverless Land** (https://serverlessland.com/), composed of the latest information, blogs, videos, code, and learning resources for serverless in AWS. It is always a good starting point whenever you are planning to build a serverless application.

Compared to traditional deployment strategies, serverless implies a different paradigm and a good understanding of the core services is key. AWS offers a serverless developer guide (https://docs.aws.amazon.com/serverless/latest/devguide/welcome.html), with learning paths for the core services, and is also a great resource for serverless-related information.

Lastly, as stated in the previous chapters, each AWS service has a dedicated page with all the service-related information. For example, in the case of AWS Lambda, you can access it at https://aws.amazon.com/lambda/.

Architecture

Whilst user experience and interface should be as similar as possible compared to the previous version of the recipe-sharing application developed in *Chapter 3*, the platform architecture is where the majority of the changes should be noted.

In this chapter, you will follow the same top-down approach when designing your architecture. You will be starting with the highest abstraction level and moving down to the component level architecture, where you define each of the services used and how all of them fit together to build your application.

Looking at the different architecture layers, you will follow the same structure you had in the previous chapter, with three well-defined layers, like what is shown in *Chapter 3, Figure 3.4*:

- **Presentation layer**: How to host and serve your frontend
- **Compute layer**: How to incorporate and execute business logic
- **Data layer**: Where to store and retrieve your data

The Presentation and Compute layers use an API as the interface between the two layers. The API is responsible for exposing the endpoints to perform all the actions to execute and abstract the business logic. In this case, and taking into consideration the requirements, the main update is the inclusion of the new feature for liking a recipe, as represented in *Figure 4.3*:

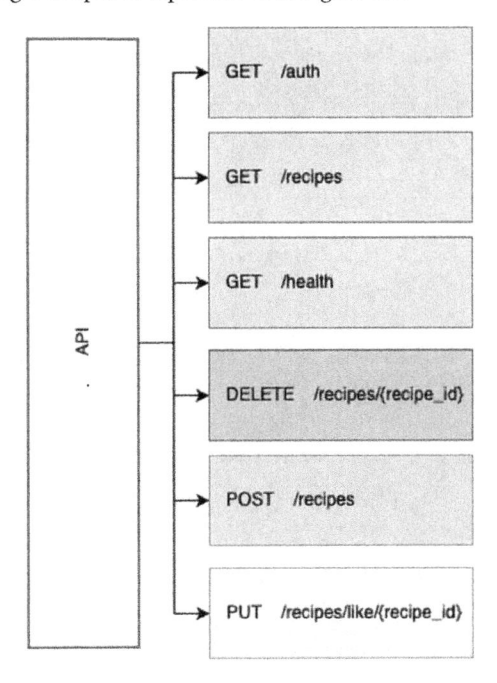

Figure 4.3 – API structure

Here is the breakdown:

- `GET /auth`: Test authorization flow
- `GET /recipes`: Get the list of recipes
- `GET /health`: Simple health check endpoint
- `DELETE /recipes/{recipe_id}`: Delete a specific recipe by its ID
- `POST /recipes`: Create a new recipe record
- `PUT /recipes/like/{recipe_id}`: increase recipes' likes

Besides the endpoint for adding likes, we also added the `/auth` endpoint, which, despite not being used for the application, serves as a learning resource for understanding the authentication and endpoint protection workflow.

Figure 4.4 represents the architecture you will implement, based on all the requirements. The frontend will use the same approach as in the previous chapter, with S3 and CloudFront for hosting and serving. The data layer will still use DynamoDB to store recipe data. However, you will introduce Amazon Cognito as an authentication service to restrict recipe management activities to authorized users. For the API, you will use Amazon API Gateway and associate it with AWS Lambda functions to implement the API endpoint functionalities.

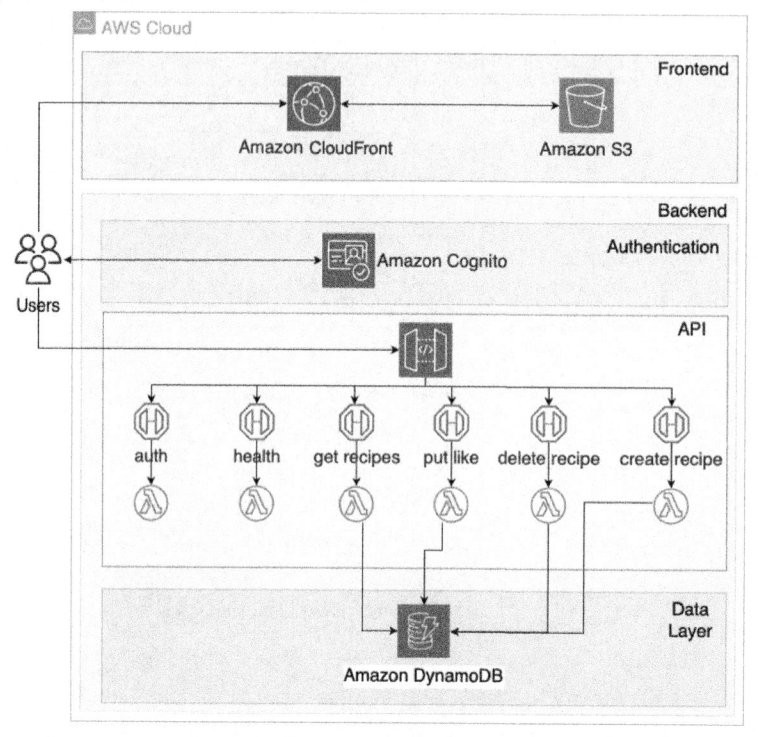

Figure 4.4 – AWS architecture for your new recipe-sharing application

Each of the services mentioned, as well as the main advantages and reasons for these choices, will be described next.

AWS services

Choosing from the vast number of services available can be challenging, and a good understanding of the requirements is key for the decision. Part of the services were covered in previous chapters, so to avoid duplication, we'll only mention the advantages for the current use case if not referenced before, and point to the relevant chapter for a detailed explanation.

Amazon Simple Storage Service (S3)

Amazon S3 is an example of a serverless technology that you should already be familiar with, as it was explained in detail in the previous two chapters. If you want to review it, we recommend checking the details in *Chapters 2* and *3*.

Amazon CloudFront

Just like Amazon S3, CloudFront has been extensively used in the previous project of this book, and it was covered in the previous AWS Services sections in both *Chapters 2* and *3*. To review it, we recommend checking the details in the previous chapters.

Amazon DynamoDB

Data requirements have been the main drivers for choosing database technologies. In this chapter, the data requirements did not change, so Amazon DynamoDB keeps being our choice. The main characteristics and advantages were described in the *AWS Services* section in the previous chapter, so if you want to get a detailed explanation and understanding of DynamoDB, we recommend reviewing that.

AWS CloudFormation

As you did in the previous chapter, you will continue to use AWS CloudFormation (CloudFormation) as your **Infrastructure as Code** (**IaC**) tool. CloudFormation was explained in detail in the previous chapter, so for a detailed explanation of the service and its advantages, we recommend reviewing that chapter.

Amazon Cognito

Amazon Cognito is a fully managed service that provides authentication, authorization, and user management for your web and mobile applications. With Amazon Cognito, you can easily implement features such as user sign-up, sign-in, and account recovery. It supports various authentication methods, including user pools (for managing your application's own user directory) and identity pools (for integrating with social media or enterprise identity providers). Amazon Cognito integrates seamlessly with other AWS services, such as Amazon API Gateway, which are also part of your serverless architecture. This integration enables you to implement serverless authentication and authorization mechanisms for your API, ensuring that only authenticated users can access and perform actions within your application.

Amazon Lambda

Amazon Lambda is a serverless computing service that allows you to run code without provisioning or managing servers. With Lambda, you can focus on writing your application code, and AWS takes care of provisioning and managing the underlying compute resources. Lambda automatically scales your code's execution in response to incoming events or requests, ensuring that your application can handle fluctuations in traffic without manual intervention.

Lambda provides support for various programming languages, with Python being one of the supported runtimes that fits your technical requirements. Furthermore, Lambda seamlessly integrates with other AWS services such as Amazon API Gateway, enabling you to create event-driven architectures and develop applications that are highly scalable, resilient to failures, and cost-effective.

API Gateway

Amazon API Gateway is a fully managed service that makes it easy to create, publish, maintain, monitor, and secure APIs at any scale. It acts as the front door for your serverless application, handling client requests and routing them to the appropriate backend services, such as AWS Lambda functions.

Amazon API Gateway supports two types of RESTful APIs: **REST APIs** and **HTTP APIs**. Choosing between the two must be based on the features supported. REST APIs provide more advanced features such as API versioning, request/response data transformations, caching, and comprehensive access control mechanisms, while HTTP can be considered if you are looking for a simplified and cost-effective option that does not require advanced features.

If you want to know how to choose between HTTP and REST APIs in Amazon API Gateway, you can access `https://docs.aws.amazon.com/apigateway/latest/developerguide/http-api-vs-rest.html`.

Coding the solution

Now is the time to put all the concepts into action by coding the solution described so far, reviewing and improving the services you already used in previous chapters, and getting familiar with the new services introduced in this architecture.

Cloning the project

As you have been doing in the previous chapter, the first step is to copy the project locally from the Git repository associated with this book. If you were following along with the previous chapter, you should have already a copy of the Git repository on your local machine. If this is not the case, you can either clone it directly from the Git repository associated with this book or download it as a ZIP file.

Navigate to the `chapter4/code` folder. Inside, you will find two subfolders, as shown in *Figure 4.5*:

- `frontend`: Contains the code for your frontend.
- `platform`: Contains a CloudFormation template to deploy the main infrastructure for your application.

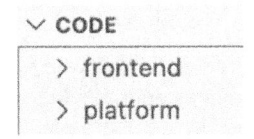

Figure 4.5 – Chapter 4 folder structure

Solution deployment

Now, it is time to deploy all your application infrastructure through the CloudFormation template called `ch4-application-template.yaml`, which is located in the `/platform` subfolder of your `chapter4/code` folder (`chapter4/code/platform/ch4-application-template.yaml`).

In *Table 4.1*, you can see all the resources created by your CloudFormation template, but feel free to explore the code itself and try to map it to the architecture presented in *Figure 4.4*.

Template	ch4-application-template.yaml
Frontend	CloudFront and S3
Backend	• 1 HTTP API with 6 endpoints • 6 lambda functions, one for each endpoint • 1 Cognito user pool
Data store	DynamoDB

Table 4.1 – CloudFormation template details

From the console, go to the CloudFormation service (`https://console.aws.amazon.com/cloudformation/`) and select the region where you want your application. You can select the AWS region in the drop-down menu located in the upper-right corner of your console window, as shown in *Figure 4.6*.

Figure 4.6 – Console access to CloudFormation

> **Why is important to choose a region?**
>
> In AWS, services can be classified as either regional or global based on their availability and data replication mechanisms. Regional services are deployed and operate within a specific AWS region, while global services are designed to provide a consistent experience across multiple regions.
>
> CloudFormation is an example of a regional service. Thus, it is crucial to pick the right region because it ensures that your resources are deployed closer to your target users, providing lower latency and the best user experience.

To proceed with stack creation, follow these steps:

1. Click on **Create Stack**.
2. In the **Prerequisite – Prepare template** section, select **Choose an existing template**.
3. In the **Specify template** section, choose **Upload a template file**.
4. Click on **Choose file**.
5. Select the template from the `chapter4/code/platform` folder.
6. Click **Next**. Your **Create Stack** window should look like *Figure 4.7*.

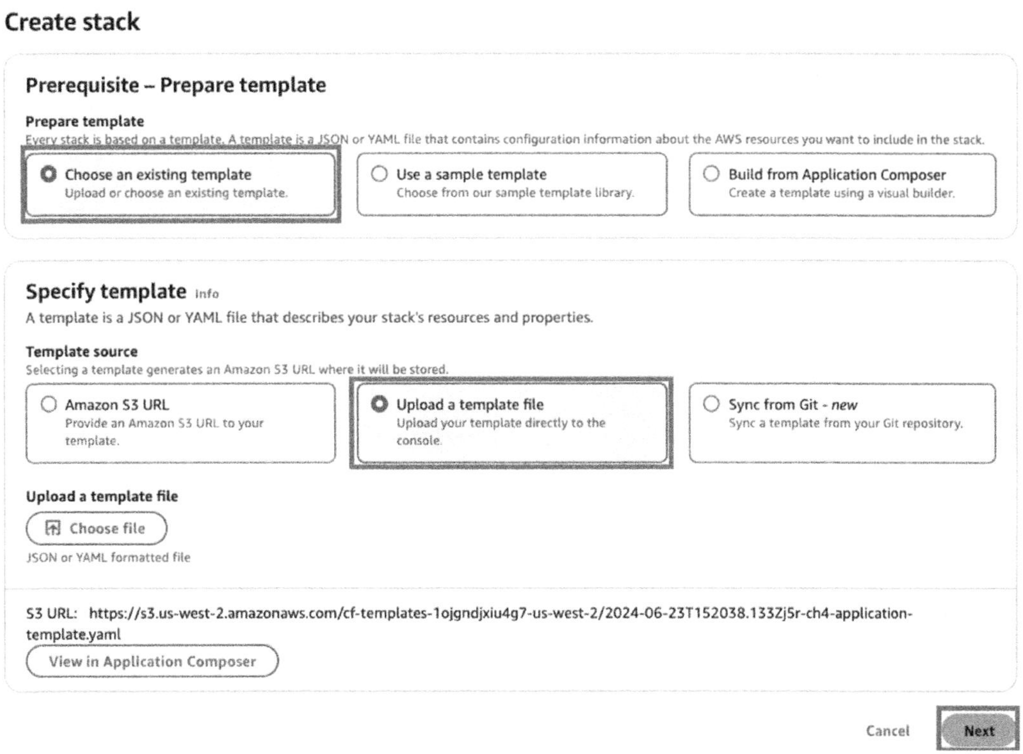

Create stack

[Figure 4.7 – A CloudFormation Create stack form]

The next step is to configure the parameters in your CloudFormation stack. In *Table 4.2*, you can find a detailed explanation of each parameter.

Parameter	Description
APIName	The name you want to associate with your API
UserEmail	The email you associate with your user must be valid, as you will receive a temporary password and need to verify the email later
UserPoolName	The name you will give to your Cognito User Pool
Username	Later, this is the username you will use to log in to your application

Table 4.2 – CloudFormation templates parameters

An example of the parameters windows is shown in *Figure 4.8*.

Specify stack details

Provide a stack name

Stack name

[chapter-4]

Stack name must be 1 to 128 characters, start with a letter, and only contain alphanumeric characters. Character count: 9/128.

Parameters

Parameters are defined in your template and allow you to input custom values when you create or update a stack.

APIName
API Name

[ch4-api]

UserEmail
The email for the initial user

[jonhdoe@example.com]

UserPoolName
The name for the Cognito User Pool

[chapter4-userpool]

Username
The username for the initial user

[admin]

Cancel Previous **Next**

Figure 4.8 – Stack parameters in CloudFormation

You can proceed until the last page. Acknowledge the creation of the IAM Roles that will be used to provide access to the lambda functions for performing operations to the DynamoDB table, namely, to delete a recipe, and click **Submit**.

Capabilities

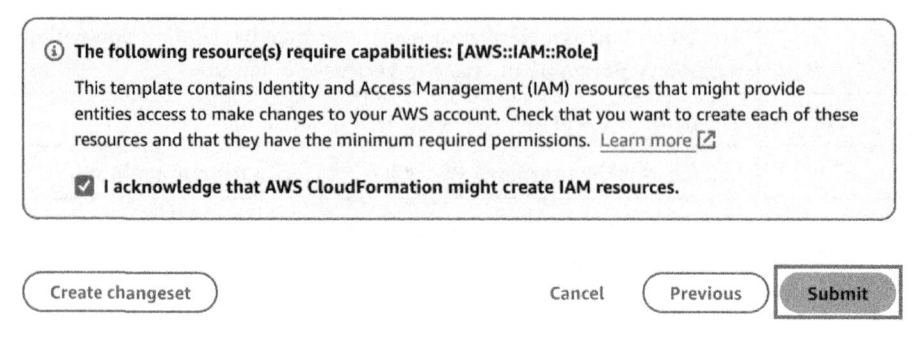

ⓘ **The following resource(s) require capabilities: [AWS::IAM::Role]**

This template contains Identity and Access Management (IAM) resources that might provide entities access to make changes to your AWS account. Check that you want to create each of these resources and that they have the minimum required permissions. Learn more ↗

☑ I acknowledge that AWS CloudFormation might create IAM resources.

Create changeset   Cancel   Previous   **Submit**

Figure 4.9 – CloudFormation stack submission

Wait until the stack status changes to **CREATE_COMPLETE**, as depicted in *Figure 4.10*. This will mean that all the resources are provisioned and you can now proceed.

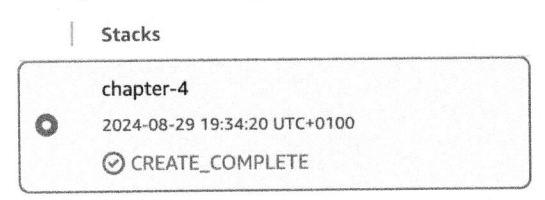

Stacks

chapter-4
2024-08-29 19:34:20 UTC+0100
⊘ CREATE_COMPLETE

Figure 4.10 – CloudFormation Stack Created status

In our case, it took around five minutes for the stack to be deployed but take into consideration that this may vary.

> **Important note**
>
> If you have been following along with the previous chapter (*Chapter 3*) and forgot to clean up all the resources created in that chapter, you may encounter issues when attempting to deploy the CloudFormation template in this chapter. The deployment may fail because in AWS, DynamoDB table names must be unique within a region in a single account. Since this chapter is an evolution of the previous one, we used the same table name for storing the recipes.
>
> To resolve this issue, please ensure that you have properly cleaned up and deleted all the resources in the previous chapter, as described in the *Clean up* section, before proceeding with this one.

Frontend configuration and deployment

With all the AWS services provisioned, it's now time for configuring your frontend and deploying the files.

Navigate to the `.../frontend/src/configs` folder, and you will find two files:

- `aws-exports.ts`: This file is used to configure your authentication with data from the Cognito user pool.
- `configs.tsx`: This file is used to configure your application, namely the API URL to use.

Let's look at them in detail.

aws-exports.ts

This file is composed of four configuration variables:

- `AWS_PROJECT_REGION`: The region you deployed your solution
- `AWS_COGNITO_REGION`: Your Cognito user Pool region
- `AWS_USER_POOLS_ID`: The ID of your user pool
- `AWS_USER_POOLS_WEB_CLIENT_ID`: The client ID of your Cognito User Pool application

configs.tsx:

This config file is composed of seven configurations:

- `CONFIG_MAX_INGREDIENTS`: Max ingredients in a recipe
- `CONFIG_MAX_STEPS`: Max steps in a recipe
- `CONFIG_MAX_RECIPES`: Max recipes supported
- `CONFIG_USER_PAGE_TITLE`: Title for user page
- `CONFIG_ADMIN_PAGE_TITLE`: Title for admin page
- `CONFIG_appConfig`: Object with page title and icon (icons in `/frontend/public/`)
- `CONFIG_API_URL`: API endpoint

All the mandatory values needed as part of the configuration files can be found in the **Outputs** tab of the CloudFormation template you just deployed.

To access it, follow these steps:

1. Go to the CloudFormation console at `https://console.aws.amazon.com/cloudformation/`.
2. Click on your stack.
3. On the right menu, select the **Outputs** Tab, as shown in *Figure 4.11*.

Coding the solution

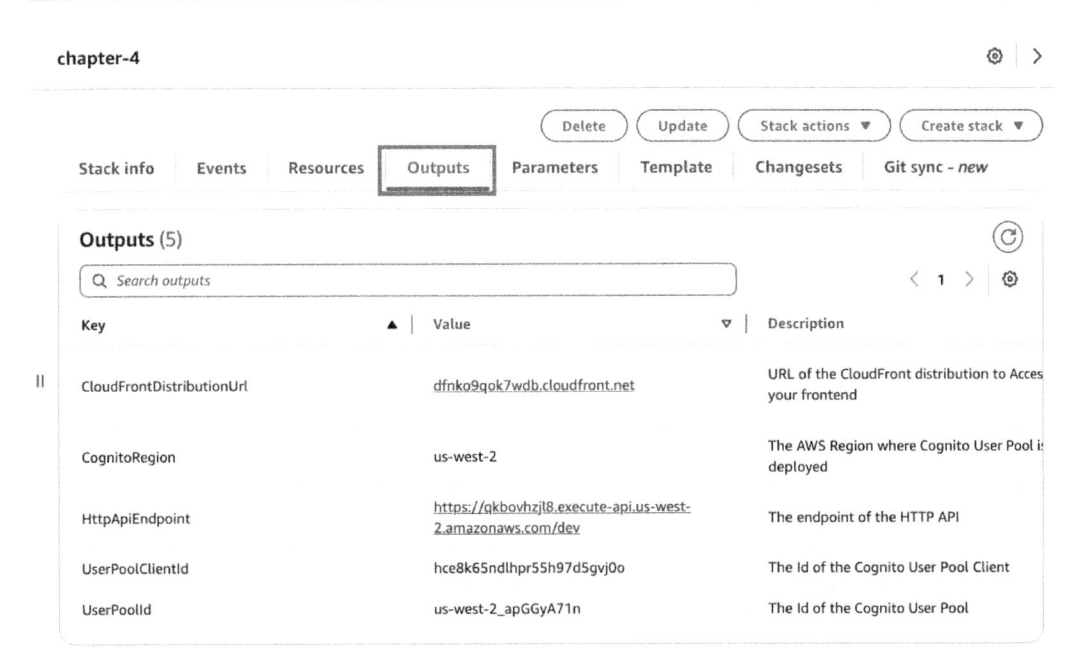

[CloudFormation console screenshot showing chapter-4 stack Outputs tab with 5 outputs:]

Key	Value	Description
CloudFrontDistributionUrl	dfnko9qok7wdb.cloudfront.net	URL of the CloudFront distribution to Access your frontend
CognitoRegion	us-west-2	The AWS Region where Cognito User Pool is deployed
HttpApiEndpoint	https://qkbovhzjl8.execute-api.us-west-2.amazonaws.com/dev	The endpoint of the HTTP API
UserPoolClientId	hce8k65ndlhpr55h97d5gvj0o	The Id of the Cognito User Pool Client
UserPoolId	us-west-2_apGGyA71n	The Id of the Cognito User Pool

Figure 4.11 – CloudFormation Outputs tab

Table 4.3 maps the Stack outputs with the configuration files' parameters (`aws-exports.ts` and `config.tsx`).

File	Parameter	Cloudformation Stack outputs
aws-exports.ts	aws_project_region	CognitoRegion
	aws_cognito_region	CognitoRegion
	aws_user_pools_id	UserPoolId
	aws_user_pools_web_client_id	UserPoolClientId
configs.tsx	CONFIG_API_URL	HttpApiEndpoint

Table 4.3 – Mapping between CloudFormation Outputs and aws-exports.ts parameters

Paste the values in each of the files respectively, and by the end, your parameters' `aws-exports.ts` file should look like *Figure 4.12*.

```ts
frontend > src > configs > TS aws-exports.ts > ...
1   export const amplifyConfig = {
2       aws_project_region: '[CognitoRegion]',
3       aws_cognito_region: '[CognitoRegion]',
4       aws_user_pools_id: '[UserPoolId]',
5       aws_user_pools_web_client_id: '[UserPoolClientId]',
6   };
```

Figure 4.12 – Example of a configuration file (aws-exports.ts)

and `config.tsx` file should look like *Figure 4.13*.

```tsx
frontend > src > configs > configs.tsx > ...
1    export const CONFIG_MAX_INGREDIENTS = 20;
2    export const CONFIG_MAX_STEPS = 10;
3    export const CONFIG_MAX_RECIPES = 4;
4    export const CONFIG_ADMIN_PAGE_TITLE = "Admin";
5    export const CONFIG_USER_PAGE_TITLE = "User Page";
6    export const appConfig = {
7        title: "CHAPTER_4",
8        iconFileName: "ch4_link.png",
9    };
10
11   export const API_URL = "https://XXXXXX.execute-api.us-west-2.amazonaws.com/dev";
```

Figure 4.13 – Example of configuration file (config.tsx)

4. Save the files.

Once you've updated the configuration files, you can initiate the `build` process to transform the code into a web-ready bundle that can be served to browsers. In our example, we utilized npm as the package manager, so you'll need to install the dependencies and kick off the `build` process:

```
$ npm install && npm run build
```

Note that the previous command should be run at the root of the `frontend` folder. To test whether you are at the root, you can use the following command:

```
$ pwd
.../chapter4/code/frontend
```

The result is a folder with the files needed to be copied to our S3 buckets. The folder name may vary but is typically `build/` or `dist/`. It is created at the frontend root, as you can see in *Figure 4.14*.

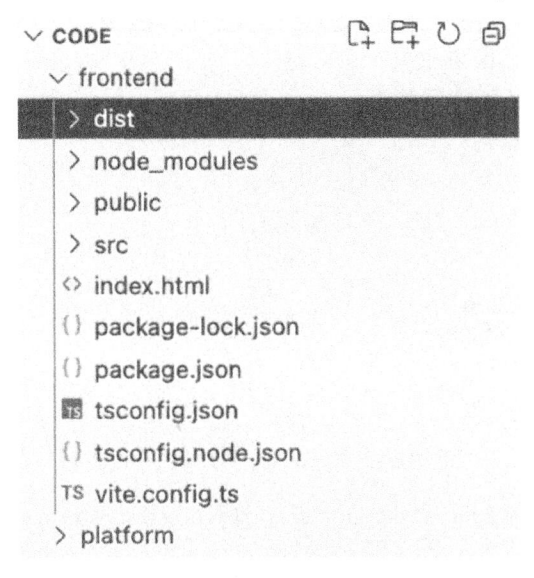

```
∨ CODE
  ∨ frontend
    > dist
    > node_modules
    > public
    > src
    <> index.html
    {} package-lock.json
    {} package.json
    TS tsconfig.json
    {} tsconfig.node.json
    TS vite.config.ts
  > platform
```

Figure 4.14 – Frontend folder structure

Now, the last step is to copy the build folder to S3, with the following instructions:

1. Locate the S3 bucket.
2. First, you need to find the S3 bucket that you created earlier using the CloudFormation template. The name of the bucket should start with `frontend-chapter-4-`, followed by a random string of characters (e.g., `frontend-chapter-4-XXXXX`). Click on its name to open it.
3. Add files from the `dist` folder.
4. Inside the S3 bucket, click on the **Upload** button. This will allow you to upload files from your local machine to the S3 bucket.
5. Add the necessary content to the bucket.
6. First click on **Add Files**, locate the `dist` folder on your local machine, select all the files inside the folder, and confirm. Next, on the S3 console, click **on Add folder**, locate the `dist` folder on your local machine, select the `assets` folder, and confirm.

7. Optionally, you can just drag the content to the S3 window, but regardless of the method you use, your S3 **Upload** window should look like *Figure 4.15*.

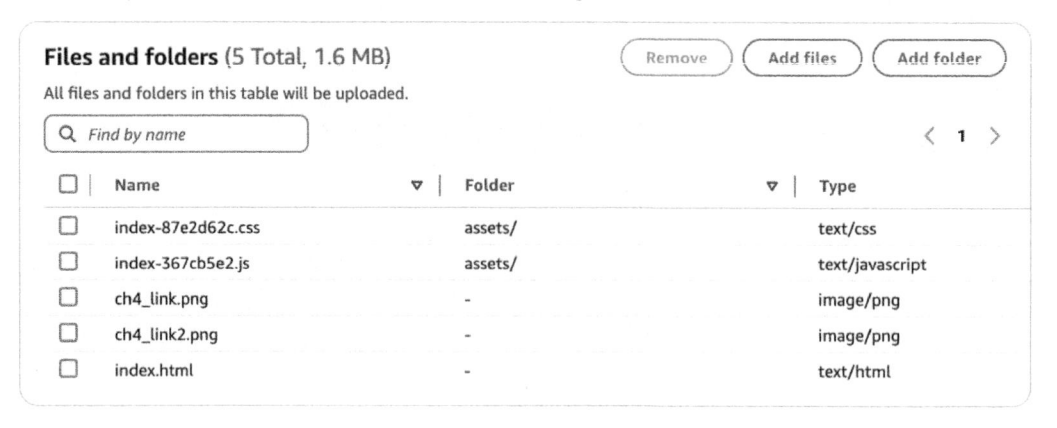

Name	Folder	Type
index-87e2d62c.css	assets/	text/css
index-367cb5e2.js	assets/	text/javascript
ch4_link.png	-	image/png
ch4_link2.png	-	image/png
index.html	-	text/html

Figure 4.15 – Frontend files uploaded to S3

File names are auto-generated by the `build` process, so your names are probably different than the ones in the preceding figure. Make sure that you have the following files:

- `index.html`
- `index-XXXXXX.css`
- `index-XXXXXX.js`
- Static files you may have included in your application, for example, images

8. After that, at the bottom, click on **Upload**.

You've just finalized all the deployment and configuration of your application, and now it is time to test it.

Test and explore your application

This last section is all about testing and exploring your application, and we divided it into two parts: backend and frontend. Unlike the previous chapter, let's start with the frontend!

We've made the CloudFront URL available as an output in the CloudFormation Stack, so you can get it with the `CloudFrontDistributionUrl` output.

You can also get the value directly from the console:

1. Go to the CloudFront console at `https://console.aws.amazon.com/cloudfront/`.
2. Click on **Distributions** on the left menu.
3. Select the distribution you created.
4. Copy the **Distribution domain name** value from the **Details** section, as depicted in *Figure 4.16*.

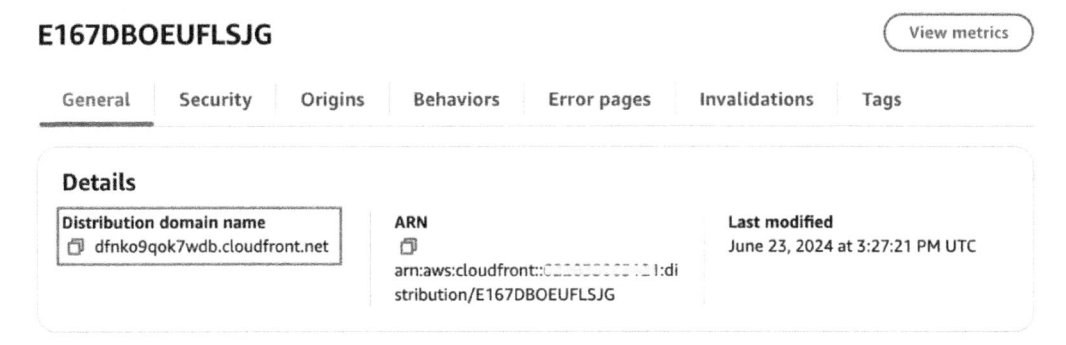

Figure 4.16 – CloudFront distribution console

5. If you copy and paste the URL into the browser, you should be able to access your newly created application, as is shown in *Figure 4.17*.

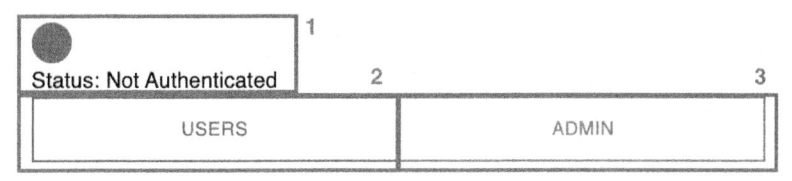

Figure 4.17 – Application frontend example

Your new application is composed of three elements:

- **Status (Not Authenticated)**: This component will help you understand whether you are authenticated by changing the description and color. Also, if you are authenticated, it will highlight and show your current access token.
- **USERS**: Navigate to the **Users** page.
- **ADMIN**: Navigate to the **Admin** page.

Let us have a look.

Admin page

One of the improvements of this new solution is the authentication. To test it, navigate to the admin page, and you should be prompted to authenticate, as you can see in *Figure 4.18*.

Figure 4.18 – Authentication form

With the deployment of the application CloudFormation template, you should have received an email similar to *Figure 4.19* to the user email you defined as a parameter during the stack deployment process, with a temporary password for the username you also defined.

From: "no-reply@verificationemail.com" <no-reply@verificationemail.com>
Date: Saturday, 20 April 2024 at 20:20
To: "YOUR_EMAIL" <youremail@yourdomain>
Subject: Chapter4 - Your temporary password

Hello YOUR_USERNAME from Recipe Sharring Serverless Application. Your temporary password is YOUR_PASSWORD

Figure 4.19 – Temporary password email example

Use these values as your username and password and continue. You should be prompted to define a new password, so proceed with it and click on **Change password**.

You have your new password defined, so the last step is to verify your email for account recovery purposes.

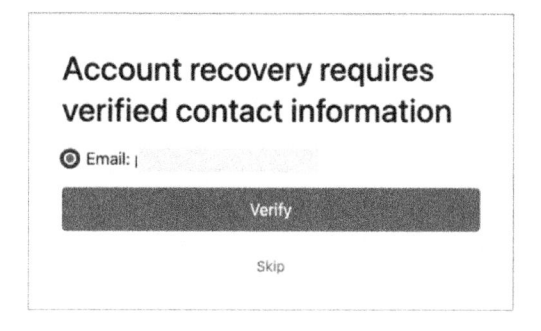

Figure 4.20 – Email verification form

Select your email address and click on **Verify**. With this action, you should receive a new email containing your verification code, as shown in *Figure 4.21*.

Figure 4.21 – Account verification email example

Paste the verification code and proceed. You have now finalized the authentication setup, and your interface should look like *Figure 4.22*.

Figure 4.22 – Admin page after authentication

108   Building a Serverless Recipe-Sharing Application

As you can see, the authentication status component has changed color and is now saying that you are authenticated as your username. In our case, that username is `admin`. Also, if you hover over the access token, you will be able to access the current access token.

Figure 4.23 – Tooltip with access token

Feel free to navigate the application by clicking the left arrow and going back to the admin page, and you will see that you will remain authenticated until you sign out. Back to the admin console; start by creating some recipes to explore the user experience.

Note that we added a new functionality to our application, as per the requirements, giving the ability for users to like our recipes. Additionally, we can sort our recipes by likes and, for example, delete the recipes with few likes, as shown in *Figure 4.24*.

Figure 4.24 – Admin user experience with number of likes per recipe

User page

The **User** page is like in the previous chapter, but we have added the new feature of likes for the recipes.

Navigate to the **User** page, choose a recipe, and click **Like**. This should increase the number of likes of the specific recipe, as shown in *Figure 4.25*.

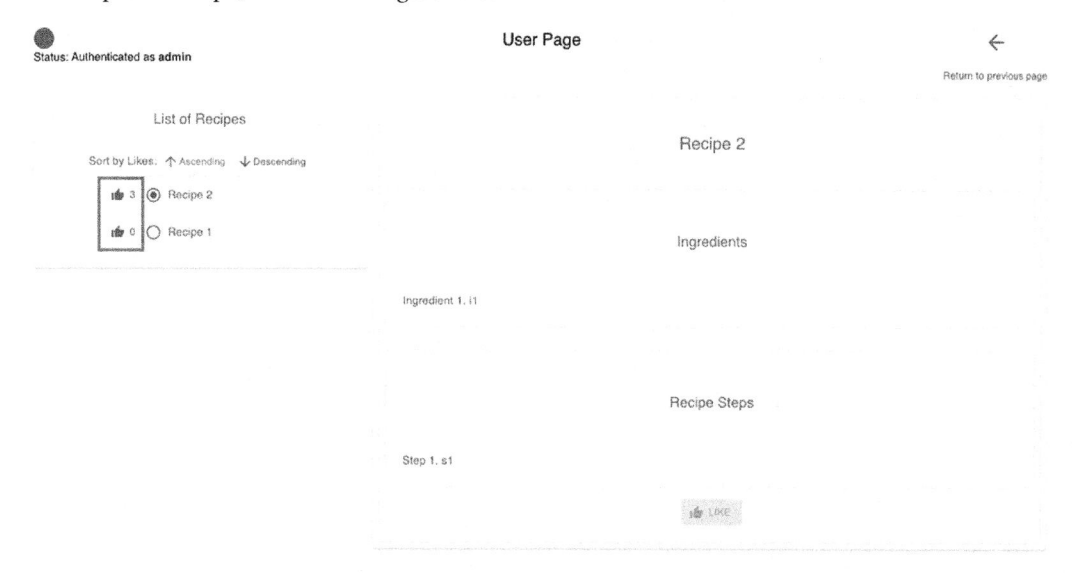

Figure 4.25 – Example of adding a like to a recipe as a regular user

If you want to play around with the likes functionality, just refresh the page and the like button will be available again. Lastly, try to change the sort to choose the most popular recipe according to user feedback.

Testing and exploring the backend

Your backend is now built with an HTTP API gateway with a Lambda function for each endpoint responsible for executing the associated action. For example, let's explore the `delete` function:

```
import json
import boto3
dynamodb = boto3.resource('dynamodb')
table = dynamodb.Table('recipes')
def lambda_handler(event, context):
    try:
        recipe_id = event['pathParameters']['recipe_id']
        response = table.delete_item(
                Key={'id': recipe_id}
                )
```

```
            return {
                "statusCode": 200,
                "body": json.dumps({"message": "Recipe deleted
successfully"})}
        except Exception as e:
            return {
          "statusCode": 500,
          "body": json.dumps({"message": f"Error deleting recipe: {e}"})
```

The delete function is responsible for deleting a specific recipe in DynamoDB based on the ID.

So, for every execution, the API gateway will trigger the Lambda function associated. In this case, the function will grab recipe_id from the path and call the delete_item API for your table.

Go ahead and explore the other examples:

1. Navigate to the API Gateway console at https://console.aws.amazon.com/apigateway.
2. Select your API with the name you gave as part of the CloudFormation Stack parameters.
3. Select the option API: [your API name].
4. Click on **Integrations** from the left menu.
5. Select the route you want to explore.
6. Click on the blue arrow on the **Lambda Function** field. This will redirect you to the Lambda page of your specific Lambda function.

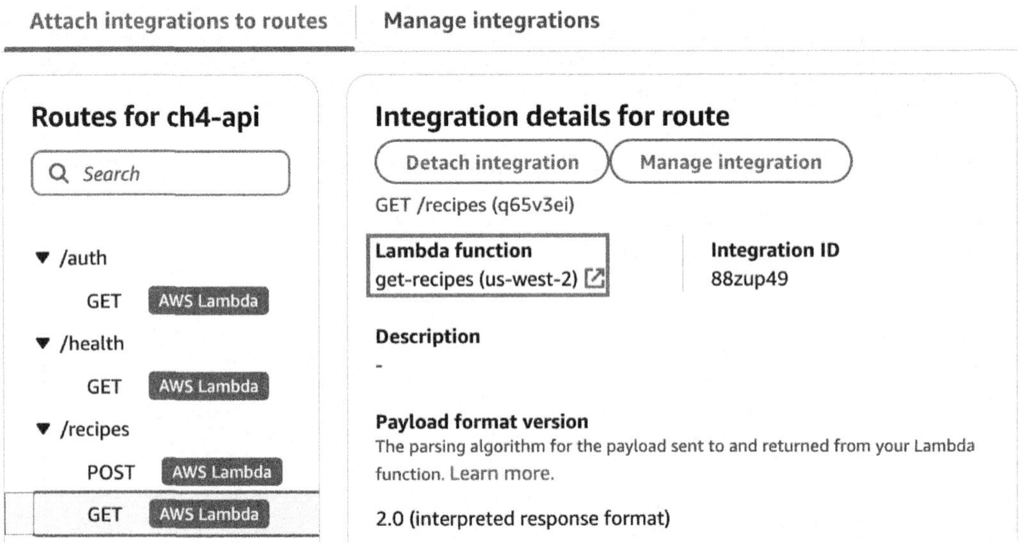

Figure 4.26 – Lambda function access through API Gateway console

Your application is protected by Cognito authentication since you cannot access the admin page without being authenticated. However, what would happen if a user tried to directly access the API?

That is where API authorization comes into the picture. For this application, we have already configured authentication for the specific routes defined in the requirements sections, and you can explore it in the API Gateway console:

1. Navigate to the API Gateway console `https://console.aws.amazon.com/apigateway`.
2. Select your API with the name you gave as part of the CloudFormation Stack parameters.
3. Select the option API: `[your API name]`.
4. Click on **Authorization** from the left menu.

You should see something that looks like *Figure 4.27*, with two endpoints with an authenticator associated. In this case, that's **JWT Auth**.

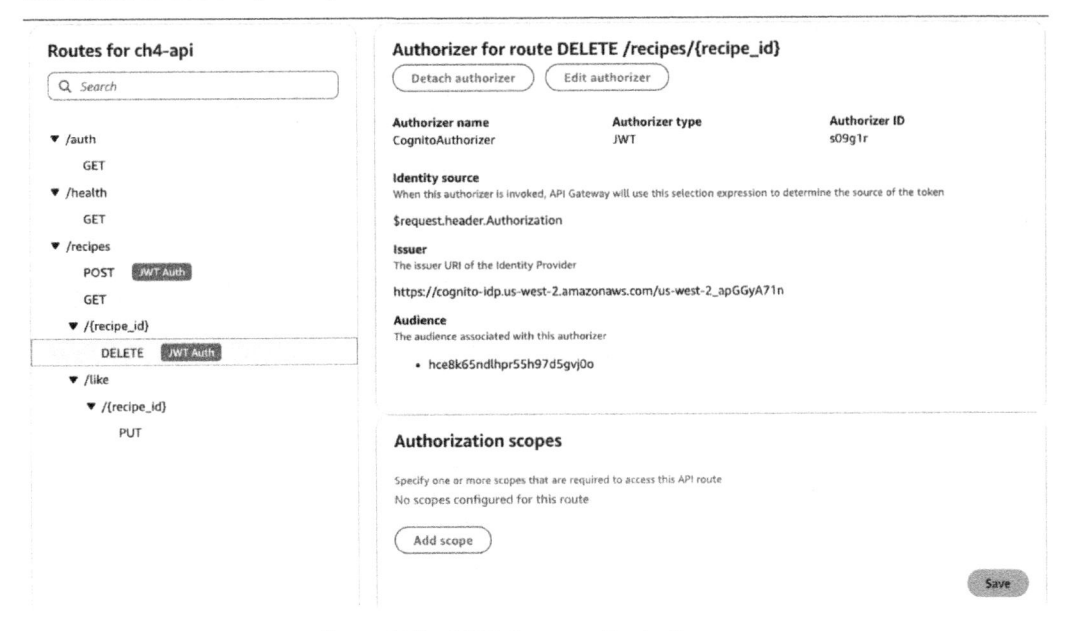

Figure 4.27 – API Gateway authorization pane

From the authorizer details on the right, you can see that it expects an authorization token in the **Authorization** header and will verify it based on your Cognito user pool configuration.

To understand the behavior, we have created the `/auth` route that, at this moment, does not require authorization, meaning it is publicly accessible. We will make some changes to understand how to make it a protected route and require an authorization token.

For this example, we used `curl`, but you can perform the same test with other tools, for example, Postman:

1. Perform a Get request to the `API_URL/auth` endpoint. You should have this value in your `config.tsx` file, but in case you do not have it available, you can access your **Outputs** tab from the CloudFormation console:

   ```
   $ curl -i YOUR_API_URL/auth
   HTTP/2 200
   ...
   {"message": "You've passed the authentication token"}
   ```

2. Change the authorization for this route to require the **Authorization** header:

   I. Access the **Authorization** pane of your API.

   II. Select the GET method under the /auth route.

   III. On the **Select an authorizer to view its details** dropdown, select **CognitoAuthorizer**.

   IV. Click on **Attach Authorizer**.

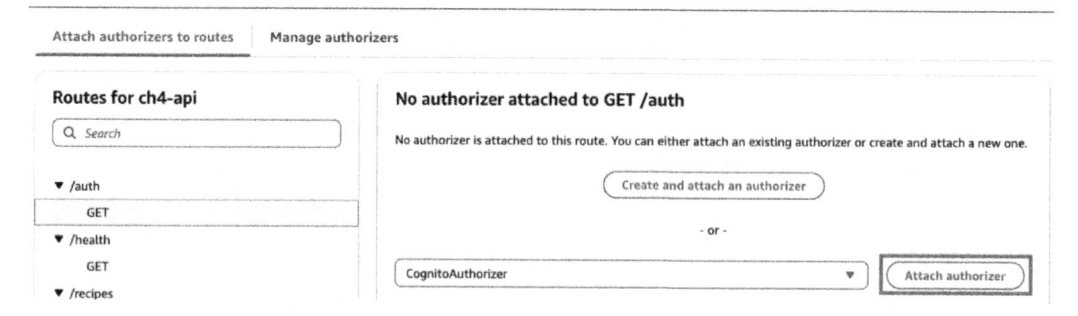

Figure 4.28 – Authorizer attachment process

Your **Authorization** menu should now include the **JWT Auth** mark in front of the **/auth | GET** option, as shown in *Figure 4.29*.

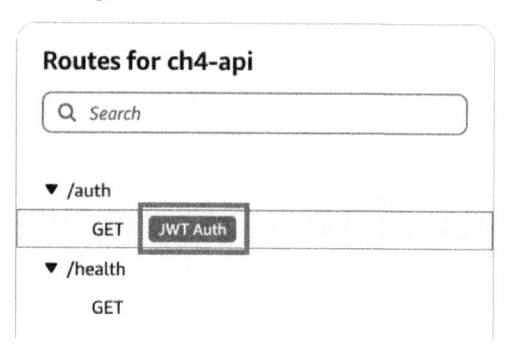

Figure 4.29 – Routes Authorizers' page

3. Perform the request again and confirm that we get an `Unauthorized` response:

   ```
   $ curl -i YOUR_API_URL/auth
   HTTP/2 401
   ...
   {"message": "Unauthorized"}
   ```

   Since you've changed /auth to require the authorization token and you are trying to perform the request without providing it, you are getting an `Unauthorized` response.

4. Change the request to include the authorization token. To get the authorization token, follow these steps:

   I. Go to your application in your browser.

   II. Navigate to the **Admin** console.

   III. If you are not authenticated, proceed with the sign-in process.

   IV. On the **Admin** page, hover over the access token and copy the full access token, as shown in *Figure 4.23*.

Now try to perform the same request but pass the `Authorization` header with the value you copied from your admin console:

```
$ curl -H "Authorization: YOUR_JWT_TOKEN" -i YOUR_API_URL/auth
HTTP/2 200
...
{"message": "You've passed the authentication token"}
```

With this change, you are able to perform requests to this route again.

Try to change a single character in your long JWT and you will note that modifying even a single character in your token means it will become invalid and any requests associated with that token will be rejected because the signature verification will fail, preventing unauthorized access.

Clean up

One of the main advantages of using serverless technologies is that they provide a pay-as-you-go model by design, meaning you only pay for what you use. However, in the long term, you may incur costs if you leave the application up and running, so it is recommended to clean your infrastructure if you are not using it anymore. Since we deployed it with an IaC, the clean-up process is very straightforward, and is composed of two steps:

1. Empty the bucket:

   I. Go to the S3 console in your AWS account.

II. Select your frontend s3 bucket (the name of the bucket should start with `frontend-chapter-4-`, followed by a random string).

III. Click on **Empty**; This will delete all the content inside your bucket.

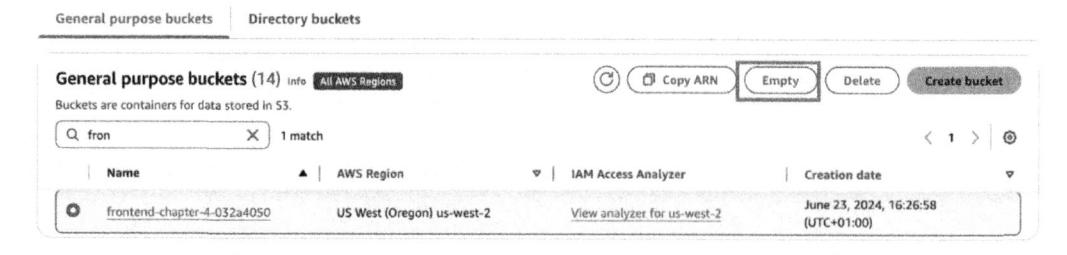

Figure 4.30 – Process of emptying an S3 bucket

2. Delete the CloudFormation stack:

   I. Go to the CloudFormation console in your AWS account.

   II. Select the stack you created.

   III. Click on **Delete**.

Note: If you don't see your CloudFormation stack on the list, try to change the region in the upper-right corner and select the region where you deployed your application. After that, you should proceed with the deletion process described and represented in *Figure 4.31*.

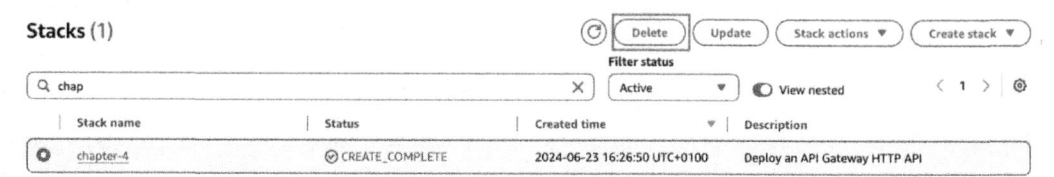

Figure 4.31 – CloudFormation Stack deletion

With the previous steps, you successfully removed all the resources created for the recipe-sharing application.

Rearchitecting your recipe-sharing application using serverless technologies has been an exciting experiment. However, as with any project, there are always opportunities for improvement. The next section will explore potential enhancements and future considerations to further refine your serverless recipe-sharing application.

Future work

Congratulations, you have built a new version of your recipe-sharing application with solely serverless technologies and you can now scale based on utilization without worrying about your application's infrastructure. This new recipe-sharing application already incorporates some of the future work highlighted in the previous chapter, for example, authentication or utilization of secure protocols, but there is always room for improvement.

Enrich your application with media content

So far, your application shows a set of ingredients and steps, which is the minimum required to follow a recipe. However, the first thing people look for is a photo of the expected result and your application still lacks this feature. As future work, you could invest in adding photos and videos to your recipe to improve the user experience and enrich the recipe content.

User profile

With your current authentication mechanism, only authorized users can manage the recipes, but for the end users, you have almost no visibility of their preferences and profiles. The likes feature gives you a notion of how popular a recipe is, but that does not mean it fits everyone's preferences. For example, a user may have some food restrictions and if you could offer a more customized experience, this would probably increase your application's popularity. As a future project, you could invest in letting your users create their own profiles, with their own preferences and food restrictions, and shortlist recipes based on their preferences.

In the last chapter, there was already a long list of possible improvements. Most of those still apply to this version of your application, for example, caching the content or defining a monitoring and logging platform, so we only focused on two additional features to add to the current list of future work.

Figure 4.32 demonstrates how your architecture could look based on the two proposed improvements we highlighted.

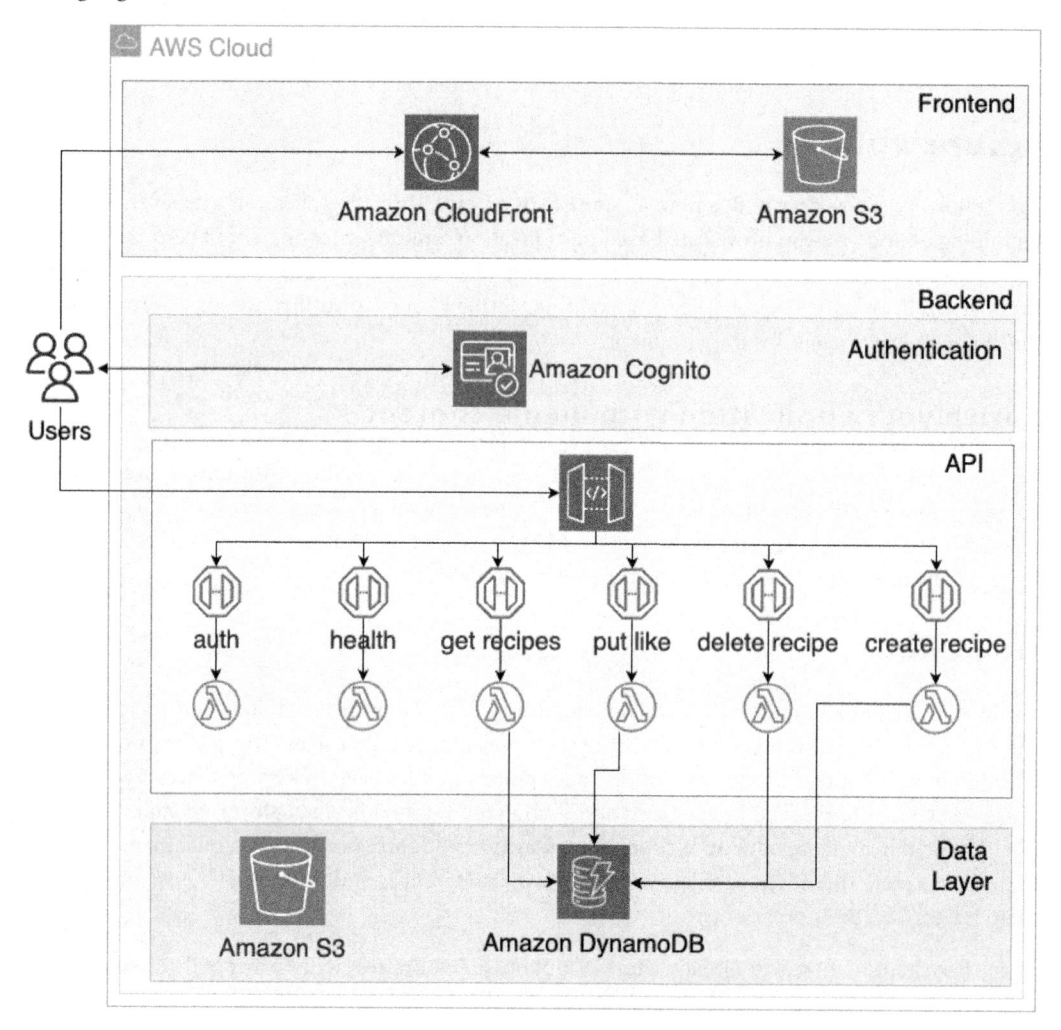

Figure 4.32 – Final architecture

Note that an Amazon S3 bucket was added to the data layer, which will be responsible for storing all the media content related to each recipe. As a learning exercise, think about how you can store the paths of the recipe photos and try to implement them.

As a hint, you could follow the same logic you have currently for ingredients and steps, and store the paths of each media file in an array inside the recipe document...

Summary

In this chapter, you invested in rearchitecting your previous application, and it is now more robust and feature-rich. Moreover, you focused only on serverless technologies such as Amazon API Gateway for our API, Amazon Cognito for the authentication layer, and Amazon Lambda for compute, and it should be clear how these technologies offer advantages in terms of scalability, cost efficiency, and operational effort. For the unchanged components such as Amazon S3 and Amazon CloudFront for the frontend, or Amazon DynamoDB as the data layer, you were able to practice and review it, so you should be more proficient with them.

In the next chapter, you will explore machine learning using AWS technologies to develop an image analyzer.

5
Implementing an Image Analyzer to Detect Photo Friendliness

This chapter is focused on the value that **machine learning** (**ML**) can bring to your applications. You are going to build another serverless application, but this time, you will take advantage of AWS-native ML services instead of complex programming logic.

You are going to build your application using Python and architecture using Terraform.

This chapter covers the following main topics in order:

- What you are going to build – a photo quality analyzer
- How you are going to build it – using serverless AWS services
- Building it – using Terraform and Python
- How to improve the application – using ML, advanced security features, and custom domain names

By the end of this chapter, you will have your own application that uses ML to identify if a photo is professional-looking enough for a profile picture. This is an introduction to more advanced ML applications that you will see in *Chapter 7*.

Technical requirements

To implement your own photo analyzer following these chapter instructions, you will need access to an AWS account.

This chapter has a dedicated folder in the GitHub repository of this book, where you will find the code snippets required to follow along: `https://github.com/PacktPublishing/AWS-Cloud-Projects/tree/main/chapter5/code`.

Scenario

You work for a marketing company. Your company receives customers' information and photos, curates them, and creates social media profiles for them.

However, your clients complain that they are not getting enough hits. After a study, the data science team attributes the lack of hits to unprofessional-looking photos.

You are tasked to create a system that identifies if a photo is professional-looking enough before it is uploaded to social media.

Requirements

You want to build something that evaluates if a photo is professional-looking. But what does it mean to be professional-looking? You decide that professional-looking photos require the subject to be smiling and have their eyes open.

How can you identify these characteristics in a photo? It is not an easy task to program logic that identifies specific characteristics in photos, especially when photos can come in so many file formats. An ML model has the best odds of yielding good results.

Because of the security compliance standards your company is subject to, your solution should not store personal information.

This application, unlike the others you built in previous chapters, does not require a user interface. It does, however, require that it integrates with existing applications at your marketing company.

All of these requirements can be translated into functional, non-functional, data, and technical requirements.

Functional requirements

Functional requirements define the specific features, functionalities, and capabilities that the solution must provide, which, in this case, are the following:

- Ability to recognize if a photo is good enough for a profile picture
- Interactable with other applications
- Support for multiple photo formats: `.png`, `.jpeg`

Non-functional requirements

Non-functional requirements define the qualitative attributes that the solution must provide, which, in this case, are the following:

- Highly-available
- Low-cost
- Scalable – up to 20 requests per second

Data requirements

Data requirements define data sources, processing, governance, and compliance needs, which, in this case, is the following:

- Must not store any personal data

Technical requirements

Technical requirements define specific technologies, programming languages, frameworks, and tools that the solution must use or integrate with, which, in this case, are the following:

- Must integrate with multiple other Python applications
- New infrastructure must be provisioned using Terraform
- The classification algorithm must use ML

Architecture patterns

Starting in the AWS Architecture Center, you can search for `image recognition` or `image classification`. The results, unfortunately, do not output any reference architecture. However, a prescriptive guidance document named *Image classification solutions on AWS* stands out (`https://docs.aws.amazon.com/prescriptive-guidance/latest/image-classification/introduction.html`).

Although the focus of this document is to identify objects in images, it also applies to your use case. For the image analysis, AWS recommends you follow one of four approaches:

- Use a pre-trained managed solution, for example, Amazon Rekognition
- Fine-tune a managed solution, for example, Amazon Rekognition Custom Labels
- Train a model using a no-code solution, for example, Amazon SageMaker Canvas
- Manually train a model on your own

For each of these options, they detail benefits and drawbacks, such as flexibility, effort, and cost. You can contrast these with your requirements.

Architecture

A possible agnostic architecture, applying what you have learned in previous chapters, looks like *Figure 5.1*. Different applications connect to a frontend component, which handles connection termination, SSL certificates, and so on, and orchestrates and load balances backend connections where the submitted photos are parsed and analyzed.

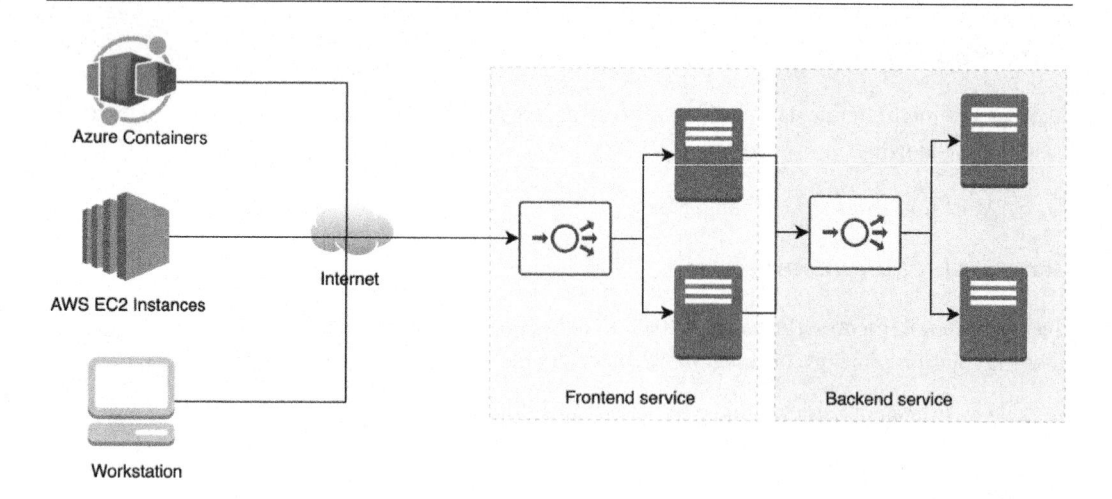

122   Implementing an Image Analyzer to Detect Photo Friendliness

Figure 5.1 – Photo classification architecture

A diagram using AWS services looks like the one in *Figure 5.2*: a three-component diagram, with API Gateway, Lambda, and Rekognition. Different types of applications will connect to API Gateway using HTTPS, invoking a Lambda function, which queries Rekognition for image analysis and parses the response accordingly.

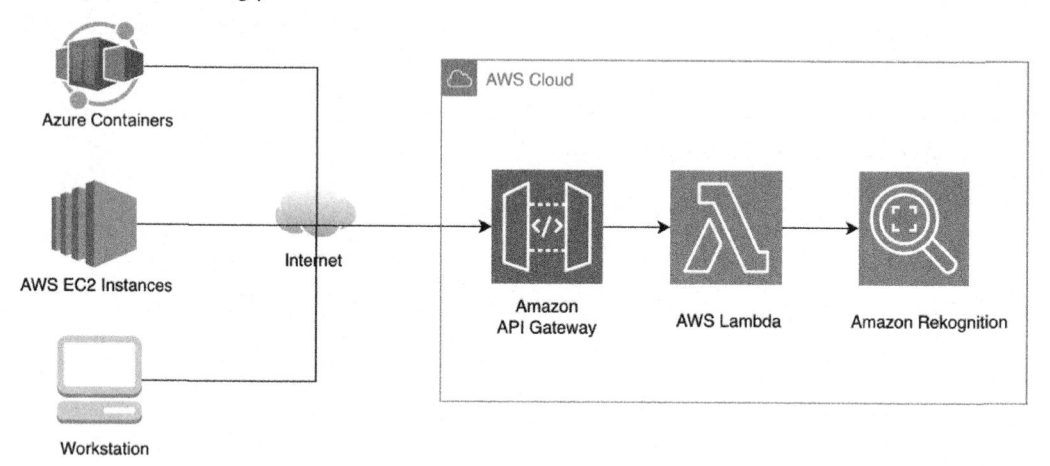

Figure 5.2 – Photo classification architecture on AWS

In the following section, you will find a detailed explanation of why Rekognition is the better tool for this use case. For now, trust us.

In this architecture, you collapse the frontend and the backend in API Gateway and Lambda.

You might be asking yourself, "Why can't I allow my consuming applications to interact with Rekognition directly?" You can't do this for several reasons:

- It requires all consuming applications to have access to AWS credentials
- It does not allow for parsing and customization of the response
- It does not allow custom authentication/authorization

As shown, your consumer applications can be any type, and be anywhere; they can be virtual machines on EC2, containers on other cloud providers, or simply your workstation.

AWS services

This architecture uses three services, but you have used two of them before. In this section, you will understand how they address this project's requirements.

Amazon Rekognition

For this use case, you don't want to create programming logic to identify photo features, so you choose to implement the same functionality using ML.

As mentioned in the AWS prescriptive guidance, you can create your own model from scratch. But how does it compare with using a pre-trained managed service?

First, before comparing the two, you need to identify a service that can handle the task. AWS has a vast suite of AI and ML services:

- **Amazon Rekognition**: A computer vision service that is designed to analyze images and videos for various use cases, such as facial analysis, object detection, and text recognition.
- **Amazon Transcribe**: An **automatic speech recognition** (**ASR**) service that converts audio files to text.
- **Amazon Translate**: A neural machine translation service that can translate text between multiple languages.
- **Amazon Comprehend**: A **natural language processing** (**NLP**) service that can extract insights and relationships from unstructured text data.
- **Amazon Kendra**: An intelligent search service that can be used for indexing and searching multimedia content, including images and videos.
- **Amazon Lex**: A service for building conversational interfaces and chatbots, using natural language understanding and automatic speech recognition.
- **Amazon Polly**: A text-to-speech service that can convert text into lifelike speech.

Amazon Rekognition seems like a perfect fit. Its main capabilities are as follows:

- **Facial analysis**:
    - Detect and analyze faces in images and videos.
    - Identify facial attributes, such as gender, age range, emotions, and facial hair.
    - Recognize and identify faces by comparing them against a user-provided dataset of faces.
    - Detect unsafe content in images or videos based on explicit or suggestive content.

- **Object and scene detection**:
    - Detect and label objects, people, text, scenes, and activities in images and videos.
    - Identify objects and concepts with high accuracy.
    - Provide bounding boxes around detected objects and scenes.

- **Text recognition**:
    - Detect and recognize text in images and videos.
    - Extract textual content from different surfaces and orientations.

- **Moderation**:
    - Detect and filter out explicit or suggestive content in images and videos.
    - Automatically flag inappropriate or offensive content.

> **Important note**
> Take into consideration that when using Amazon Rekognition or any facial recognition technology, it's crucial to consider privacy and ethical concerns, as well as compliance with relevant laws and regulations.

So, should you use Rekognition facial analysis capabilities or build your own model? Both approaches are valid, and the main comparison points are as follows:

- **Ease of use**:
    - Rekognition is a fully managed service, which means you don't have to worry about setting up and maintaining the underlying infrastructure or training models. It provides an API to analyze images.
    - Training your own ML model requires expertise in data preparation, model architecture selection, training techniques, and deployment strategies. It involves a significant learning curve and hands-on work. It also requires vast amounts of data.

- **Customization and control**:

  - Rekognition offers pre-trained models. While it provides some customization options, such as creating custom collections for facial recognition, the level of customization is limited.

  - Training your own model allows you to have complete control over the model architecture, training data, and fine-tuning processes. This enables you to tailor the model specifically to your use case and achieve higher accuracy for specialized tasks.

- **Data privacy and security**:

  - Using Rekognition, your data – images, in this case – is sent to AWS for processing, which can raise data privacy and security concerns.

  - When training your own model, you have complete control over the data and can ensure that sensitive information never leaves your environment, providing better data privacy and security.

- **Scalability and performance**:

  - Rekognition is a highly scalable service that can handle large volumes of data and concurrent requests.

  - Training and deploying your own model at scale can be challenging, as it requires provisioning and managing compute resources, optimizing performance, and handling infrastructure-related tasks.

- **Cost and resource management**:

  - Rekognition follows a pay-as-you-go pricing model, where you pay for API requests. This is cost-effective for smaller workloads or intermittent usage.

  - Training your own model requires upfront investment in hardware resources, as well as ongoing costs for managing and maintaining the infrastructure.

In summary, Rekognition provides a convenient and scalable solution for common computer vision tasks, but with limited customization options. Training your own ML model offers more flexibility and control but requires significant expertise, data, and resources.

In this case, Rekognition is the winner. You do not have thousands of images labeled with the features you want to identify, nor do you have the data science knowledge or time to build an end-to-end ML framework.

Relating it to your requirements, Rekognition is a highly available scalable service, that supports up to 100 requests per second. It supports both the `.jpeg` and `.png` image formats and does not store your submitted images. It also qualifies as low-cost; in the N. Virginia region, it costs a tenth of a cent, 0.001$, to analyze 1 image. Because of its pay-as-you-go model, you will only pay if you analyze images; sitting idle has no cost.

Amazon API Gateway and AWS Lambda

In the *Architecture* section of this chapter, you learned why interacting directly with Rekognition was not ideal. However, you ask yourself, "What indirection layer should I use?"

You could use Lambda directly.

Lambda allows you to parse requests and Rekognition responses. Using Lambda function URLs, you will be able to access your function from other applications using HTTPS (see `https://docs.aws.amazon.com/lambda/latest/dg/lambda-urls.html`). However, Lambda function URLs only support IAM authentication or no authentication, and one of your requirements was not to have AWS credentials spread everywhere.

Or, maybe, you could use only API Gateway. As you learned in the previous chapter, it provides you with a unique domain name that you can interact with through HTTP and a multitude of features. However, it comes with drawbacks, too; although you can do some request and response mapping, it is hard to implement programming logic. Rekognition will not return a good/bad photo diagnosis, but rather a list of image attributes that you must parse to compute a decision.

There is a blocking limitation for the API Gateway-only approach. API Gateway does not integrate directly with all AWS services, more specifically it does not integrate directly with Rekognition. For this, you need to use a Lambda integration.

For this project, your indirection layer should be a combination of both.

> **Important note**
> Lambda function URLs are fit for use cases where you need a single function with a public endpoint that doesn't require advanced API Gateway functionalities, such as request validation, throttling, custom authorizers, custom domain names, and caching.
>
> They are a great way to invoke your Lambda functions during testing.
>
> You could use them for this chapter's use case, however, to mimic a real project, you won't.

API Gateway together with Lambda will allow you to do the following:

- **Control access to your services by authenticating and authorizing requests**: You can configure API keys, IAM roles, and other custom authentication mechanisms.

- **Simplify API versioning and life cycle management**: You can create and deploy multiple versions of your Rekognition integration API, and manage the transition between versions seamlessly.

- **Implement built-in request throttling and rate limiting capabilities**: This helps to protect your backend services, such as Rekognition, from being overwhelmed by excessive requests, which could lead to service disruptions and higher costs.

Relating it to your requirements, Lambda and API Gateway allow you to receive requests from many types of applications using a well-known and accepted protocol, HTTPS, integrate with Rekognition for image analysis, process the response into a diagnosis of good/bad photos in a pay-as-you-go serverless manner without storing the image in any of the underlying architecture components. You can do all of this using highly available and scalable components.

Coding the solution

Congratulations again – you designed an architecture that meets all your company's requirements. Now, it's time to build it. During this chapter, we are going to use the AWS N. Virginia region. You can change the Terraform variable to your preferred region.

Building the infrastructure

The solution requirements mandated that the infrastructure be built using Terraform because the IaC language is already being used in the company.

In this book's GitHub repository, in the `chapter5/code` folder, you will find the following files: `interact.py`, `lambda.tf`, `apigw.tf`, `badphoto.png`, `goodphoto.jpeg`, and a Python subdirectory.

Start by focusing on the two terraform files: `apigw.tf` and `lambda.tf`. Recall that your architecture had three components. You don't need to create your own Amazon Rekognition because it is **Software as a Service (SaaS)**, and because of that, it doesn't have a Terraform resource representation.

> **Important note**
> Although many people use a `main.tf` file to describe their infrastructure in Terraform, Terraform considers all files with a `.tf` extension in the directory. Filenames do not matter.

Start by exploring the `lambda.tf` file. Inside, you will find five resource definitions; `aws_lambda_function` is the one that creates your lambda function named `Detection_Lambda_Function`.

```
data "aws_iam_policy" "rekognition_policy" {
  arn = "arn:aws:iam::aws:policy/AmazonRekognitionReadOnlyAccess"
}
resource "aws_iam_role_policy_attachment" "codedeploy_service_role_policy_attach" {
    role       = aws_iam_role.lambda_role.name
    policy_arn = "${data.aws_iam_policy.rekognition_policy.arn}"
}
data "archive_file" "zip_the_python_code" {
    type        = "zip"
    source_file = "${path.module}/python/rekognition.py"
```

```
    output_path = "${path.module}/python/rekognition.zip"
}
resource "aws_lambda_function" "terraform_lambda_func" {
    filename                       = "${path.module}/python/
rekognition.zip"
    function_name                  = "Detection_Lambda_Function"
    role                           = aws_iam_role.lambda_role.arn
    handler                        = "rekognition.lambda_handler"
    runtime                        = "python3.8"
    depends_on                     = [aws_iam_role_policy_attachment.
attach_iam_policy_to_iam_role]
}
```

In this same Terraform file, `lambda.tf`, you also create an IAM role named `Detection_Lambda_Function_Role`, which has two IAM policies attached: `aws_iam_policy_for_terraform_aws_lambda_role` and `AmazonRekognitionReadOnlyAccess`. This is necessary for your Lambda function to be able to access other AWS services, in this case, Rekognition and CloudWatch Logs. Notice how the IAM policies are based on the least privilege principle, allowing the Lambda function only read access to the required services.

Because your marketing company is already using Python, you also choose Python for your Lambda function. Maintaining a single, or few, programming languages helps with developer productivity. You will dive deeper into the application code in the next section, but note how this Terraform project handles code deployment; it's using a `.zip` file. This Lambda function uses Python 3.8 as runtime, but by the time you are reading this, you might have to upgrade it to a higher version. If that's the case, simply change the runtime variable.

In the second Terraform file, `apigw.tf`, you will find eight resources. An API gateway, to work, has to have multiple components: stages, resources, and methods. Also, it needs permissions to interact with other components, in this case, your Lambda function.

```
resource "aws_api_gateway_rest_api" "my_api" {
  name = "my-api"
  description = "My API Gateway"

  endpoint_configuration {
    types = ["REGIONAL"]
  }
}
resource "aws_api_gateway_resource" "root" {
  rest_api_id = aws_api_gateway_rest_api.my_api.id
  parent_id = aws_api_gateway_rest_api.my_api.root_resource_id
  path_part = "friendly"
}
```

The first two Terraform resources, my-api and root, create a regional API gateway named my-api, and a /friendly resource path on the root resource. This will be accessible at API_Gateway_URL/friendly, as you will see later.

The four following resources in apigw.tf define a POST method for the /friendly resource path:

```
resource "aws_api_gateway_method" "proxy" {
  rest_api_id = aws_api_gateway_rest_api.my_api.id
  resource_id = aws_api_gateway_resource.root.id
  http_method = "POST"
  authorization = "NONE"
}
resource "aws_api_gateway_integration" "lambda_integration" {
  rest_api_id = aws_api_gateway_rest_api.my_api.id
  resource_id = aws_api_gateway_resource.root.id
  http_method = aws_api_gateway_method.proxy.http_method
  integration_http_method = "POST"
  type = "AWS"
  uri = aws_lambda_function.terraform_lambda_func.invoke_arn
}
resource "aws_api_gateway_method_response" "proxy" {
  rest_api_id = aws_api_gateway_rest_api.my_api.id
  resource_id = aws_api_gateway_resource.root.id
  http_method = aws_api_gateway_method.proxy.http_method
  status_code = "200"
}
resource "aws_api_gateway_integration_response" "proxy" {
  rest_api_id = aws_api_gateway_rest_api.my_api.id
  resource_id = aws_api_gateway_resource.root.id
  http_method = aws_api_gateway_method.proxy.http_method
  status_code = aws_api_gateway_method_response.proxy.status_code
  depends_on = [
    aws_api_gateway_method.proxy,
    aws_api_gateway_integration.lambda_integration
  ]
}
```

This code creates four components, as shown in *Figure 5.3*: **Method request**, represented by the aws_api_gateway_method resource, **Integration request**, represented by the aws_api_gateway_integration resource, **Integration response** represented by the aws_api_gateway_integration_response resource, and **Method response**, represented by the aws_api_gateway_method_response resource.

This is where you can do things such as request and response processing. In this case, you define the method request as a `POST` method without authentication, and the integration request type as Lambda. You don't alter the response of the Lambda, just proxy it back.

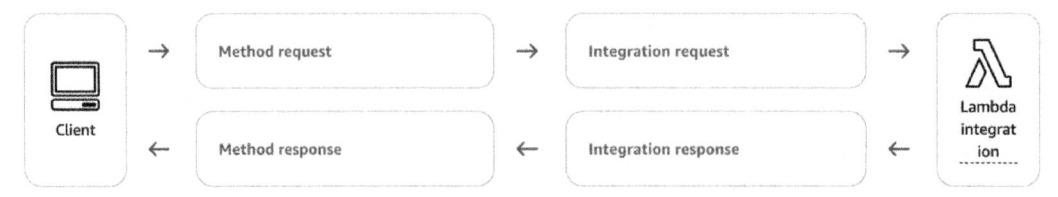

Figure 5.3 – API gateway method settings

At the end of `apigw.tf`, you will find a resource named `apigw_lambda`, which alters your Lambda permissions to allow the API gateway to invoke it.

In your favorite terminal, navigate to the `chapter5/code` folder, run the following Terraform command, and confirm. This will create all the resources mentioned in this section:

```
$ terraform apply
```

If your `apply` command is successful, it should output something like the following:

```
aws_iam_policy.iam_policy_for_lambda: Creation complete after 1s
[id=arn:aws:iam::381672823963:policy/aws_iam_policy_for_terraform_aws_
lambda_role]
aws_api_gateway_rest_api.my_api: Creation complete after 1s
[id=2g9sm87cnd]
aws_iam_role.lambda_role: Creation complete after 1s [id=Detection_
Lambda_Function_Role]
aws_api_gateway_resource.root: Creation complete after 1s [id=064211]
aws_iam_role_policy_attachment.codedeploy_service_role_policy_attach:
Creation complete after 1s [id=Detection_Lambda_Function_Role-
20240401171553538300000001]
aws_iam_role_policy_attachment.attach_iam_policy_to_iam_role:
Creation complete after 1s [id=Detection_Lambda_Function_Role-
20240401171553543900000002]
aws_api_gateway_method.proxy: Creation complete after 0s [id=agm-
2g9sm87cnd-064211-POST]
aws_api_gateway_method_response.proxy: Creation complete after 0s
[id=agmr-2g9sm87cnd-064211-POST-200]
aws_lambda_function.terraform_lambda_func: Creation complete after 15s
[id=Detection_Lambda_Function]
aws_api_gateway_integration.lambda_integration: Creation complete
after 0s [id=agi-2g9sm87cnd-064211-POST]
aws_lambda_permission.apigw_lambda: Creation complete after 0s
[id=AllowExecutionFromAPIGateway]
```

```
aws_api_gateway_integration_response.proxy: Creation complete after 0s
[id=agir-2g9sm87cnd-064211-POST-200]
aws_api_gateway_deployment.deployment: Creation complete after 1s
[id=g5m5qa]
Apply complete! Resources: 13 added, 0 changed, 0 destroyed.
Outputs:
deployment_invoke_url = "https://2g9sm87cnd.execute-api.us-east-1.
amazonaws.com/dev"
```

Note down your deployment URL. You will use it later.

Open your AWS console and navigate to API Gateway, Lambda, and IAM to verify everything that was created.

Understanding the image analyzer code

The Terraform infrastructure code you deployed in the previous section created a Lambda function with application logic. Open the `rekognition.py` file in the directory named `python` of the `chapter5/code` folder.

You will find boilerplate code, as in the previous chapter, to integrate with the Lambda ecosystem. But more interesting than that is the way it interacts with the Rekognition `DetectFaces` API (see https://docs.aws.amazon.com/rekognition/latest/APIReference/API_DetectFaces.html).

The code calls the `DetectFaces` API and parses the response to make sure the photo does not contain more than one person, and that the person is smiling and has their eyes open:

```
rekognition_response = rekognition.detect_faces(
Image=image, Attributes=['ALL'])

if len(rekognition_response['FaceDetails']) != 1:
    raise ValueError(
        'Please upload a picture with only one face')

smile = rekognition_response['FaceDetails'][0]['Smile']
eyesOpen = rekognition_response['FaceDetails'][0]['EyesOpen']

result = 'Bad Profile Photo'

if smile['Value'] == True and eyesOpen['Value'] == True:
    result = 'Good Profile Photo'
```

The Rekognition `DetectFaces` API also returns a list of emotions identified in the person's photo. The script is set up to save the list in a variable named `Emotions`:

```
#'HAPPY'|'SAD'|'ANGRY'|'CONFUSED'|'DISGUSTED'|'SURPRISED'|'CALM'|
'UNKNOWN'|'FEAR'
Emotions = rekognition_response['FaceDetails'][0]['Emotions']
```

Enhance the script to take the person's emotions into consideration before making the final verdict of a good or bad photo.

Testing your application

Congratulations, you have a working photo identification application in AWS, which identifies if a photo is professional-looking enough for social media.

Figure 5.4 shows what you've deployed so far. An API Gateway endpoint with a `dev` stage, configured with a `/friendly` resource path that supports the `POST` method. This method invokes a Lambda, written in Python, that calls the Rekognition `DetectFaces` API and parses the results.

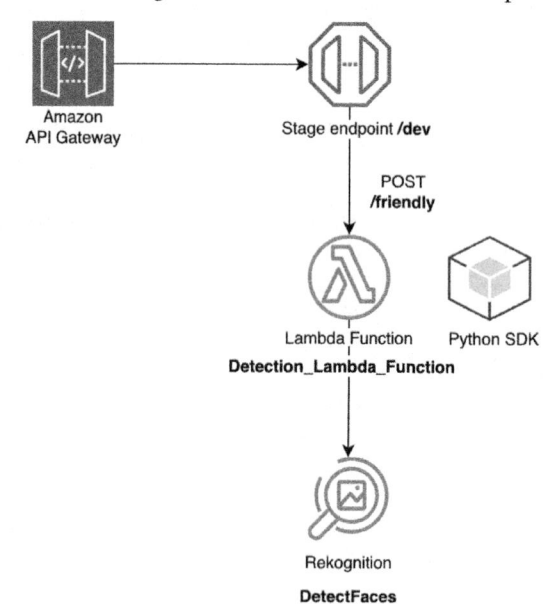

Figure 5.4 – Image analyzer API architecture

However, you have not really tested it. How do you know it works?

This application does not have a user interface like the previous ones. Nonetheless, there are multiple ways to interact with these types of HTTP applications, for example: using a terminal tool, such as `curl`, using an application, such as Postman, or using another application, such as a Python script.

Start with Postman. Postman is an API platform for building and using APIs. If you do not have it installed, install it and open it.

Select POST as the method and paste your previously noted deployment URL, followed by `/friendly` at the end of it in the URL field. Navigate to the body section, select `raw`, and paste the following code:

```
{ "image": "b64" }
```

You are missing images to test this application. Recall that your Lambda function received an image as an input. You will find two images in the `chapter5/code` folder: `goodphoto.jpeg` and `badphoto.png`.

To send images over the wire, the easiest way is to use `base64` encoding. Open your favorite terminal, navigate to where the images are located, and run the `openssl` command, replacing the `<infile>` and `<outfile>` variables with `badphoto.png` and `badphoto.txt` respectively. This command creates a new file named `badphoto.txt`. Inside, you will find the `base64` representation of your image:

```
openssl base64 -A -in <infile> -out <outfile>
```

Go back to Postman and replace the body with your generated `base64` encoding. Send the request. The result should look like *Figure 5.5*. You receive a `200 OK` status code, with a `Bad Profile Photo` response in the body.

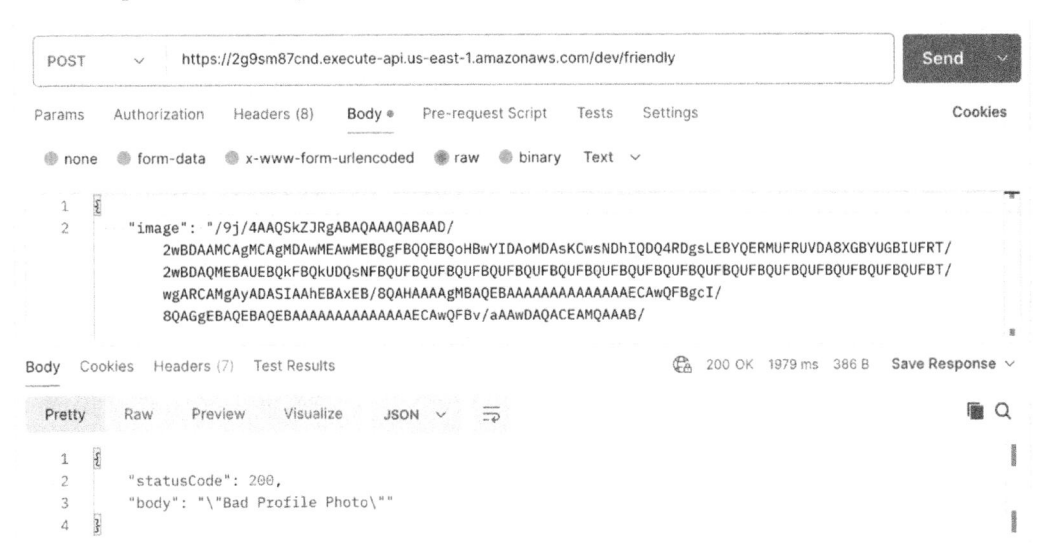

Figure 5.5 – Postman configuration

Do it again, this time with the good photo in the same directory, and observe how the response is different. You can also do it more times with photos of yourself or friends.

However, the initial focus of this project was to be integrated with other applications, many of them Python applications. Open the `interact.py` file located in the `chapter5/code` folder.

In this file, you will find a Python application that reads two arguments, `url` and `image`, from the standard input and sends a `POST` request to the received URL, with the image encoded in `base64` in the body:

```python
def analyze_image(url, image):

    with open(image, 'rb') as image_file:
        image_bytes = image_file.read()
        data = base64.b64encode(image_bytes).decode("utf8")
        payload = {"image": data}

    response = requests.post(url, json=payload)
    return response.json()


def main():
    try:
        parser = argparse.ArgumentParser(usage=argparse.SUPPRESS)
        parser.add_argument("url", help="The url of your API Gateway")
        parser.add_argument("image", help="The local image that you want to analyze.")
        args = parser.parse_args()
        result = analyze_image(args.url, args.image)
```

From your terminal, in the `chapter5/code` directory, test this application using the following syntax. You will only need to replace `invoke_url` with your own. This application converts the image into `base64` for you, so you don't need to use the `openssl` tool:

```
$ python3 interact.py invoke_url goodphoto.jpeg
```

This application returns the response to your terminal window. Other applications, more complex ones, could just parse it and make a decision based on it. For example, when someone tries to upload a photo, block the upload.

Cleaning up

This architecture does not cost you anything if no requests are made. All services used are paid for by the request and have no provisioning cost. Nonetheless, it is a good practice to delete the solution when you are done using it.

To delete all the resources, run the following command in the `chapter5/code` directory and confirm:

```
$ terraform destroy
```

Terraform keeps a state file of its deployed resources, and it will only delete the ones it is managing. If you have other resources manually deployed on the same account, those will not be deleted.

Future work

There is only so much a book chapter can cover. Your project works and covers the requirements. It identifies if a photo is professional-looking enough, but you can still improve it.

Implementing authentication and authorization

Currently, anyone can discover and call your API gateway to verify if their photo is professional-looking. A malicious actor can take advantage of this, and you will incur high costs.

In the previous chapter, you already implemented Cognito to manage authentication and authorization. You could do the same for this application, or if your client applications also run on AWS, you could change your REST API to a private API. In this case, your API gateway will only be reachable within the VPC and no longer be internet-reachable. You can read more about it in the AWS documentation at `https://docs.aws.amazon.com/apigateway/latest/developerguide/apigateway-private-apis.html`.

Improving your security posture

You are way past the static websites you learned in *Chapter 2*. This chapter's application receives users' input. This is a potential attack vector, as a malicious persona can upload custom software to exploit vulnerabilities.

One way to mitigate this is to attach a WAF with security policies to your API gateway and benefit from all its security features described in *Chapter 2*.

To implement it, follow the AWS documentation: `https://docs.aws.amazon.com/apigateway/latest/developerguide/apigateway-control-access-aws-waf.html`.

Implementing custom names

You are calling your API using the URL given to you by AWS. It's not a human-friendly name.

To change this, you will need to have your own domain name and create a certificate.

In *Chapter 3*, you did this for a load balancer. API Gateway also supports custom domain names and certificates.

To implement it, follow the AWS documentation: `https://docs.aws.amazon.com/apigateway/latest/developerguide/how-to-custom-domains.html`.

Improving the image analysis algorithm

Currently, your algorithm detects if the photo has a single person, if that person has their eyes open, and if they are smiling. If you implemented the emotions functionality, that is also taken into consideration for the final verdict.

However, consider the following scenario: a photo of a fully naked person with their eyes open and smiling. Is it a professional-looking photo? Your algorithm thinks so.

You've already exhausted all the useful `DetectFaces` Rekognition API response fields. However, you can use other APIs to enhance your solution.

For example, `DetectModerationLabels` detects if images contain inappropriate or offensive content. Examples include explicit nudity, violence, hate symbols, and drugs. You can see all the supported content and how to use it on AWS documentation, `https://docs.aws.amazon.com/rekognition/latest/dg/procedure-moderate-images.html`.

To implement it, you could follow different two approaches depending on your preference:

- Chain API calls on your already existing Lambda and mash all the results into a decision.
- Create a different API resource, for example, `/moderate`, and a different Lambda function, and chain calls from the consuming client applications.

Your application is synchronous. If you add a lot of different functionality to do the image verification, the response latency will increase, and your user experience will feel degraded.

You can change your clients' expectations to submit a photo and wait to receive the verdict at a later date. Then, transform your application into an asynchronous processing application where you chain a bunch of verifications, and deliver the decision at the end.

Hosting your own ML model

What if the functionality you are looking for does not exist in a managed service? Or, maybe it exists, but it does not yield the results you are looking for. For example, let's say you want to identify if the photo was taken by a professional photographer.

In these cases, you can train and host your own ML models.

As briefly mentioned before in this chapter, training your own ML models requires expertise in data engineering, model training, and selection and deployment strategies.

If you already have this expertise, or, if you want to practice, create a model using Amazon SageMaker and call it from your API gateway in a new resource path. This integration will also require a Lambda function.

SageMaker is a fully managed AWS service that aims to simplify and streamline the entire ML workflow, from data preparation to the deployment and operation of ML models.

Summary

In this chapter, you saw how AI and ML can help you solve problems that are traditionally hard for regular programming to solve. You, again, followed a structured methodology to approach the project, starting from the requirements, checking for reusable assets, and lastly, architecting.

This time, you built using Terraform.

You dove deep into application logic using Python to retrieve and parse API responses. Then, again, for testing.

At the end of this chapter, you have multiple ideas that you can implement on your own using the AWS documentation to improve this chapter's project. You can now, confidently, take advantage of AI/ML in your future projects.

In the next chapter, you are going to continue to learn about ML systems, this time applied to dynamic content translation. But that is not all; you will also start your journey into CI/CD tooling.

6
Architecting a Content Translation Pipeline

In this chapter, you are going to have your first contact with **Continuous Integration and Continuous Delivery (CI/CD)**. You are going to build an event website that automatically renders in your users' preferred language but deploys it in an automated fashion unlike you have done so far.

Just like in the previous chapter, you are also going to use AWS machine learning services, Python, and Terraform.

In summary, this chapter covers the following main topics:

- What you are going to build – a multilingual web application using a CICD pipeline
- How you are going to build it – using S3, CloudFront, Lambda@Edge, Translate, and CICD tooling
- Building it – using Terraform and Python
- How to improve the application – adopting CICD for infrastructure and supporting more languages

By the end of this chapter, you will have hands-on experience with AWS CI/CD services and be able to build your own application pipelines.

Technical requirements

This chapter has a dedicated folder in the GitHub repository of this book, where you will find the code snippets required to follow along: https://github.com/PacktPublishing/AWS-Cloud-Projects/tree/main/chapter6/code.

To follow along, you will need access to an AWS account.

Scenario

Your company hosts tech events, such as conferences and webinars, in North America. Your marketing colleagues publicize these events, individually, on various social media platforms. However, they think it would be beneficial to have a single page where people can find all the upcoming events.

You are tasked to create a **proof of concept** for this functionality as a web application.

In a conversation with a senior leader, she mentions that accessibility is a company tenet. She also mentions that although all your company events are streamed in multiple languages, they are always only advertised in English. This is reflected in their attendance numbers.

Requirements

You need to build an application that shows all the upcoming company events and takes the user to the event's registration page. Language accessibility is important; the application should dynamically render in the user's preferred language.

Since events keep happening, and new ones are scheduled, you need a mechanism to make changes.

Cloud costs at the company are at an all-time high. This application should be as low-cost as possible while maintaining high availability. If people try to access it, and it is down, that will reflect in lower event attendance. However, you do not want to contribute to even higher cloud costs.

You can format the requirements into various categories: functional, non-functional, and technical.

Functional requirements

Functional requirements define the specific features, functionalities, and capabilities that the solution must provide. In this case, those are as follows:

- Display company future events
- Ability to create, edit, and delete events
- Ability to roll back to previous versions
- Support for images and text
- Interfaces must adapt to users' preferred languages

Non-functional requirements

Non-functional requirements define the qualitative attributes that the solution must provide. In this case, those are as follows:

- Low cost
- Low latency in North America

- High availability
- Ease of maintainability

Technical requirements

Technical requirements define specific technologies, programming languages, frameworks, and tools that the solution must use or integrate with. In this case, those are as follows:

- Must integrate with Terraform codebase
- Must use an automated mechanism for content translation

Architecture patterns

Navigate to the AWS Architecture Center and search for `content localization`. You will find *Guidance for Automated Language Translations on AWS* and *Content Localization on AWS* reference architecture.

The reference architecture is for a solution that creates multi-language subtitles, while the guidance is focused on translation product information that sits in databases. Although these are not exact matches, you can see a pattern: both take advantage of Amazon Translate for the actual content translation.

Before moving on, search for `CICD`. This returns plenty of results. Explore them. A particularly interesting one is **CI/CD for .NET Applications on AWS Fargate**. It uses CodeCommit as a code repository, CodeBuild to build the artifacts, and finally, ECS to deploy them. All these are orchestrated as CodePipeline stages.

At the time of writing this, CodeCommit was deprecated by AWS.

None of the architectures are an exact match to your requirements. You must design it yourself.

Architecture

There are separate ways to render a webpage in the users' preferred languages. You can use specific framework tools, such as `i18n` in React, or infrastructure redirection, such as `Lambda@Edge`.

> **Important note**
> This is a practical AWS book, not a specific web framework one, so this chapter implements the infrastructure redirection method.

However, how do you identify a user's preferred language? You can add a button at the top for the user to choose the language. This is a common approach. However, you can do better. You will make it automatically detect the users' preferences based on request properties.

After deciding how you want to implement the language rendering, and going back to the solution requirements, you will notice that they are similar to *Chapters 2* and *3*. However, since this is a proof of concept, and you want to minimize time to market, you decide to re-use the static architecture, with a configuration that automatically detects the language property and sends the appropriate resources. Using AWS services, the architecture looks like *Figure 6.1*. Use two or more S3 buckets to store your application pages (in this case, English and Spanish), and CloudFront with `Lambda@Edge` to inspect users' requests and fetch specific language assets.

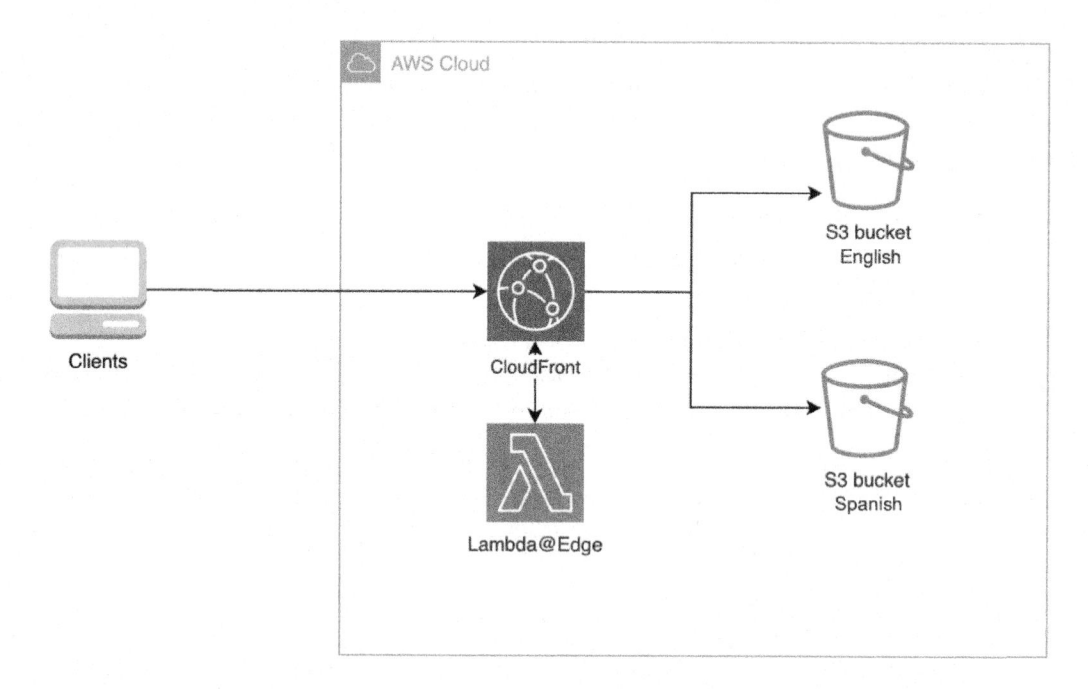

Figure 6.1 – Multilingual static website architecture

This architecture works, but it does not fulfill all requirements, such as ease of maintainability or automatic translation. You can add, alter, and delete events; however, in *Chapter 2*, it was a single bucket. In this new architecture, every time you want to make a change, you must replicate it to all the buckets. You are also missing an automated mechanism to create translated content. Although you can use S3 object versioning to support rollbacks, it is not an ideal mechanism, especially when you must keep your content in sync in multiple different buckets.

As you previously saw in the Architecture Center, CI/CD can help with building and pushing changes to applications. In this case, you could store your web application files in a code repository and use a CICD pipeline to orchestrate the translation and synchronization of your content to multiple buckets. *Figure 6.2* shows what it looks like using AWS services. The application administrator, Admin, stores the application files in English in a GitHub repository. Changes to the repository trigger a CodePipeline that interacts with Amazon Translate to generate translated versions of the files and deploys them in their respective buckets. The GitHub repository is depicted inside the AWS cloud, but it lives outside. This was just for ease of representation.

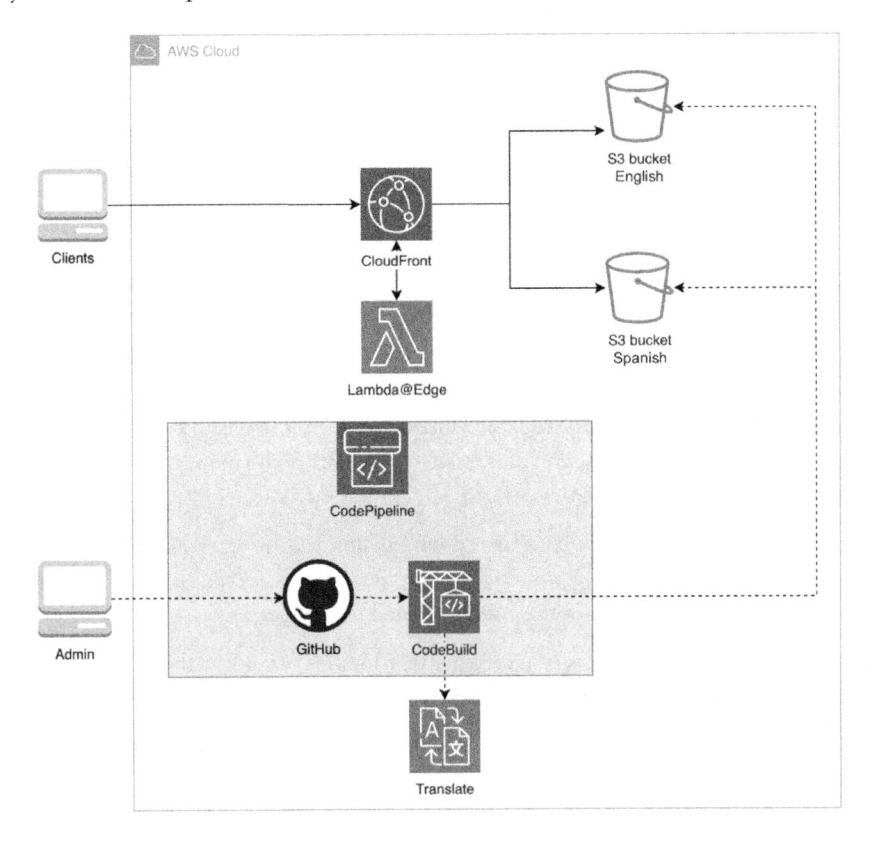

Figure 6.2 – Multilingual website with a content translation pipeline architecture

Using this architecture, the administrator only makes changes in a single place, in a single language. Although the example shows Spanish, modifications can be propagated to any number of configured languages.

AWS CI/CD services are one of many options. You can also implement this architecture using 3rd party CI/CD tools. Examples include Jenkins, GitHub Actions, or GitLab CI/CD.

AWS services

This architecture uses four new services. In this section, you will learn what these new services do, and why they address your requirements.

Other services, such as S3 or CloudFront, were already deployed previously. Refer to the previous chapters for an in-depth explanation of their functionality.

Lambda@Edge

You already learned about Lambda in other chapters, but Lambda@Edge is different. Instead of running in an AWS region, these special lambdas run at AWS edge locations when you associate them with CloudFront distributions.

The main idea behind Lambda@Edge is to bring compute capabilities closer to your users, enabling operations such as modifying requests or responses at the edge, exactly what you want to do.

Lambda@Edge functions are tightly integrated with CloudFront. The functions can be triggered in response to four types of events:

- **Viewer request**: This event is triggered when a viewer requests content from your CloudFront distribution. A Lambda@Edge function at this event can modify the request headers or the requested object path before it is sent to the origin.

- **Origin request**: This event is triggered when CloudFront needs to request content from your origin. A Lambda@Edge function at this event can modify the request headers or the requested object path before it is sent to the origin.

- **Origin response**: This event is triggered when CloudFront receives the response from your origin server. You can use a Lambda@Edge function at this event to inspect and modify the origin's response before it is cached and returned to the viewer.

- **Viewer response**: This event is triggered before CloudFront returns the requested content to the viewer. A Lambda@Edge function at this event can modify the CloudFront response headers or the response body before it is sent to the viewer.

In your case, you want to change the object path based on users' requests. The Origin Request trigger fits.

These special lambdas are used in many other use cases such as adding HTTP security headers, blocking unwanted requests, redirecting to different pages, A/B testing, and others.

There is no free tier, but these lambdas are priced at $0.0000006 per request plus $0.00005001 for every GB-second. You can see the details on the AWS website at `https://aws.amazon.com/lambda/pricing/`.

Amazon Translate

You need an automated translation mechanism. Amazon Translate is that and more. It is a managed API-based service that supports 75 different languages. It uses machine learning to provide high-quality translations on-demand, meaning pay-per-translation.

It supports both text and document translation. In your case, you will send HTML documents. However, depending on the web application framework, you might need to send text excerpts. If you are using React with i18n, you will need to create `translation.json` files.

There are other third-party translation services. However, Translate is well-integrated into the AWS ecosystem. You can use IAM roles with temporary credentials for access instead of usernames and passwords, and your data does not have to travel through the internet.

If you are a new user, it also includes a free tier.

AWS CodePipeline and AWS CodeBuild

You need something to tie all your components together and orchestrate the steps.

AWS CodePipeline is a fully managed **Continuous Delivery/Deployment** (**CD**) service that helps you automate your application and infrastructure updates. However, before diving into CodePipeline benefits and how it ties to your requirements, what is CI/CD?

CI/CD is a software development practice that aims to automate and streamline the entire process of building, testing, and deploying applications.

Continuous Integration (**CI**) refers to the practice of frequently merging code changes into a central repository. Whenever developers push code changes, the CI process automatically builds the application, runs unit tests, and checks for any integration issues.

CD is the next step after CI. CD focuses on automating the entire software release process, including building, testing, and packaging an application. The goal is to ensure that the application is always in a releasable state and can be deployed quickly and safely with minimal manual intervention. Continuous deployment is an extension of continuous delivery. In this practice, every code change that passes the automated tests and checks is automatically deployed without manual intervention. In your project, you will use continuous deployment.

A typical CI/CD process involves the following components:

- **Code repository**: This is a place where developers commit code changes, in your case GitHub.
- **CI tooling**: These are tools that compile source code, run tests, and produce ready-to-deploy software packages. Popular CD tools include TravisCI or AWS CodeBuild.
- **Continuous delivery tooling**: These are tools that automatically detect code changes, retrieve the latest version from your repository, and execute a series of steps. Popular CD tools include Jenkins, GitHub Actions, AWS CodePipeline.
- **Continuous deployment tooling**: This is a tool that automates the deployment of an application after it is built and tested, they implement popular deployment strategies such as blue-green, canary, and others. Popular tools include AWS CodeDeploy or Ansible.

CI/CD practices aim to deliver software faster, more reliably, and with higher quality by automating the entire process from code commit to deployment. They eliminate manual effort, reduce the risk of human errors, and enable teams to release updates more frequently and consistently. In your case, it enables you to have a single code repository in English and deploy to multiple buckets in multiple languages.

CodePipeline is a viable choice for continuous delivery. It has a free tier, integrates natively within the AWS ecosystem, has an easy-to-understand syntax, and is an AWS project.

Since your deployment targets are S3 buckets, you will not need a traditional continuous deployment tool. You are doing continuous deployment, meaning that if you make a change in your code repository, that change will be pushed directly into your web application. However, you will be using a continuous integration tool, CodeBuild, to achieve it.

Are you confused? CodeBuild is a fully managed continuous integration service that compiles source code, runs tests, and produces packages. In your case, a deployment is copying files to S3 buckets. CodeBuild can do that. CodeBuild reads and executes the instructions from a build specification file, `buildspec.yml`, in a configurable environment, for example, a Linux virtual machine or a Docker container.

Traditional continuous deployment tools are aimed at applications that require traditional compute environments such as virtual machines. If you were implementing this web application with an API backend as you did in *Chapter 3*, you would take advantage of these tools.

In the *Building the CI/CD pipeline* section of this chapter, you will see each of these tools in more detail and interact with them.

Coding the solution

This solution has two parts: the web application and the CI/CD pipeline. You will build them sequentially.

During this chapter, you are going to deploy your resources to the **N. Virginia** region.

Building the web application

In this section, you will build the architecture discussed in *Figure 6.1* using Terraform.

If you have not yet done so, clone the book's repository from `https://github.com/packtpublishing/aws-cloud-projects`. Navigate to the `chapter6/code` folder.

In this folder, you will find multiple files and folders:

```
.
├── app
│   ├── index.css
│   ├── index.html
│   └── translate.py
├── buildspec.yml
├── ch2-files
│   ├── index.css
│   └── index.html
```

```
├── cicd.tf
├── dev.tfvars
├── infrastructure.tf
├── lambda
│   ├── lambda.py
│   └── lambda.zip
└── variables.tf
```

Open `infrastructure.tf` in your favorite code editor and examine the code carefully. This code creates two S3 buckets with *Chapter 2*'s HTML and CSS files inside, a CloudFront distribution that uses OAC to connect to S3, a Lambda@Edge function that triggers on origin requests, and roles with permissions for all these components' interactions to work.

There are snippets worth highlighting, for example, how the bucket names are input variables:

```
resource "aws_s3_bucket" "english-bucket" {
  bucket = var.en_bucket_name
}
resource "aws_s3_bucket" "spanish-bucket" {
  bucket = var.es_bucket_name
}
```

You must define these variables yourself in `dev.tfvars`. They are pre-populated. However, you must change them to different values because bucket names are unique. You will refer to this file at runtime:

```
en_bucket_name = "my-english-assets-bucket"
es_bucket_name = "my-spanish-assets-bucket"
```

It is also worth highlighting some of your CloudFront variables: the `PriceClass_100` price class, the forwarded headers, and the low TTL cache values:

```
resource "aws_cloudfront_distribution" "s3_distribution" {
  origin {
    domain_name              = aws_s3_bucket.english-bucket.bucket_regional_domain_name
    origin_access_control_id = aws_cloudfront_origin_access_control.oac.id
    origin_id                = local.s3_origin_id
  }
  enabled             = true
  default_root_object = "index.html"
  default_cache_behavior {
    allowed_methods  = ["DELETE", "GET", "HEAD", "OPTIONS", "PATCH", "POST", "PUT"]
    cached_methods   = ["GET", "HEAD"]
    target_origin_id = local.s3_origin_id
```

```
    forwarded_values {
      query_string = false
      headers       = ["Accept-Language"]
      cookies {
        forward = "none"
      }
    }
    lambda_function_association {
      event_type   = "origin-request"
      lambda_arn   = aws_lambda_function.terraform_lambda_func.qualified_arn
    }
    viewer_protocol_policy = "allow-all"
    min_ttl                 = 0
    default_ttl             = 1
    max_ttl                 = 1
  }

  price_class = "PriceClass_100"

  restrictions {
    geo_restriction {
      restriction_type = "none"
    }
  }
  viewer_certificate {
    cloudfront_default_certificate = true
  }
}
```

Of the requirements, your company only expects viewers in North America. CloudFront has different pricing strategies, whereby it does not distribute your content to all edge locations. This price class distributes your content only in North American and European edge locations, making data transfers cheaper. This does not mean users from other locations cannot access your content, it just means it will travel through the internet instead of the backbone AWS network.

The cache is lowered to a time to live between 0 and 1. It makes CloudFront fetch the assets from the origin after one second. This configuration helps you test and troubleshoot the solution without having to wait for cache timeouts. You can increase it afterward.

Lastly, there's the **Accept-Language** forwarded header. There are separate ways to implement what a user's preferred language is. For example, you can use the user's IP address to infer their country, or CloudFront-added headers such as **CloudFront-Viewer-City** or **CloudFront-Viewer-Country-Name**. In this project, you will use the Accept-Language header because you consider that even though a person might be physically located in a country, they may not be able to speak that country's language. This happens often while traveling.

The Accept-Language header indicates users' language preferences. It is a list. Browsers set this value according to users' settings. In Chrome, the setting is under the **Languages** section, as shown in *Figure 6.3*.

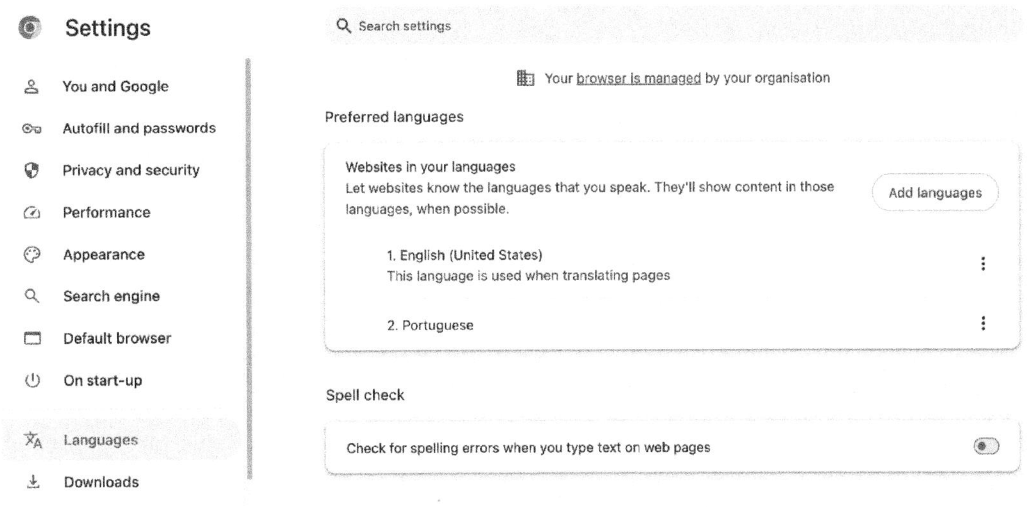

Figure 6.3 – Google Chrome Languages settings UI

In CloudFront, you must forward this header so it can be evaluated by the Lambda@Edge function.

Move on to the Python code, `lambda.py`, inside the `lambda` folder. This code will power your Lambda@Edge function. Although short, the code in this function parses the Accept-Language header and checks whether the first value on the list starts with **es**. If it does, it changes the origin to the bucket where the Spanish version of the assets is:

```
import re

def handler(event, context):
    request = event['Records'][0]['cf']['request']

    viewerCountry = request['headers'].get('accept-language')
    if viewerCountry:
        countryCode = viewerCountry[0]['value']
        if re.match(r'^es', countryCode):
            domainName = "my-spanish-assets-bucket.s3.us-east-1.amazonaws.com"
            request['origin']['s3']['domainName'] = domainName
```

```
                request['headers']['host'] = [{'key': 'host', 'value':
domainName}]

    return request
```

You need to alter this code with your own **domainName** parameter. This is the URL for your Spanish assets S3 bucket. This code uses the first value on the list because the Accept-Language header is ordered by users' preferences.

Terraform reads all `.tf` files in a directory and applies the required changes to your infrastructure. You could run these Terraform modules individually by refactoring the code and moving it to a separate directory. However, it is a best practice to maintain all project assets in a single Terraform state file. For now, do not run the Terraform `apply` command. You will do it in the next section.

Building the CI/CD pipeline

In the previous section, you learned about how to build the architecture discussed in *Figure 6.1*. In this section, you will learn about the CI/CD components, and build the complete *Figure 6.2* architecture using Terraform.

Open `cicd.tf` in your code editor. This Terraform file creates a CodeStar connection to a GitHub repository, an S3 bucket with the value of the `codepipeline_bucket_name` variable in the `dev.tfvars` file, a CodeBuild project using `buildspec.yml`, a CodePipeline with two stages (*Source* and *Build*), and roles and policies for all the components to interact with each other successfully.

CodeStar is the simplest. It is just a connection to a GitHub code repository. However, for this to work, you must create your own GitHub repository. If you are not familiar with the process, you can follow this guide. Learn how to create a new repository and commit your first change in five minutes at https://docs.github.com/en/repositories/creating-and-managing-repositories/quickstart-for-repositories.

In this repository, you will save your website files. After creating your repository, alter the `github_repository_url` variable in `dev.tfvars` to match your GitHub URL.

Look at the CodePipeline piece. It creates a pipeline with two stages but notices how each stage's artifacts are connected through the `input_artifacts` and `output_artifacts` variables. This functionality makes sure you have what was built previously available in the next stages. It uses an S3 bucket as you can see in the `artifact_store` variable:

```
resource "aws_codepipeline" "codepipeline" {
  name     = "tf-test-pipeline"
  role_arn = aws_iam_role.codepipeline_role.arn
  artifact_store {
    location = aws_s3_bucket.codepipeline_bucket.bucket
```

```
      type       = "S3"
    }
    stage {
      name = "Source"
      action {
        name              = "Source"
        category          = "Source"
        owner             = "AWS"
        provider          = "CodeStarSourceConnection"
        version           = "1"
        output_artifacts  = ["source_output"]
        configuration = {
          ConnectionArn    = aws_codestarconnections_connection.
codestar_connection.arn
          FullRepositoryId = var.github_repository_url
          BranchName       = "main"
        }
      }
    }

    stage {
      name = "Build"

      action {
        name              = "Build"
        category          = "Build"
        owner             = "AWS"
        provider          = "CodeBuild"
        input_artifacts   = ["source_output"]
        output_artifacts  = ["build_output"]
        version           = "1"
        configuration = {
          ProjectName = "event-website"
        }
      }
    }
}
```

The first stage clones the repository, and the second stage triggers a CodeBuild project.

Now, shift your attention to the CodeBuild piece. It uses a compute environment of Lambda, meaning it uses a lambda function to run the instructions instead of an EC2. The instructions that CodeBuild executes are defined in a `buildspec` YAML file:

```
resource "aws_codebuild_project" "translate" {
  name         = "event-website"
  service_role = aws_iam_role.codebuild.arn

  artifacts {
    type = "CODEPIPELINE"
  }

  environment {
    compute_type = "BUILD_LAMBDA_2GB"
    image        = "aws/codebuild/amazonlinux-x86_64-lambda-standard:python3.12"
    type         = "LINUX_LAMBDA_CONTAINER"
  }

  source {
    type      = "CODEPIPELINE"
    buildspec = file("buildspec.yml")
  }
}
```

Open `buildspec.yml`. You can see what five commands CodeBuild will execute. In summary, CodeBuild will copy the contents of the local directory to each of the buckets, then execute a Python function. Lastly it copies the resulting file of that Python function to the Spanish bucket:

```
version: 0.2
phases:
  build:
    commands:
        - ls
        - aws s3 sync . s3://my-english-assets-bucket
        - aws s3 sync . s3://my-spanish-assets-bucket
        - python translate.py en es index.html
        - aws s3 cp es-index.html s3://my-spanish-assets-bucket/index.html
```

You need to replace the URLs with your own for all AWS S3 commands.

Why does CodeBuild have files in the local directory? This is because CodeBuild is executed after pulling from GitHub in CodePipeline. Now, open `translate.py` in the app folder.

> **Important note**
> The `s3 sync` command synchronizes directories to and from S3 by recursively copying files. It only transfers changed files.

Remember, the goal of this pipeline was to propagate changes made to the website's source code; you do that with the `s3 sync` command. However, you also wanted to have the assets automatically translated to Spanish and propagated to a different bucket. This is what `translate.py`, leveraging Amazon Translate, does. The code calls the `translate_document` API with `index.html` as data and creates a local document with the result:

```python
import boto3
import argparse

parser = argparse.ArgumentParser()
parser.add_argument("SourceLanguageCode")
parser.add_argument("TargetLanguageCode")
parser.add_argument("SourceFile")
args = parser.parse_args()

translate = boto3.client('translate')

localFile = args.SourceFile
file = open(localFile, "rb")
data = file.read()
file.close()


result = translate.translate_document(
    Document={
            "Content": data,
            "ContentType": "text/html"
        },
    SourceLanguageCode=args.SourceLanguageCode,
    TargetLanguageCode=args.TargetLanguageCode
)
if "TranslatedDocument" in result:
    fileName = localFile.split("/")[-1]
    tmpfile = f"{args.TargetLanguageCode}-{fileName}"
    with open(tmpfile, 'w') as f:
        f.write(result["TranslatedDocument"]["Content"].decode('utf-8'))

    print("Translated document ", tmpfile)
```

The code is extendable. It reads the input and output language, as well as the file to be translated from the execution arguments.

In the `app` folder, you will also find new `index.css` and `index.html` files. These are your new website assets. Explore these in your local workstation to see what the website will look like.

Now that you know all the solution components and how they are represented in Terraform, it is time to create them. Run `terraform apply` with your variable file:

```
terraform apply -var-file="dev.tfvars"
```

A successful execution should output `Apply Complete!`.

There is one manual step you must do before it all works: give permissions to CodePipeline to access your GitHub repository:

1. Navigate to the **CodePipeline** console at `https://us-east-1.console.aws.amazon.com/codesuite/settings/`.
2. Under **Settings**, select **Connections**.
3. You will find the `app-dev-codestar` connection with the **Pending** status. Select it and click **Update pending connection**.
4. On the popup, select **Install a new App**, as shown in *Figure 6.4*, and log in using your GitHub credentials.

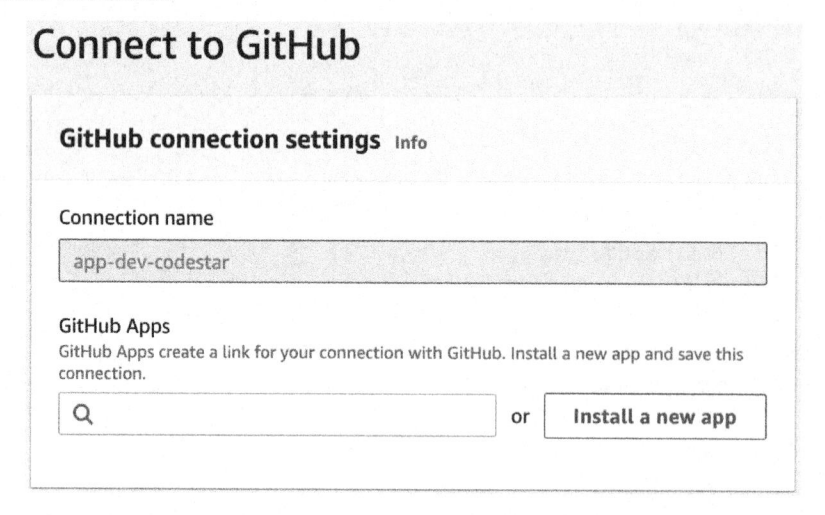

Figure 6.4 – Connect to GitHub AWS Menu

Your `app-dev-codestar` connection should now show the **Available** status.

Testing the solution

Navigate to the CloudFront console and extract your distribution's URL. Visit it, and what do you see? It should be *Chapter 2*'s frontend.

The files in your S3 buckets were not changed. To trigger a change, you first need to upload the application files to your GitHub repository.

There are multiple ways to do this. It is Git compatible, so you can clone the repository, and add your files that way. Another way is to manually upload the three files using the GitHub Console.

Using the Git method, execute the following commands, from within the `app` folder, replacing the URL with your own:

```
$ ls
index.css    index.html    translate.py
$ git clone  https://github.com/IvoP1/chapter6-repo.git
Cloning into 'chapter6-repo'...
warning: You appear to have cloned an empty repository.
$ cp index.html index.css translate.py chapter6-repo/
$ cd chapter6-repo
$ chapter6-repo git:(main) X ls
index.css    index.html    translate.py
$ chapter6-repo git:(main) X git add .
$ chapter6-repo git:(main) X git commit -m "1 version"
$ chapter6-repo git:(main) git push
You are pushing to the remote origin at  https://github.com/IvoP1/chapter6-repo.git
Enumerating objects: 5, done.
Counting objects: 100% (5/5), done.
Delta compression using up to 12 threads
Compressing objects: 100% (5/5), done.
Writing objects: 100% (5/5), 2.52 KiB | 2.52 MiB/s, done.
Total 5 (delta 0), reused 0 (delta 0), pack-reused 0
remote: Validating objects: 100%
To  https://github.com/IvoP1/chapter6-repo.git
 * [new branch]      main -> main
   chapter6-repo git:(main)
```

Navigate to your distribution's URL. You should now see the new website, either in English or in Spanish depending on your browser preferences. *Figure 6.5* shows a side-by-side comparison. Try both.

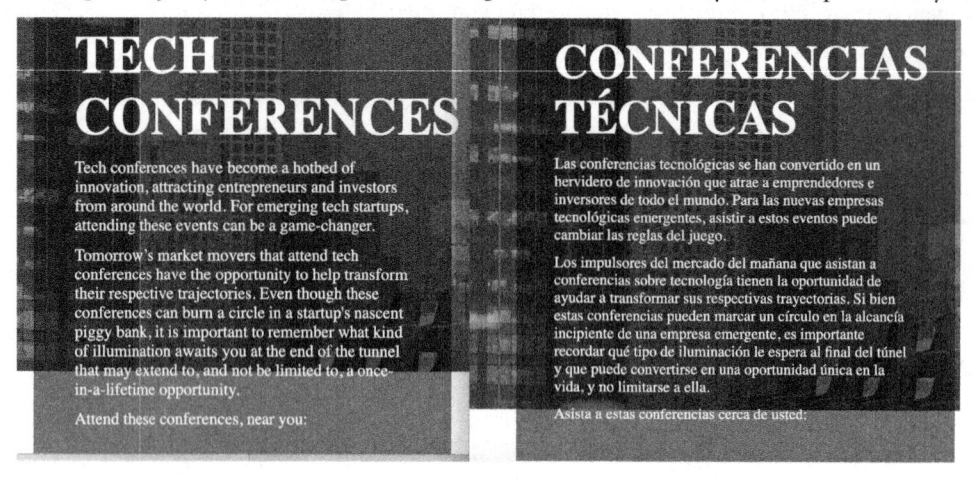

Figure 6.5 – Side-by-side comparison of English and Spanish web application versions

Navigate to the CodePipeline and CodeBuild consoles and explore the outputs.

Make any changes to your `index.html` or `index.css` local files and upload the newer versions to git. Verify how that triggers your CodePipeline.

Cleaning up

As you saw in the previous chapter, cleaning up using Terraform is simple. You use the `destroy` command.

However, in this architecture, there are three caveats you need to have in mind:

- S3 buckets cannot be deleted if they have objects inside. Before running the `terraform destroy` command, you must manually, or programmatically, empty all the buckets. There are three buckets: Spanish assets, English assets, and CodePipeline artifacts.

- Lambda@Edge functions can take a few hours to be deleted. This is an AWS limitation highlighted in their documentation by the following quote; "Wait a few hours after deleting the function association so that the Lambda@Edge function replicas can be cleaned up. After that, you will be able to delete the function by using the Lambda console, AWS CLI, Lambda API, or an AWS SDK." (https://docs.aws.amazon.com/AmazonCloudFront/latest/DeveloperGuide/lambda-edge-delete-replicas.html).

- You created your own GitHub repository outside Terraform. You have to delete that manually.

With the previous in mind, run the `terraform destroy` command. It will delete everything but the Lambda function, assuming your buckets are empty. A few hours later, you can delete the Lambda function manually.

Future work

Your proof of concept was a success; now you must take it into production. This section inspires you with some enhancements.

Implementing custom names

The usual enhancements apply here. A friendly DNS name is not only good for remembrance but also security, so folks do not connect to a different web application by mistake.

If you own a domain name and a certificate, like you learned about in *Chapter 3*, you should configure them in this application too. With this architecture, this is done at the CloudFront level.

Expanding your application functionality

Although this web application fulfills all the requirements, it could support many more languages. Modify the solution to work with at least one more language.

For this, you will need to create a new bucket and change the Lambda@Edge code to look for different header values.

You can find out what is the header value for each language at `https://learn.microsoft.com/en-us/graph/search-concept-acceptlanguage-header`.

Adopting CI/CD for infrastructure code

You have built many infrastructure components throughout the chapters of this book. CI/CD, as you have learned in this chapter, also applies to IaC. Instead of running IaC commands from your terminal, for example, `terraform apply`, you can and should do it from a CI/CD tool.

This approach has several benefits:

- **Scoped access**: Human operators only have access to the CI/CD tools, and do not have direct access to infrastructure
- **Better traceability**: Knowing who did what, when
- **Standardization**: No more "it works on my machine" comments

If you are interested in this topic, AWS has in-depth guidance on it at `https://docs.aws.amazon.com/prescriptive-guidance/latest/patterns/create-a-ci-cd-pipeline-to-validate-terraform-configurations-by-using-aws-codepipeline.html`.

Summary

In this chapter, you built a dynamic rendering web application that takes users' preferences into account to deliver a better user experience. Although you built it to adapt to your users' preferred languages, the same approach can be used to adapt applications based on other information such as websites visited or device type.

To build this application, you used an advanced CloudFront dynamic rendering functionality using Lambda@Edge and a machine learning algorithm powered by Amazon Translate.

The second part of this chapter was focused on CI/CD. You took advantage of AWS-native services to build a fully automated pipeline that received English assets, translated them, and deployed them to the web application. CI/CD is widely leveraged in most applications today.

The chapter finished with homework: tasks that you can implement on your own to sharpen your skills while improving this project's functionalities.

In the next chapter, you will continue taking advantage of AWS machine learning services, but this time, you will build a human-like chatbot.

Part 3: Advanced Level Projects

In *Part 3* of this book, you will continue learning about new AWS architectures and services. This last part focuses on advanced capabilities such as artificial intelligence, machine learning, and data analytics. You will leverage large language models, serverless ETL tools, and AWS-native dashboards. At the end of this part, you will find extra resources that you can follow to build your next big project.

This part has the following chapters:

- *Chapter 7, Implementing a Chatbot Using Machine Learning*
- *Chapter 8, Building a Business Intelligence Application*
- *Chapter 9, Exploring Future Work*

7
Implementing a Chatbot Using Machine Learning

In the previous chapters, you already had the opportunity to experiment and familiarize yourself with **Artificial Intelligence** (**AI**) technologies for different domains. Starting with computer vision by analyzing your photos to the automation of text translation, you should, by now, have two fully functional projects that demonstrate the power of AI in modern applications, but that is just the tip of the iceberg.

In today's digital landscape, users increasingly look for engaging and interactive experiences within applications, and chatbots have emerged as a powerful way to fulfill this demand, leveraging **Natural Language Processing** (**NLP**) and conversational AI to provide personalized, real-time assistance and foster a sense of human-like interaction.

In summary, this chapter covers the following topics, in order:

- What you are going to build – a chatbot application for scheduling meetings
- How you are going to build it – using Amazon Lex
- Building it – through CloudFormation and using the AWS console
- How to improve the solution – extend your chatbot with additional features from Amazon Lex

Throughout this chapter, you will improve your knowledge of AI technologies and explore the use case of developing a chatbot to help schedule meetings without any human interaction. By the end of the chapter, you will understand how Amazon Lex works and, more importantly, how to incorporate a chatbot into your own projects.

Technical requirements

To set up your own chatbot application, you will require access to an AWS account. This book has a dedicated folder within its GitHub repository where you can find the necessary code snippets to follow along: `https://github.com/PacktPublishing/AWS-Cloud-Projects/tree/main/chapter7/code`.

Scenario

After successfully building and deploying several applications leveraging cloud and serverless technologies, you have become proficient in these modern architectures. However, one area that still demands critical time and effort is scheduling meetings. On average, you need three or more interactions to coordinate availability, discuss agenda items, and finalize logistics for each meeting. This back-and-forth communication can be tedious and time-consuming, often distracting you from more important tasks.

While exploring ways to optimize and accelerate these repetitive processes, you stumble upon the concept of chatbots. With your growing interest in AI and its practical applications, you realize that chatbots could be more than just conversational interfaces – they could potentially handle specific actions and automate workflows.

The idea of creating a chatbot to streamline the meeting scheduling process piques your interest. By leveraging NLP and conversational AI, a well-designed chatbot could understand meeting-related requests and automatically create the meeting requests.

Excited by the potential efficiency gains and the opportunity to apply your AI knowledge, you decide to embark on a new project: developing an intelligent chatbot application to change the way you schedule meetings. With the right combination of cloud technologies, serverless architectures, and AI capabilities, you aim to create a seamless, conversational experience that can automate the entire meeting scheduling process, freeing up valuable time and allowing you to focus on more strategic tasks.

Requirements

Now you will start by gathering the requirements for this project. This exercise, aligned with what you've done so far for the previous chapters, will help you design your application and define the technical choices for the implementation.

Gathering requirements implies understanding the profiles that will be interacting with your application, the actions they will perform, and any constraints you may have from a technical and functional standpoint.

Overall, you still want to serve two different personas interacting with your application:

- **End user/meeting requester**: Part of the platform that is publicly accessible with a chatbot to help schedule meetings.
- **Admin/meeting owner**: Manage meeting requests with a calendar view of the accepted meetings.

These requirements can be translated into functional, non-functional, and data requirements.

Functional requirements

With your applications' personas well defined, you can break down the functional requirements per user type:

- **Meeting requester**:
  - Applications should be publicly available and not require authentication.
  - Responsive so anyone can interact with your application over any device.
  - Your chatbot should be able to handle small typos in the inputs.
  - Ability to understand descriptive dates such as "tomorrow" or "next Monday".

- **Meeting owner**:
  - List pending meeting requests, and the ability to approve or reject them.
  - Include a calendar with all the approved meetings where the admin can navigate.
  - The calendar should support different views by day, week, and month.
  - The admin page should only be available through authentication.
  - Conflicting meetings should not be rejected by the chatbot; if the proposed slot is already taken, the application should include a warning sign associated with the meeting request.

While listing the primary functionalities or capabilities is an effective approach to defining functional requirements, complementing them with visual representations can significantly enhance value and accelerate the development process. With this in mind, you have created two simple mockups: one for the end user interface and another for the admin interface, as depicted in *Figures 7.1* and *7.2*, respectively:

- **/home** looks like this:

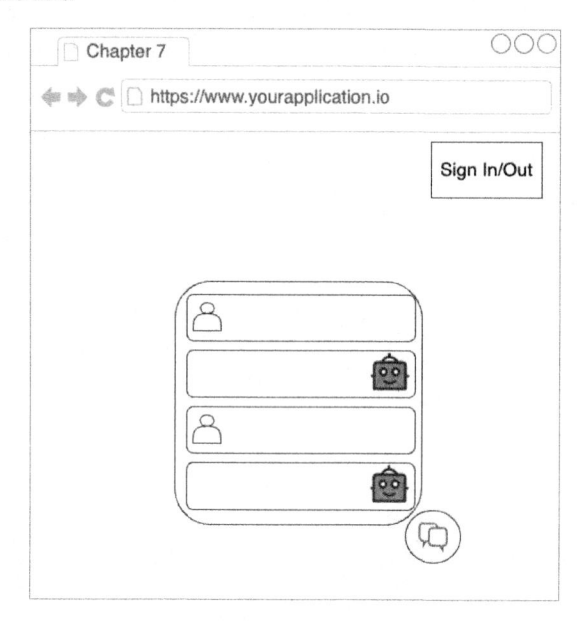

Figure 7.1 – UI mockup of the user page

- **/admin** looks like this:

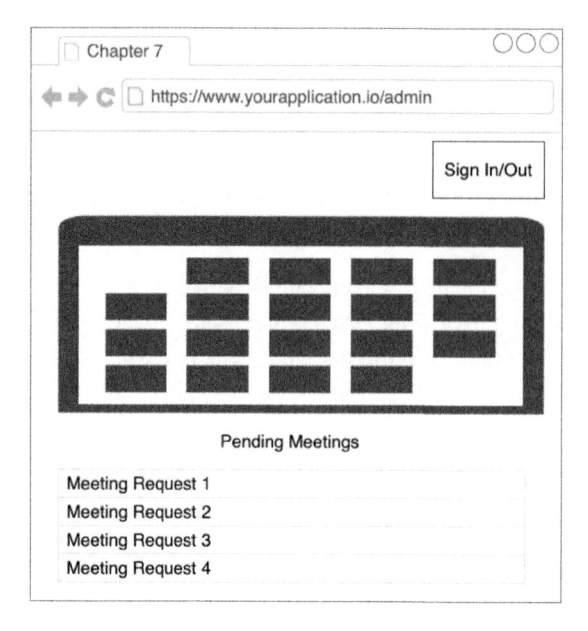

Figure 7.2 – UI mockup of the admin page

Non-functional requirements

Based on your research, you found that conversational AI is a hot topic nowadays due to the emergence of generative AI technologies and large language models specialized in chatbot development.

For this first project, you want to start with a simple solution by adopting a managed service that is easily configurable and requires the least amount of maintenance effort.

Moreover, you want to keep this solution as optimized as possible from a cost standpoint and, whenever possible, adopt serverless technologies to leverage a pure pay-as-you-go model.

Data requirements

Your application's purpose is to store and manage meetings. It is crucial to review the operations you want to perform to help you define the right data structure. Let's start with the operations you want to perform over the meeting requests:

- **Create a meeting**: Create a new meeting.
- **Get pending meeting requests**: Show a list of the meeting requests with a **Pending** status to either accept or reject, with a warning for overlapping requests.
- **Change meeting status**: Change the status of a pending meeting to accepted or rejected.
- **Check approved meetings within a time window**: The ability to get a list of the approved meetings to include in your calendar.

Considering the operations listed, a meeting can be described as `meeting_example.json`:

```
{
  "meetingId": "GUID",
  "startTime": "time when the meeting starts",
  "endTime": "time when the meeting ends",
  "duration": "duration of the meeting in minutes",
  "attendeeName": "the name of the participant",
  "email": "the email of the participant",
  "status": "meeting request status",
  "date": "meeting date",
  "isConflict": "for a meeting request, define if there is any overlap with a pre-accepted meeting"
};
```

There is no relationship between meetings, and you do not foresee any need to run complex queries, so you want to adopt a high-performing, serverless data service that supports the execution of all the enumerated actions.

Architecture patterns

AI solutions have the potential to bring significant value to businesses across various industries, but often, finding the resources to plan them from scratch can be time-consuming, expensive, and complex. As part of the AWS Solutions Library, AWS has a dedicated section called **Solutions for Artificial Intelligence** (https://aws.amazon.com/solutions/ai/), with a curated set of architectures that can help you accelerate AI adoption and decrease the time to embed it in your current products. These solutions belong to different domains, ranging from predictive analytics and computer vision to personalization and recommendation, among others. This is always a good place to start when thinking about an AI project in AWS.

More specifically, there is a subsection called **Chatbots & Virtual Assistants** (https://aws.amazon.com/solutions/ai/chatbots-virtual-assistants/). It is part of the language understanding domain, which can be a good baseline for this project.

Architecture

To architect your applications, it is key to define the building blocks that compose them. Starting from the higher level, you defined a layered approach composed of four layers:

- **Presentation layer**: How to host and serve your frontend
- **Compute layer**: How to incorporate and execute business logic
- **Data layer**: Where to store and retrieve your data
- **Chatbot layer**: Layer responsible for developing your chatbot

For the presentation layer, you decided to adopt a similar strategy to the one you used in the previous chapter and develop a single-page application in React. For your compute layer, you started by designing the API that will be the interface between your frontend and the business logic included in your compute layer. Considering your functional requirements, you listed the various actions to be performed and structured your API as represented in *Figure 7.3*:

- **GET /meetings**: Get the list of approved meetings within a time window
- **GET /pending**: Get the list of pending meeting requests
- **POST /chatbot**: Interact with the chatbot by sending the user prompts
- **PUT /status**: Change the status of a meeting request to approved or rejected

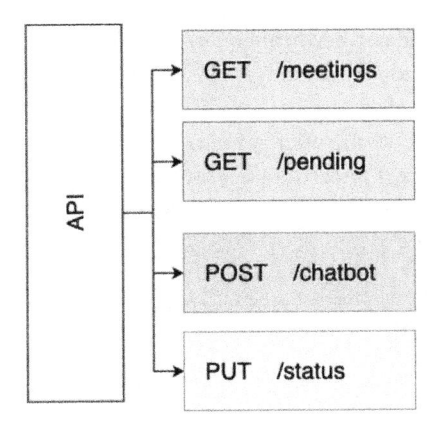

Figure 7.3 – API structure

Figure 7.4 illustrates the architecture you will implement based on all the requirements.

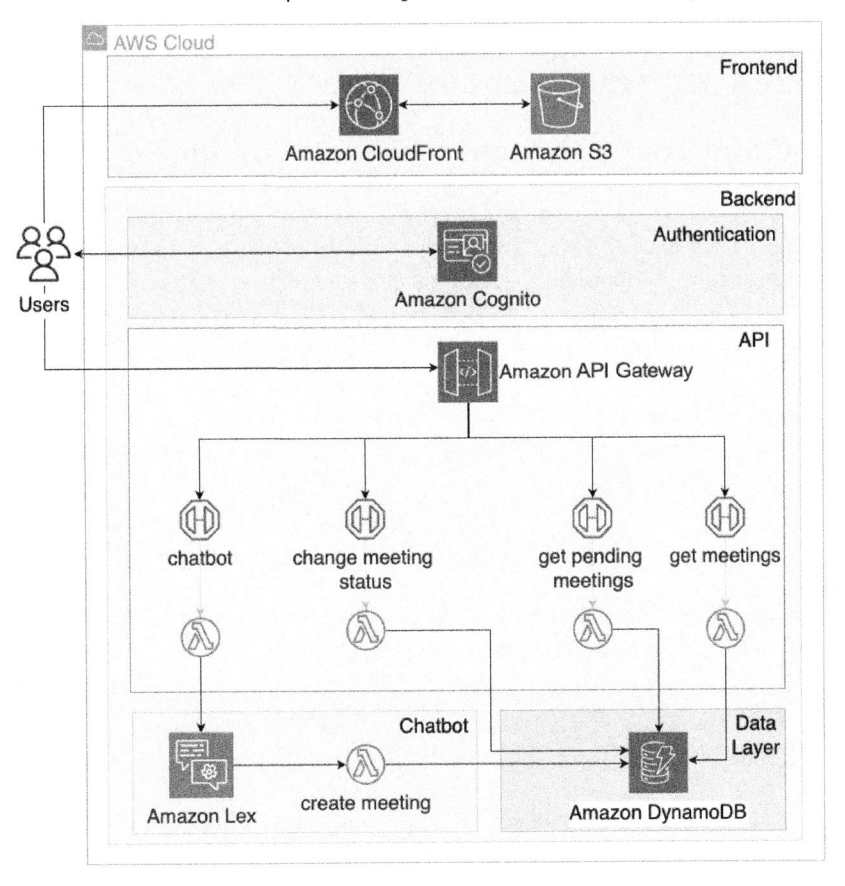

Figure 7.4 – AWS architecture for your chatbot application

The frontend will be hosted and served through a combination of S3 and CloudFront services. For the API, you will leverage Amazon API Gateway HTTP API with endpoints that map the actions you have listed. After reviewing the data requirements, you have chosen DynamoDB as your data store. The last component is the chatbot, and after conducting research, you have selected Amazon Lex as a managed solution due to its cost-effectiveness, simplicity, and overall integration with other AWS services such as Lambda functions, allowing you to extend your chatbot's capabilities and perform actions on your behalf.

Each of the services mentioned and the main advantages and reasons for these choices will be described next.

AWS services

Selecting from the extensive range of available services can be a daunting task, and a thorough understanding of the requirements is crucial for making an informed decision. Some of the services have already been covered in previous chapters, so to avoid redundancy, we will only highlight the advantages specific to the current use case if they have not been previously mentioned and provide references to the relevant chapters where you can find detailed explanations.

Amazon CloudFront and Amazon Simple Storage Service (S3)

We have extensively covered Amazon S3 and Amazon CloudFront for hosting a single-page application frontend. These two AWS services played a crucial role in the previous projects mentioned, and if you want to review them, we recommend checking *Chapters 2* and *3*.

Amazon DynamoDB

Amazon DynamoDB was introduced in *Chapter 3* as part of the first version of the recipe-sharing application. If you are not familiar with the service and its purpose, we recommend reviewing *Chapter 3*'s *AWS services* section.

Amazon Cognito, Amazon API Gateway, and Amazon Lambda

Amazon API Gateway has been used for the API layer, Amazon Lambda for the compute layer, and Amazon Cognito for authentication in previous projects due to their seamless integration. If you wish to explore any of these services in depth, detailed explanations are provided in *Chapter 4*.

Amazon Lex

Amazon Lex is an AWS service that makes it easy to build conversational interfaces, called chatbots or virtual assistants. As part of the AWS AI services, Amazon Lex simplifies and streamlines the creation of applications where users can communicate through voice or text, understand their intents, respond in a natural and human way and, most importantly, perform actions as responses to users' requests. Being a managed service, with Amazon Lex, you do not need to manage any infrastructure, and therefore, you do not have to pay for any unused capacity.

With Amazon Lex, you can leverage more than 25 languages and locales, at the time of this writing, which makes it easier to build versatile chatbots that can serve users across the world.

Amazon Lex has some basic concepts associated that are important to familiarize yourself with before configuring your chatbot:

- **Intents**: These represent the goal or action that a user wants to accomplish through their conversation with the chatbot. When you create a bot, you define the different intents it should understand and handle. In this chapter's case, an intent could be **Book Meetings**, but more complex chatbots may need to handle different actions from the users through several distinct intents. By default, Amazon Lex includes a default `AMAZON.FallbackIntent`, which is used whenever no other intent can be identified.
- **Utterances**: These are one or more sentences you need to provide when configuring each intent, which the chatbot will use to identify the intent based on the user input. For example, following the case of this chapter, the utterances associated with the Book Meetings intent could be as follows:
  - "I want to book a meeting"
  - "Help me book a meeting"
- **Slots**: Slots are pieces of information that Amazon Lex needs to gather from the user to successfully fulfill an intent. Each slot is associated with a slot type, which defines the kind of data expected for that slot. AWS already provides built-in slot types such as numbers or dates, but you can extend it by creating custom slot types. Following the example of this chapter, examples of slots could be any information needed to schedule a meeting, such as the attendee's name, the date, the time to start, and the duration of the meeting.

Besides these basic blocks, Amazon Lex integrates with other services from the AWS landscape, namely Amazon Lambda. There, you can trigger a Lambda function upon achieving a specific state, for example, the fulfillment of the intent. This integration, in the context of this project's scope, will enable you to trigger a Lambda function to store the meeting details collected during the conversation with the user in a data store of your choice.

Coding the solution

After understanding the architecture and all the AWS services that comprise it, now it's time to implement the solution based on the requirements and technologies selected.

Cloning the project

The first step is to clone the Git repository associated with this book, as mentioned in the *Technical requirements* section. If you are following along from the previous chapter, you should have it already cloned locally, but if you are just starting with this chapter, check whether you can clone it from Git or download it as a ZIP file.

Navigate to the `chapter7/code` folder, and inside you will find two subfolders:

- `frontend`: Contains the code for your frontend.
- `platform`: Includes the CloudFormation template to deploy the main infrastructure for your application.

Solution deployment

Start by deploying all your application infrastructure through the CloudFormation template found in the `/platform` folder. *Table 7.1* lists all the resources created by your template that map to the architecture presented in *Figure 7.4*.

Template	Ch7-application-template.yaml
Frontend	CloudFront and S3
Backend	DynamoDB
Authentication	Cognito User Pool
Backend	One HTTP API with four endpoints
	Four lambda functions, one for each endpoint
	One Cognito user pool
Data store	DynamoDB
Chatbot	One Lex Chatbot
	One lambda function to be triggered by the chatbot

Table 7.1 – CloudFormation template details

From the console, go to the CloudFormation service at `https://console.aws.amazon.com/cloudformation/` and select the AWS region where you want to host your application.

> **Important note – Choosing the AWS region for this project**
>
> Service availability is one of the reasons behind choosing an AWS region for your projects. Amazon Lex, the service you will use for your chatbot, is one example of a service that is not available in all AWS regions. Trying to deploy a CloudFormation template in a region where Amazon Lex is not available would cause an error. You can see the full list of AWS regions supported at `https://docs.aws.amazon.com/general/latest/gr/lex.html`.

Region selection is available through the drop-down menu located in the upper-right corner, as depicted in *Figure 7.5*

Figure 7.5 – Console access to CloudFormation and AWS Region dropdown menu

To deploy the CloudFormation stack associated with this project, follow these steps:

1. Click on **Create Stack**.
2. In the **Prerequisite – Prepare Template** section, select **Choose an existing template**.
3. In the **Specify template** section, choose **Upload a template file**.
4. Click on **Choose file**.
5. Select the template from the `chapter7/code/platform` folder.
6. Click **Next**.

Your **Create stack** window should look like *Figure 7.6*.

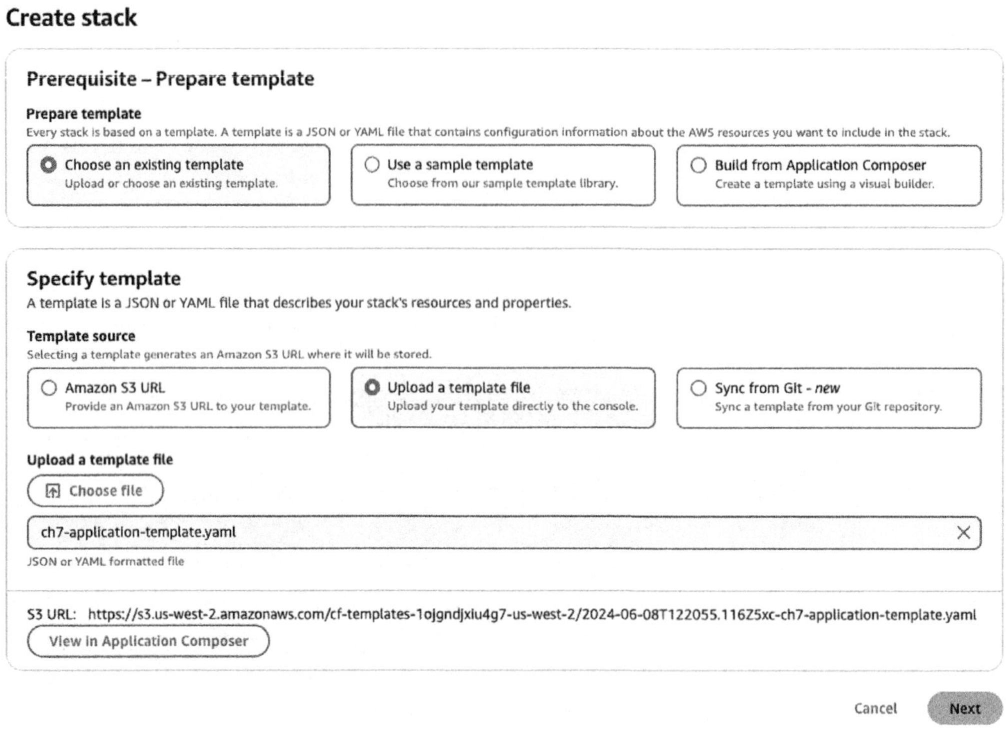

Figure 7.6 – CloudFormation Create stack form

Next, you will be asked to configure the parameters in your CloudFormation stack. In *Table 7.2*, you can find a detailed explanation of each parameter.

Parameter	Description
`APIName`	This is the project's API name.
`UserEmail`	This is the email address you want to associate with your user. This must be a valid email address because you will receive the temporary password and verify it later.
`UserPoolName`	This is the name you will give to your Cognito User Pool.
`Username`	Later in your application, this is the username you will use to log in.

Table 7.2 – CloudFormation template parameters

Figure 7.7 shows an example of how your stack configurations should look after filling out all the parameters. The values shown serve as an example; your values may differ.

Specify stack details

Provide a stack name
Stack name
```
chapter-7
```
Stack name must be 1 to 128 characters, start with a letter, and only contain alphanumeric characters. Character count: 9/128.

Parameters
Parameters are defined in your template and allow you to input custom values when you create or update a stack.

APIName
API Name
```
meety-api
```

UserEmail
The email for the initial user
```
email@email.com
```

UserPoolName
The name for the Cognito User Pool
```
chapter7-userpool
```

Username
The username for the initial user
```
admin
```

Cancel   Previous   Next

Figure 7.7 – Stack parameters in CloudFormation

You can click **Next** and proceed to the last page, where you will be requested to acknowledge the creation of IAM roles. This notification is related to the roles to be created and associated with each of the lambda functions, to provide the minimum permissions to interact with the DynamoDB table where the meetings are stored.

Click **Submit** and wait until the stack status changes to **CREATE_COMPLETE**, as depicted in *Figure 7.8*.

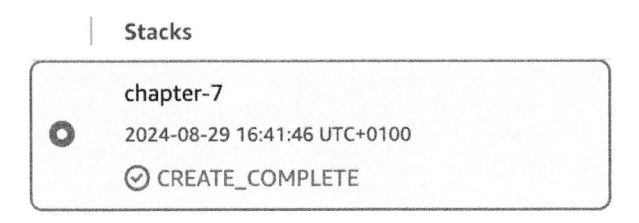

Stacks

chapter-7
2024-08-29 16:41:46 UTC+0100
⊘ CREATE_COMPLETE

Figure 7.8 – CloudFormation stack created status

This will mean that all the resources are provisioned, and you can now proceed.

Frontend configuration and deployment

Now that all the necessary AWS services have been provisioned, it is time to configure your frontend application and deploy the files.

Navigate to the `.../frontend/src/configs` folder, and you will find two files:

- `aws-exports.ts`: Configure your application authentication, with data from the Cognito User Pool. This file is composed of four configuration variables:

  - `AWS_PROJECT_REGION`: The region where you deployed your solution
  - `AWS_COGNITO_REGION`: Your Cognito user Pool region (the same as the previous variable)
  - `AWS_USER_POOLS_ID`: The ID of your user pool
  - `AWS_USER_POOLS_WEB_CLIENT_ID`: The client ID of your Cognito User Pool application

- `configs.tsx`: Define the URL of your API to be used in your application. The `configs.tsx` file is composed of one configuration variable:

  - `CONFIG_API_URL`: API endpoint

To simplify the process of obtaining these values, we have already included them in the **Outputs** section of our **CloudFormation** template. To access it, follow these steps:

1. Go to the CloudFormation console at `https://console.aws.amazon.com/cloudformation/`.
2. Click on your stack.
3. On the right menu, select the **Outputs** tab, as shown in *Figure 7.9*.

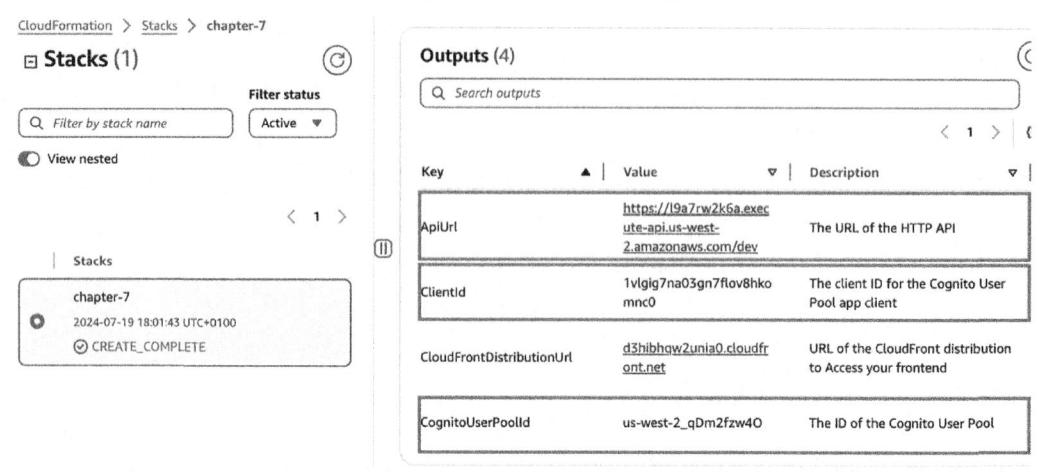

Figure 7.9 – CloudFormation stack Outputs tab

Table 7.3 maps the Stack outputs with the configuration files:

File	Parameter name	Cloudformation stack outputs
aws-exports.ts	aws_user_pools_id	UserPoolId
	aws_user_pools_web_client_id	ClientId
configs.tsx	API_URL	CognitoUserPoolId

Table 7.3 – Mapping between CloudFormation outputs and aws-exports.ts parameters

4. Save the files.

By the end, your configuration files should look like this:

configs.tsx

```
export const API_URL = '[ApiUrl CloudFormation Output]';
```

aws-exports.tsx

```
export const amplifyConfig = {
  aws_project_region: 'AWS Region code where you deployed your application. E.g.: us-west-2',
  aws_cognito_region: ' AWS Region code where you deployed your application. E.g.: us-west-2',
  aws_user_pools_id: '[UserPoolId CloudFormation Output]',
  aws_user_pools_web_client_id: '[ClientId CloudFormation Output]',
};
```

After updating the configuration files, you can begin the build process to convert the code into a web-optimized bundle that can be served to browsers. In our example, we used npm as the package manager, so you'll need to install the dependencies and start the build process:

```
$ npm install && npm run build
```

> **Note**
> The previous command should be executed in the root directory of the frontend folder. To verify whether you are at the root, use the following command:
> ```
> $ pwd
> .../chapter7/code/frontend
> ```

The `build` process generates a folder containing the files that need to be uploaded to our S3 buckets. The folder name may vary, but it is typically `build/` or `dist/`, and it is created within the `root` directory of the frontend application.

The last step is to copy the build folder to S3, with the following instructions:

1. Firstly, you need to locate the S3 bucket that you created earlier using the CloudFormation template. The bucket's name should start with `frontend-chapter-7-` followed by a random sequence of characters (e.g., `frontend-chapter-7-XXXXX`).
2. Click on the bucket's name to open it.
3. Within the S3 bucket, locate and click on the **Upload** button. This action will enable you to transfer files from your local machine to the S3 bucket.
4. Click on **Add Files** and navigate to the `dist` folder on your local machine. Select all the files inside the folder and confirm (you should have two files at the root of the `dist` folder: `index.html` and `penguin.png`).
5. Next, click on **Add folder**, locate the `dist` folder on your local machine, select the `assets` folder, and confirm.
6. Now your S3 **Upload** window should look like *Figure 7.10*.

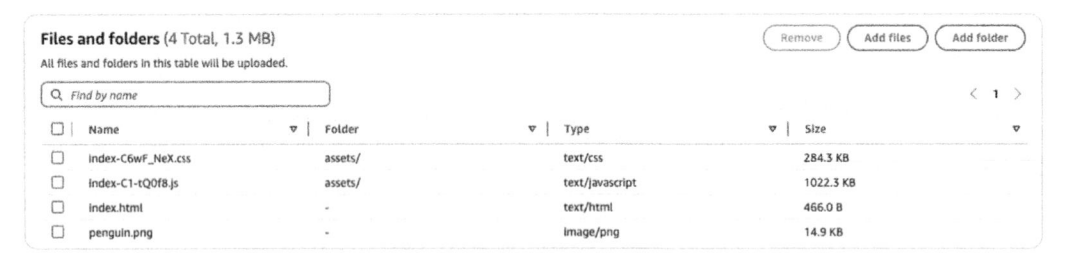

Name	Folder	Type	Size
index-C6wF_NeX.css	assets/	text/css	284.3 KB
index-C1-tQOf8.js	assets/	text/javascript	1022.3 KB
index.html	-	text/html	466.0 B
penguin.png	-	image/png	14.9 KB

Figure 7.10 – Frontend files uploaded to S3

Note that the file names are automatically generated during the build process, so the names you see might differ from the ones shown in the preceding figure. However, ensure that you have the following files:

- `index.html`
- `assets/index-XXXXXX.css`
- `assets/index-XXXXXX.js`
- Static files you may have included in your application, for example, images

7. Scroll down to the bottom of the page and click on **Upload**.

You have now completed the deployment and configuration process for your application, and you can proceed to the chatbot setup.

Amazon Lex configuration and build

You are almost done, and the only step left is the configuration of your chatbot. Most of the configurations were already performed by the CloudFormation template, and you were just left with the lambda function integration to perform the actions based on the conversation.

To finalize it, follow these steps:

1. Go to the Amazon Lex console in the region where you deployed the CloudFormation stack at `https://console.aws.amazon.com/lexv2/home?`.
2. On the left menu, select **Bots**.
3. In the **Bots** list, select **MeetyBot**, as shown in *Figure 7.11*.

Figure 7.11 – Amazon Lex bot selection

4. Under the **Deployment** section, select **Aliases** and click on **TestBotAlias**, as depicted in *Figure 7.12*.

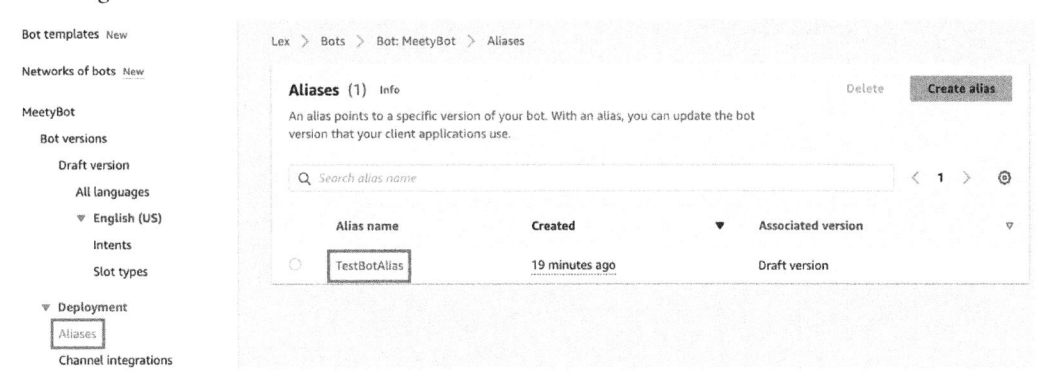

Figure 7.12 – Amazon Lex bot alias section

5. From the **Languages** list, select **English (US)**.
6. In the **Lambda function** configuration menu, select `bot-function-meety` as the source, and `$LATEST` as the version, as shown in *Figure 7.13*.

7. Click **Save**.

Figure 7.13 – Lambda function selection for your chatbot

The last step is to configure the triggering of the function whenever the BookMeeting intent is fulfilled. For that, do the following:

1. On the left menu, select **Intents** under the **English (US)** menu.
2. Click on the **BookMeeting** intent.
3. Scroll down to the **Fullfilment** section and click on the toggle button to make it active. This will ensure the lambda function is triggered every time this intent is fulfilled. You can see the expected status in *Figure 7.14*.

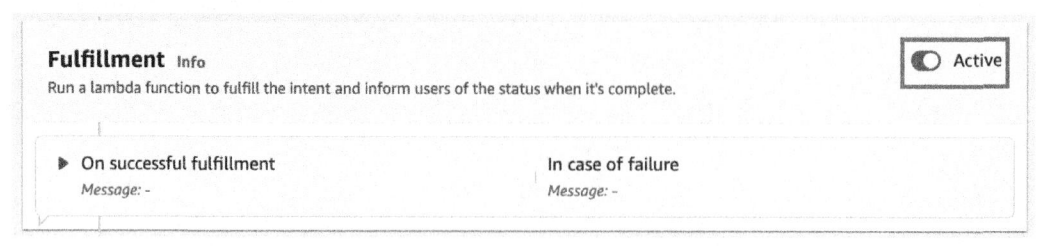

Figure 7.14 – Amazon Lex chatbot – fulfillment configuration

4. Click on **Save Intent** in the bottom right.
5. Select **Build** in the top right.

   The build process of your chatbot should take around two minutes. Wait until you see a green banner with a success message, as shown in *Figure 7.15*.

   > ✓ Successfully built language English (US) in bot: MeetyBot

   Figure 7.15 – Success message from the Amazon Lex build process

Congratulations! You have successfully finished the deployment and configuration of your application, and you should now have a fully functional project. It is time to test it out!

Test and explore your application

By now, everything should be ready to be tested. To access your application, do the following:

1. Go to the CloudFront console at `https://console.aws.amazon.com/cloudformation/`.
2. Select the stack you deployed as part of this chapter.
3. Go to the **Outputs** tab.
4. Click on the `CloudFrontDistributionUrl` value as shown in *Figure 7.16*.

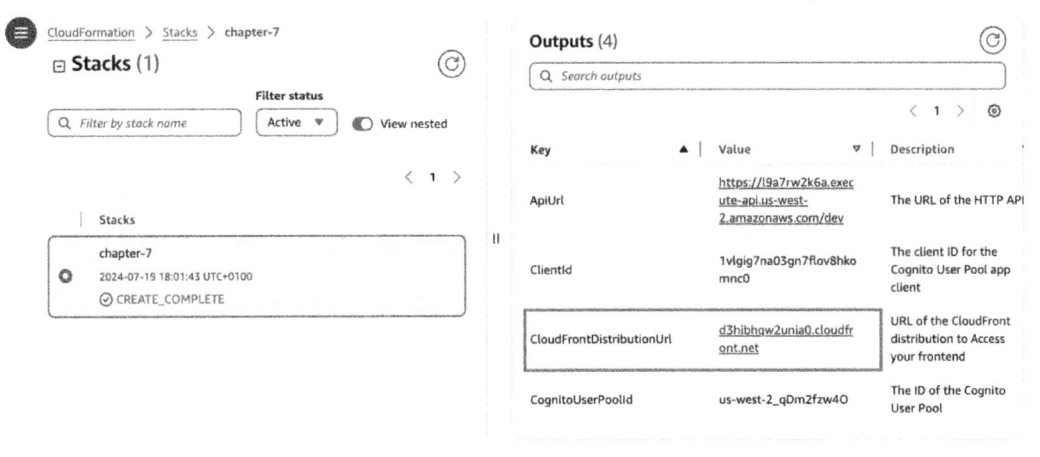

Figure 7.16 – CloudFormation Outputs tab

This should redirect you to your application, which is expected to be like *Figure 7.17*.

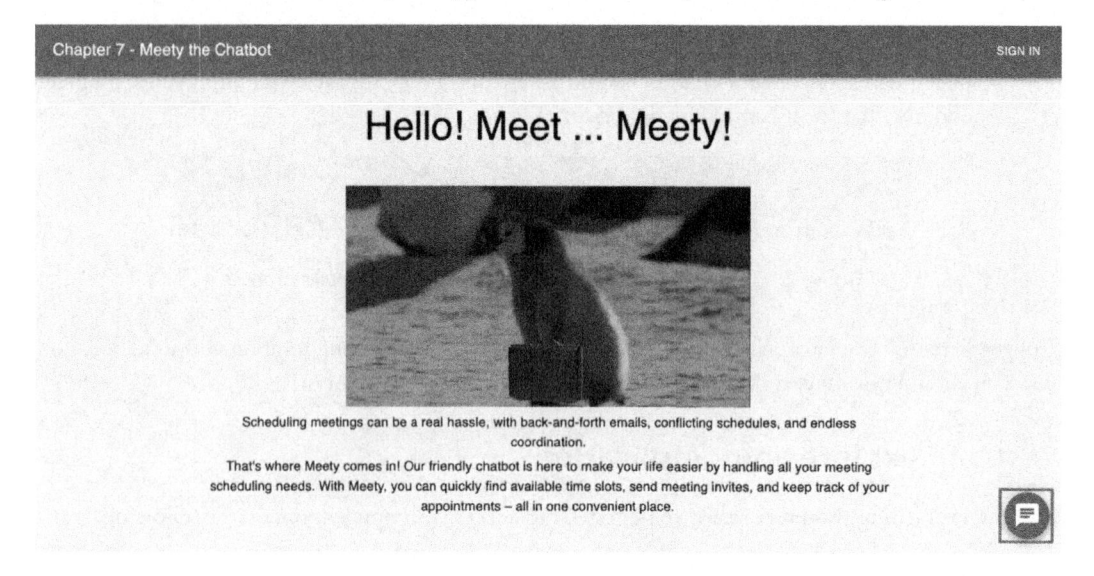

Figure 7.17 – Application homepage

This is the page where users can interact with a chatbot to schedule meetings. By clicking on the chat icon, you will be able to initiate a conversation.

As discussed in the *AWS services* section, utterances are predefined within an intent to help identify and understand the user's request.

This chapter's CloudFormation template creates a chatbot composed of three intents:

- **StartMeety**: This is the first intent responsible for the welcome message
- **BookMeeting**: The intent responsible for booking a meeting
- **FallbackIntent**: Default intent to be triggered whenever no other intent can be identified based on the user input

Explore and customize your chatbot

To explore the utterances, responses, and logic of each of the intents, do the following:

1. Navigate to the Amazon Lex console in the region where you deployed the CloudFormation stack at `https://console.aws.amazon.com/lexv2/home?`.
2. On the left menu, select **Bots**.
3. Select **MeetyBot**.
4. Under **English (US)**, click on **Intents**.

Your console should look like *Figure 7.18*.

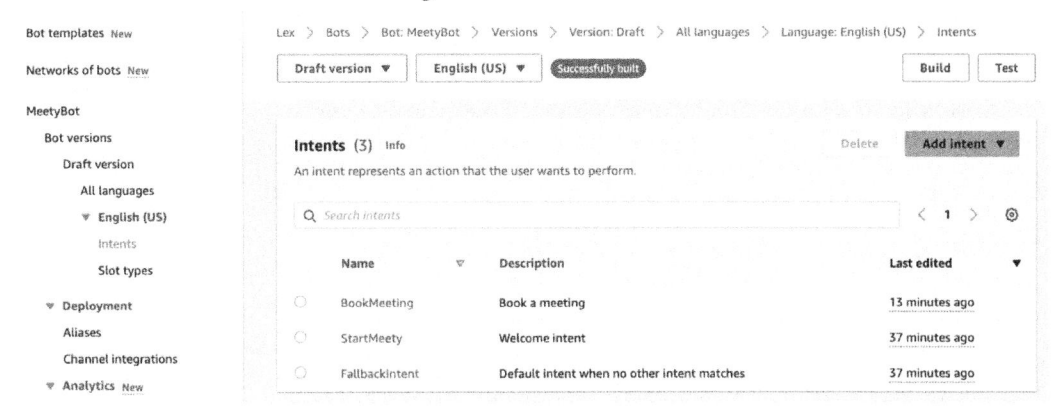

Figure 7.18 – Amazon Lex Bot Intents section

5. Click on the **StartMeety** intent.
6. Scroll down to the **Sample utterances** section to review the pre-defined utterances for this intent, as shown in *Figure 7.19*.

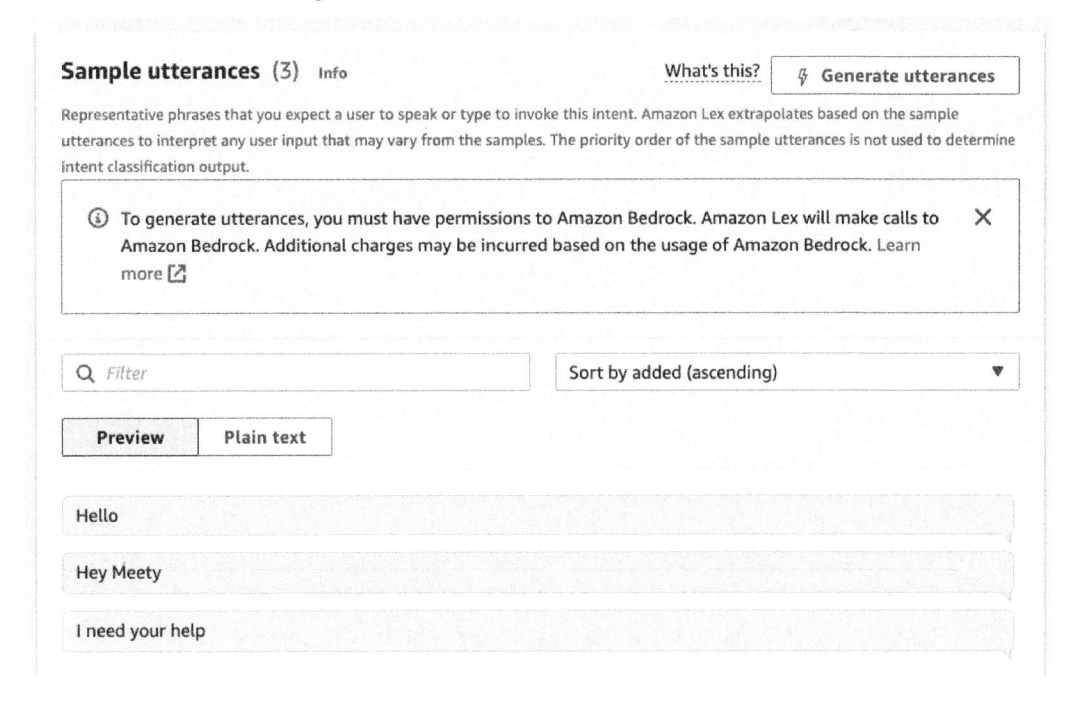

Figure 7.19 – Amazon Lex chatbot intent sample utterances

These are currently the ones available to identify the StartMeety intent, but feel free to add others or customize the existing one at will. After any change, ensure you save the intent and rebuild the chatbot, as described in the previous section.

Do the same exercise for the BookMeeting intent. In this case, Amazon Lex expects different utterances, and unlike the StartMeety intent, it also includes five slots as the pieces of data needed to fulfils the intent:

- **FullName**: The name of the attendee
- **MeetingDate**: The date the user wants to meet
- **MeetingStime**: The start time of the meeting
- **MeetingDuration**: The duration of the meeting, which should be either 30 or 60 minutes
- **AttendeeEmail**: The email the user wants to use to be contacted

We recommend spending some time exploring each slot and the prompt used by the chatbot to request it. As mentioned earlier, feel free to customize the prompts and slots according to your preference.

After getting familiar with all the configurations of your chatbot, you can proceed and start a conversation in your application to book a meeting.

Test your chatbot

With your chatbot and its intents configured, now it is time to test its behavior in your application:

1. Begin by using one of the utterances defined in the StartMeety Intent, and take note of the chatbot's response.

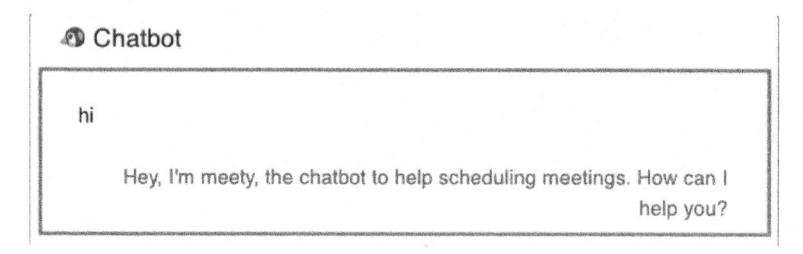

Figure 7.20 – Initial chatbot response from the StartMeety intent

Here, you can see that, based on the input that matches one of the sample utterances of the StartMeety intent, the chatbot responded with a welcome message as configured in the intent.

In this example, you can see that the chatbot identified and acknowledged the intent and replied accordingly.

2. Next, you can respond with one of the utterances defined in the BookMeeting intent, so the chatbot can identify it.

Figure 7.21 – BookMeeting intent conversation flow

The chatbot identified the intent and started asking questions to gather the slot values with the objective of fulfilling it. Note that the chatbot was able to interpret the **tomorrow** statement based on the current date.

3. As part of the BookMeeting intent, your chatbot is configured to perform a confirmation before proceeding. Here, a user can either proceed or cancel the request, as shown in *Figure 7.22*.

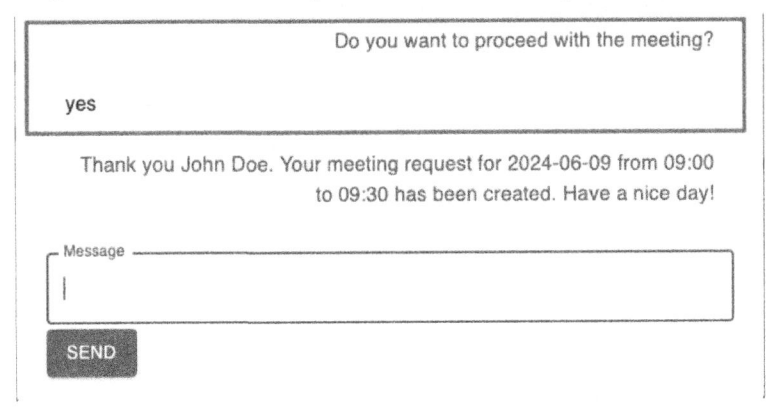

Figure 7.22 – Chatbot confirmation prompt

4. Upon confirmation, your intent reached the fulfillment state, and as per the bot configuration, the `bot-function-meety` lambda function was triggered. The lambda function has three main actions:

- Evaluate whether there are any previously accepted meetings that could conflict with the proposed meeting time, according to the slot values provided.
- Create the meeting request and store it in the DynamoDB table.
- Respond with a customized message to the end user acknowledging the meeting request.

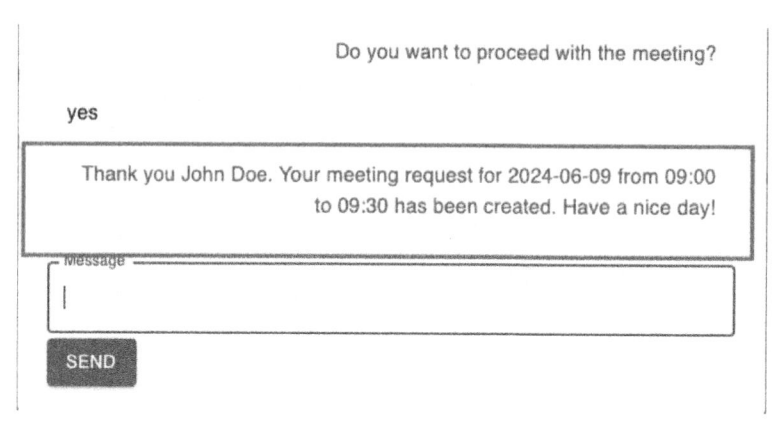

Figure 7.23 – Chatbot final response

If you want to explore the lambda function code in detail, follow these steps:

I. Go to the AWS Lambda console in the region where you deployed the CloudFormation stack at `https://console.aws.amazon.com/lambda/`.

II. On the left menu, select **Functions**.

III. Click on the `bot-function-meety` function.

IV. Scroll down to the **Code Source** section, and you will find all the code included in this lambda function.

You have already examined how a user can initiate meeting requests through conversations with your chatbot. Now, it is time to delve into the **Admin** page, where you can review the accepted meetings in your calendar and manage the pending meeting requests.

Manage meeting requests through the admin portal

So far, you have tested your chatbot, namely its capabilities to handle meeting requests with a human-like conversation, and now you will explore how to manage the requests created.

During the process of deploying your CloudFormation stack, you should have received an email like the one in *Figure 7.24* with your username and a temporary password. This will be needed to finalize the authentication process and access the **Admin** page.

From: "no-reply@verificationemail.com" <no-reply@verificationemail.com>
Date: Saturday, 8 June 2024 at 15:06
To: "YOUR NAME " <youremail@yourdomain>
Subject: Chapter7 - Your temporary password

Hello YOUR_USERNAME from the Chatbot Application. Your temporary password is YOUR_TEMPORARY_PASSWORD

Figure 7.24 – Email with a temporary password

To access the admin portal and manage the meeting requests, follow these steps:

1. From your application's homepage, click on **Sign In**.
2. Fill out the **Username** and **Password** fields with the values from the email you received and confirm.
3. Set up a new password and proceed.
4. Select your email and click on **Verify**. You will now receive an email with a temporary code.
5. Copy the verification code from your email and paste it into the confirmation form.

You have now finalized the authentication setup, and your interface should look like *Figure 7.25*.

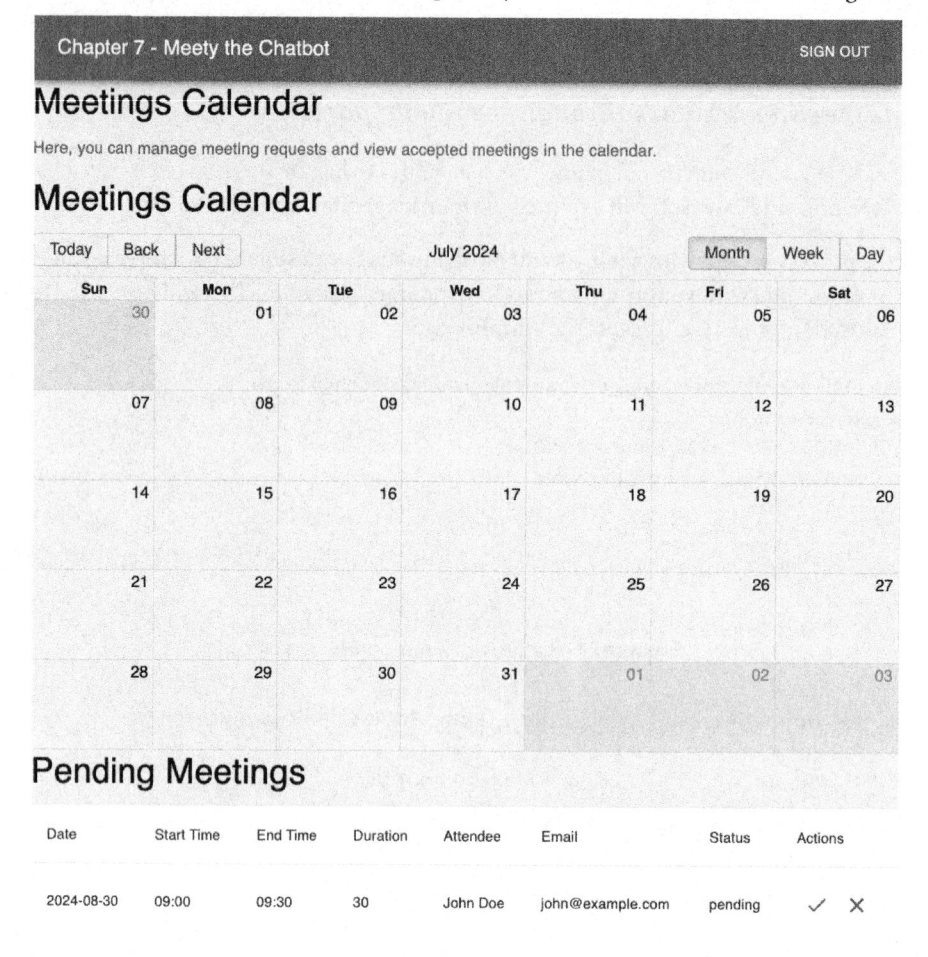

Figure 7.25 – Admin page for managing meeting requests

The admin page is divided into two distinct sections:

- Meetings calendar, which displays all the accepted meetings.
- Pending meetings section, which presents a list of meeting requests awaiting your action.

Within the **Actions** column, you have two buttons available: **Accept** and **Reject**. Clicking the **Accept** button will update the meeting request's status to **Accepted**, while selecting the **Reject** button will mark it as **Rejected**. To observe the functionality, try accepting a meeting request and watch it appear in the **Meetings Calendar** calendar.

One of the functional requirements stated that you should receive a notification when a new meeting request overlaps with a previously accepted meeting. To test this behavior, perform the following steps:

1. Open a new tab in your browser with the homepage (you can copy the URL from the **Admin** page and delete the `/admin`).
2. Attempt to schedule a meeting during the same time slot as an already accepted meeting.
3. Refresh the **Admin** page to display the new meeting request.

You can verify that the new request now displays a warning icon and a tooltip indicating that it conflicts with a previously accepted meeting, as illustrated in *Figure 7.26*.

Pending Meetings

Date	Start Time	End Time	Duration	Attendee	Email	Status	Actions
2024-07-20	09:00	10:00	60	Anna	anna@email.com	pending	✓ ✗ ⚠

Figure 7.26 – Conflicting meeting warning

You now have a fully operational web application with a chatbot that can schedule meetings based on a conversation with an end user. Additionally, you can consult a calendar with all the meetings that happened in the past and manage your agenda for the upcoming meetings.

Clean up

Aligned with your non-functional requirements, all the components of this architecture benefit from a pay-as-you-go model, meaning you pay only for what you use. Nevertheless, if you leave an application running for an extended period, you may incur unnecessary costs. Therefore, it is recommended to clean up your infrastructure when it is no longer in use. Since you deployed the application using IaC, the cleanup process is straightforward and involves two steps:

1. Empty the S3 bucket:

    I. Go to the S3 console in your AWS account.

    II. Select your frontend S3 bucket (the name of the bucket should start with `frontend-chapter-7-`, followed by a random string).

III. Click on **Empty**; this will delete all the content inside your bucket.

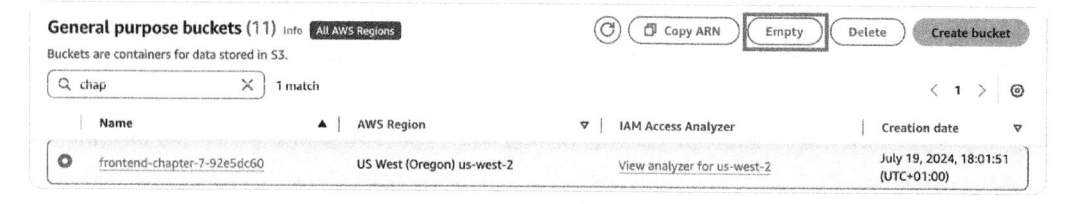

Figure 7.27 – Process of emptying an S3 bucket

2. Delete the CloudFormation stack:

    I. Navigate to the CloudFormation service console within your AWS account, ensuring you are in the same region where the initial deployment took place.

    II. Select the stack you created.

    III. Click on **Delete**, as shown in *Figure 7.28*.

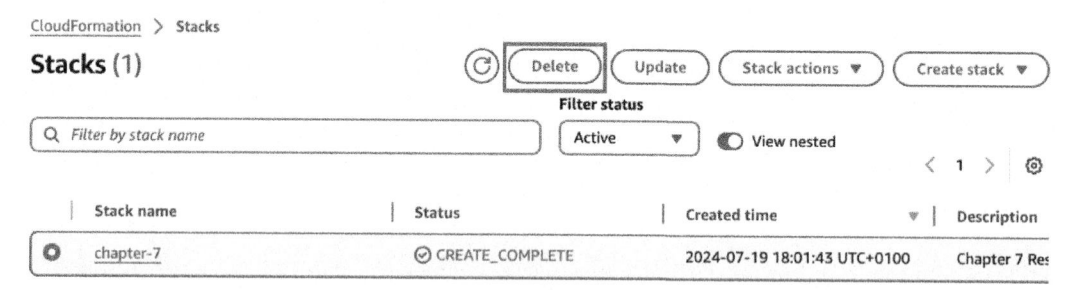

Figure 7.28 – CloudFormation stack deletion

With these actions, all the resources created for this chapter should be deleted.

While this project provides a solid foundation for your chatbot application, there are several enhancements and future considerations that can further improve its functionality and user experience. These will be presented in the next section.

Future work

Congratulations on successfully implementing the chatbot application! You have taken a significant step in harnessing the power of AWS for building intelligent conversational interfaces, and you now have the baseline for incorporating this technology into future projects. This project represents an initial version. We want to suggest some improvements and ideas you can implement to extend it and enrich your chatbot.

Extend the actions performed by your chatbot

Your current chatbot can detect conflicts when a user attempts to schedule a meeting but consider expanding its capabilities by implementing logic to suggest available time slots to the user. Additionally, you could introduce a scheduling window, for instance, from 9 AM to 5 PM, and only accept meeting requests within that timeframe:

```
def check_meeting_slot(prop_date, prop_start, prop_dur):
#check if is there any conflict by querying the dynamoDB table for
meeting already accepted at the proposed start time.
```

You could improve this function, for example, by including two new arguments:

- `min_time`: Defined by the admin, the earliest time to accept a meeting.
- `max_time`: Defined by the admin, the latest time to accept a meeting.

Now, inside your function, include the logic to test the following:

- Whether the meeting's proposed date is before `min_time`.
- Whether the meeting's end date is after `max_time`.
- Whether there is a conflict, and in case there is, query the DynamoDB table to get all the meetings happening on the proposed date and implement the logic to find an available slot considering the proposed duration.

Here is an example of the updated structure for your `check_meeting_slot` function, which incorporates the necessary parameters to extend the logic as described above:

```
def check_meeting_slot(prop_date, prop_start, prop_dur, min_time, max_time):
#future work
```

Feel free to explore and customize the `bot-function-meety` lambda function to incorporate these ideas or any other enhancements you envision for your chatbot.

Multilingual support

Currently, your chatbot only supports English, but Amazon Lex offers the capability to work with multiple languages. As a future enhancement, you could configure your chatbot to support additional languages, making it more accessible to users from different linguistic backgrounds. You can find the instructions on how to implement it in the AWS documentation at https://docs.aws.amazon.com/lexv2/latest/dg/add-language.html.

Maintain user profiles for different sessions

The CloudFormation deployment included a lambda function called `chatbot-meety`, which is responsible for interacting with your Amazon Lex chatbot by sending user inputs and receiving responses. One of the parameters when interacting with Amazon Lex is `sessionId`, which helps the service identify different conversations:

```
def lambda_handler(event, context):
...
response = bot.recognize_text(
botId = '${MeetyBot}',
botAliasId='TSTALIASID',
localeId='en_US',
sessionId='your_session_id',
text = user_input
)
...
```

Currently, this value is hardcoded. You can see this in the preceding snippet where we used the `your_session_id` string, meaning there is no way for the chatbot to handle multiple concurrent conversations. Can you think about a strategy to create a unique identifier for each session?

Summary

In this chapter, you embarked on a journey to develop an intelligent chatbot application that streamlines the meeting scheduling process. By leveraging the power of AWS services such as Amazon Lex, Lambda, API Gateway, and DynamoDB, you created a seamless, conversational experience that automates the entire meeting scheduling workflow. Specifically, in the chatbot development, you explored the intricacies of Amazon Lex, including intents, utterances, and slots, and learned how to customize and extend the chatbot's capabilities. Overall, and in the previous three chapters, you have gained knowledge in the AI field and how to adopt these technologies with AWS services.

In the next chapter, you will explore the business intelligence domain and learn how to analyze clickstream data.

8

Building a Business Intelligence Application

In today's digital era, businesses generate massive amounts of data from various sources, including websites, mobile apps, and online transactions. One such data source is **clickstream data**, which refers to the record of user interactions and activities on websites or applications. Analyzing clickstream data can provide valuable insights into user behavior, preferences, and pain points, enabling businesses to tailor their products, services, and marketing strategies to better meet customer needs.

In this chapter, we'll explore how to build a business intelligence application using native AWS services to analyze clickstream data. We'll cover the entire process, from data ingestion and storage to data transformation, querying, and visualization.

In summary, this chapter covers the following topics in order:

- What you are going to build – a business intelligence application
- How you are going to build it – using Glue, Athena, and QuickSight
- Actually building it – through CloudFormation and using the AWS console
- How to improve the solution – automate the ETL pipeline and data life cycle management

By the end of this chapter, you will have gained hands-on experience in building an end-to-end business intelligence application using AWS services to analyze clickstream data.

Technical requirements

To follow along with this chapter and implement your own business intelligence application, you need to have access to an AWS account. Additionally, this book has a dedicated folder within its GitHub repository where you can find the necessary code for provisioning all the infrastructure and the additional files that will be used throughout the chapter: https://github.com/PacktPublishing/AWS-Cloud-Projects/tree/main/chapter8/code.

Scenario

You are the owner of an e-commerce website that sells a wide range of products, from electronics to fashion items. Your website has been operational for a few years, and over time, you have managed to build a sizable customer base. However, you have noticed that your conversion rates (the percentage of visitors who make a purchase) have been stagnant, and you are unsure of the reasons behind this trend.

To improve your conversion rates and enhance the overall user experience on your website, you have decided to analyze the clickstream data generated by your users. **Clickstream data** refers to the record of user interactions and activities on your website, such as the pages visited, the links clicked, the products viewed, and the time spent on each page.

By analyzing this data, you aim to gain valuable insights into user behavior and preferences, which can help you identify potential bottlenecks, pain points, and areas for improvement in your website's user experience. Additionally, you hope to uncover patterns and trends that can guide your marketing and product development strategies, leading to increased conversions and revenue.

Requirements

As you have done until this part, gathering the requirements should be the starting point. Considering your current scenario, your objective is to analyze the clickstream data, and there are two different profiles with diverse backgrounds and technical skills that want to extract information from your data:

- **Business analysts**: Business analysts do not feel confident creating and running SQL queries and look for a more visual alternative to explore the data.
- **Technical users**: Technical users are familiar and comfortable with SQL and want to be able to run complex queries to answer specific questions.

Knowing the profiles and understanding how they will interact with your application is key for defining the functional and non-functional requirements.

Functional requirements

Functional requirements outline the essential features, functions, and capabilities that the proposed solution must deliver to meet the desired objectives. In this case, the functional requirements should do the following:

- Extract information from clickstream data
- Support geographic analysis and user distribution
- Support on-demand updates to get the most up-to-date information
- Have the ability to run ad hoc SQL queries for technical users
- Have the capacity to store the clickstream data indefinitely

Non-functional requirements

Non-functional requirements describe the qualitative characteristics and constraints that the proposed solution should adhere to, ensuring its overall quality and performance. In this specific case, the non-functional requirements stipulate the following:

- Limited maintenance effort
- Cost-effectiveness

Architecture patterns

The AWS Architecture Center (https://aws.amazon.com/architecture/) offers a set of vetted solutions developed and built by experts from both AWS and AWS Partners, which can be considered as the starting point for your projects. For this use case, AWS has available a solution from the AWS Solutions Library called **Clickstream Analytics on AWS**: https://aws.amazon.com/solutions/implementations/clickstream-analytics-on-aws/. This solution focuses on the collection, ingestion, analysis, and visualization of clickstream data from websites and mobile applications, which is in line with this project's scope.

The blueprints and solutions should be fully functional due to the regular revisions conducted by AWS, but often each project has its own peculiarities, and they may require some level of customization. Regardless, these are always valuable resources and will save some time whenever you are starting a project from scratch, namely during the architecture design phase.

Architecture

As you have been doing since the first project of this book, you adopt a top-bottom approach, starting with the requirements, which should be completely agnostic and describe the functionalities and constraints you have in your application, down to the specific services that support it.

Your business intelligence application can be decomposed into three layers, as shown in *Figure 8.1*:

Ingestion

Processing

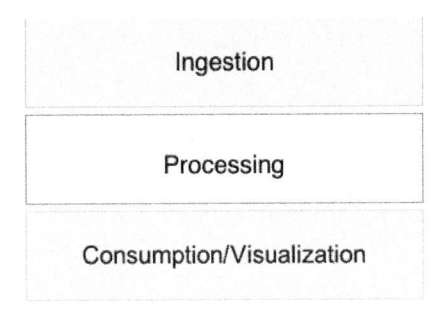

Consumption/Visualization

Figure 8.1 – Business intelligence application layers

Let us briefly go over the details:

- **Ingestion layer**: This collects and imports data from various sources into the system.
- **Processing layer**: This prepares, cleanses, and transforms the data for analysis.
- **Visualization layer**: This presents the processed data in a visually appealing and interactive manner for exploration and insights.

Comprehending the layers' purposes and their respective roles in contributing to the overall application is key for defining the suitable services to be integrated within them.

Simplicity and a minimum amount of maintenance effort are the two main pillars of your architecture considering the two types of personas you want to serve. You will need two ways of interacting with or exploring the data. Moreover, you don't want to duplicate the data and create different sources for each of the profiles that are interacting with the clickstream data; so, for the data store, you want to adopt a solution that is versatile enough to integrate with both a SQL-like engine for exploration and a business intelligence solution for visualization.

After some research, you start exploring Amazon QuickSight for the visualization layer, and Amazon Athena for running SQL queries over your clickstream data. To store the data, you decide to go with Amazon S3 since it integrates with both Amazon Athena and Amazon QuickSight and can be used without any constraints regarding the number of items to store. For the data transformations, you want a solution that does not require any infrastructure maintenance, and ideally, a tool where you could leverage your current Spark knowledge; so, you have chosen AWS Glue for your data pipelines.

Considering all the points mentioned, you produce an initial architecture, as shown in *Figure 8.2*. In summary, files are ingested into the `/raw` prefix of the bucket and processed by Glue into the `/results` prefix of the same bucket. Technical users query this data using Athena with SQL-like syntax, while business users get their insights from QuickSight in a visual format.

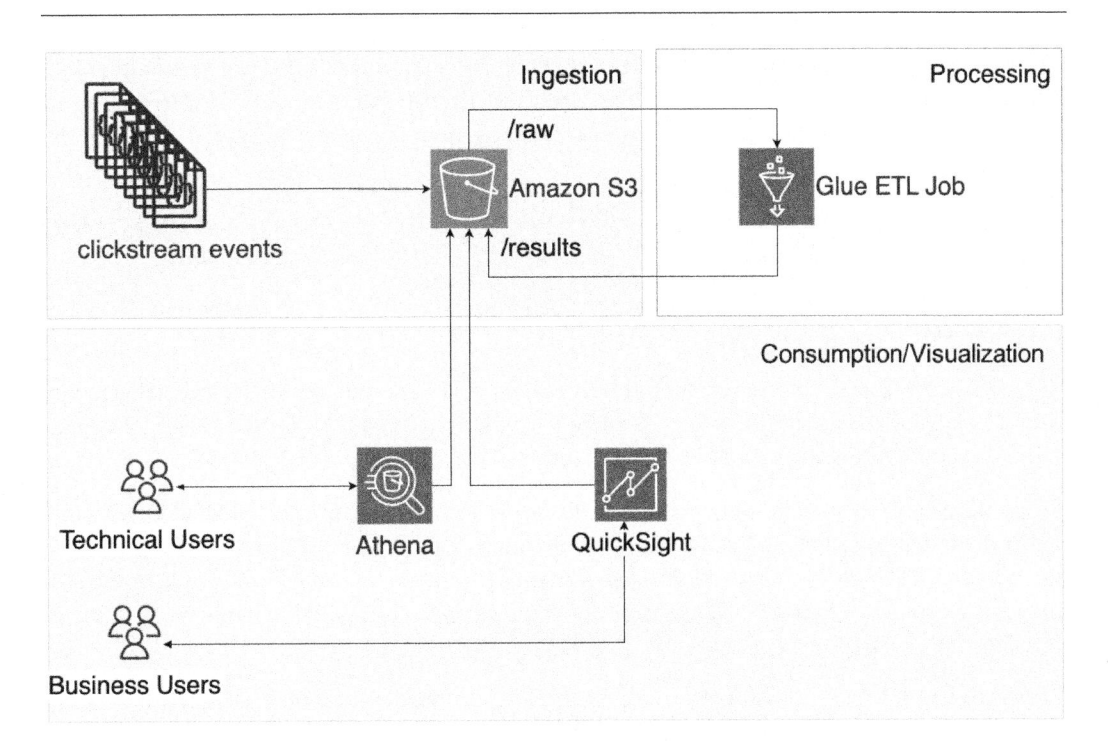

Figure 8.2 – AWS architecture for your business intelligence application

Now that you have outlined the high-level architecture, let us dive into the AWS services you have chosen to build this solution and understand how they align with the requirements that were previously established.

AWS services

As shown in *Figure 8.2*, this architecture is composed of four main services. In this section, you will explore each of the building blocks and understand how they align with the requirements.

Amazon Simple Storage Service (S3)

In your business intelligence application architecture, you need a data store to persist massive amounts of objects or events, and you discover that S3 can be the ideal solution as the foundation for your data lake. S3 is designed to offer high durability with up to 99.999999999% (11 9s) of durability, ensuring that your data remains intact and accessible even in the face of unexpected events or infrastructure failures, and high availability to guarantee a reliable solution for analytics and reporting purposes, as expected for a data lake.

Moreover, scalability and cost-effectiveness were highlighted as part of the requirements, and S3 aligns with both tenets since it can store and analyze petabytes of data without worrying about capacity constraints or infrastructure provisioning, by automatically scaling upon need, with a pay-as-you-go model.

Amazon S3 is the best fit for supporting your data lake, and you can learn more about why by reading this blog: https://aws.amazon.com/blogs/big-data/tag/data-lake/.

AWS Glue

AWS Glue is a serverless data integration service that makes it easy to discover, prepare, and combine data for analytics. In your business intelligence application architecture, AWS Glue is used for two key purposes: **extract, transform, and load** (ETL) jobs and the Glue Data Catalog.

ETL is a crucial process in data integration, where data from various sources is extracted, transformed into a desired format, and loaded into a data store for analysis or reporting; in this case, it is loaded into S3. AWS Glue provides a serverless Apache Spark environment to run ETL jobs without the need to provision or manage servers. ETL jobs in Glue can be defined using Python and executed further by Glue's Apache Spark runtime.

AWS Glue ETL jobs are highly scalable and cost-effective, as you only pay for the resources used during job execution. Additionally, Glue automatically provisions and manages the underlying Apache Spark clusters, eliminating the need for manual cluster management.

The **Glue Data Catalog** is a centralized repository that stores metadata about data sources and acts as the only source of truth for data across your organization.

In your application, the Glue Data Catalog is used to maintain metadata definitions for your data source, namely your data lake based on S3.

The Glue Data Catalog seamlessly integrates with other AWS services, such as Amazon Athena, which is part of your architecture, enabling access and query data based on the metadata stored in the catalog.

Amazon Athena

Amazon Athena is an interactive query service that makes it easy to analyze data in Amazon S3 using standard SQL. With Athena, you can run ad hoc queries or pre-defined SQL scripts directly against data stored in S3, without the need to load or transform the data into a separate data store.

Its serverless approach eliminates the need to provision and manage infrastructure, allowing you to focus on data analysis rather than infrastructure management.

As explained in the *AWS Glue* section, Athena seamlessly integrates with the AWS Glue Data Catalog, and by referencing the metadata in the Glue Data Catalog, Athena can understand the structure and location of your data in S3, enabling you to query the data using SQL without manual schema definitions.

For the technical profiles that were introduced in the *Requirements* section, Athena is a great fit since it will enable them to run queries and answer complex questions in an ad hoc way.

Amazon QuickSight

Amazon QuickSight is a cloud-based business intelligence service that enables organizations to create and deliver insightful visualizations and dashboards quickly and easily. In your business intelligence application architecture, you can leverage QuickSight as a powerful data visualization and reporting tool, empowering your business users with interactive and visually appealing dashboards for data exploration and decision-making, without the need for technical skills.

QuickSight seamlessly integrates with various data sources, including Athena, eliminating the need for complex data movement or transformation processes. By leveraging QuickSight's integration with Athena and the Glue Data Catalog, you can effortlessly visualize and explore data stored in your S3 data lake, making it easier to derive insights.

Overall, QuickSight solves the data exploration requirement for the non-technical users described in the requirements section.

Coding the solution

This project is divided into two parts; the data engineering part, where you will build the end-to-end workflow for collecting, transforming, and loading your data, and the second part, where you will build your first dashboard in QuickSight.

Section 1 – Cloning the project

To start, you will need to clone the Git repository associated with this book, as mentioned in the *Technical requirements* section. If you are following along with the previous chapters, you should already have the repository locally, but if this is not the case, you can clone it directly from Git or download it as a ZIP file if you prefer.

Navigate to the `chapter8/code` folder, and inside, you will find two subfolders:

- `platform`: This includes the CloudFormation template to deploy the main infrastructure for your application.
- `aux`: This contains a set of auxiliary files that will be used throughout the chapter.

Section 2 – Solution deployment

The first step is to deploy the necessary infrastructure to support your application. As with some of the previous chapters, this can be done through the CloudFormation template found in the /platform folder. *Table 8.1* lists all the resources created by your template that map to the architecture presented in *Figure 8.2*.

Template	ch8-application-template.yaml
Networking	1 VPC
	1 internet gateway
	1 public subnet
Data store	Amazon S3
Data processing	1 Glue database
	1 Glue table
	1 Glue job
Others	1 parameter in Parameter Store
	1 EC2 instance

Table 8.1 – CloudFormation template details

As you have done in previous chapters, you will use CloudFormation to provision the necessary infrastructure to support your application:

1. From the console, go to the CloudFormation service at https://console.aws.amazon.com/cloudformation/ and select the AWS region where you want to host your application in the upper-right corner (**Oregon**, in our case), as shown in *Figure 8.3*.

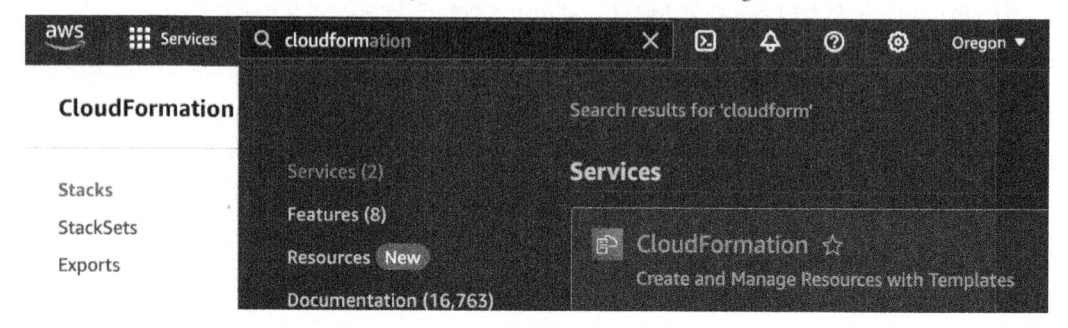

Figure 8.3 – Access to the CloudFormation console

2. Click on **Create stack**.
3. In the **Prerequisite – Prepare Template** section, select **Choose an existing template**.
4. In the **Specify template** section, choose **Upload a template file**.
5. Click on **Choose file**.
6. Select the template (`ch8-application-template.yaml`) from the `chapter8/code/platform` folder.
7. Click **Next**.

Your **Create stack** window should look like *Figure 8.4*.

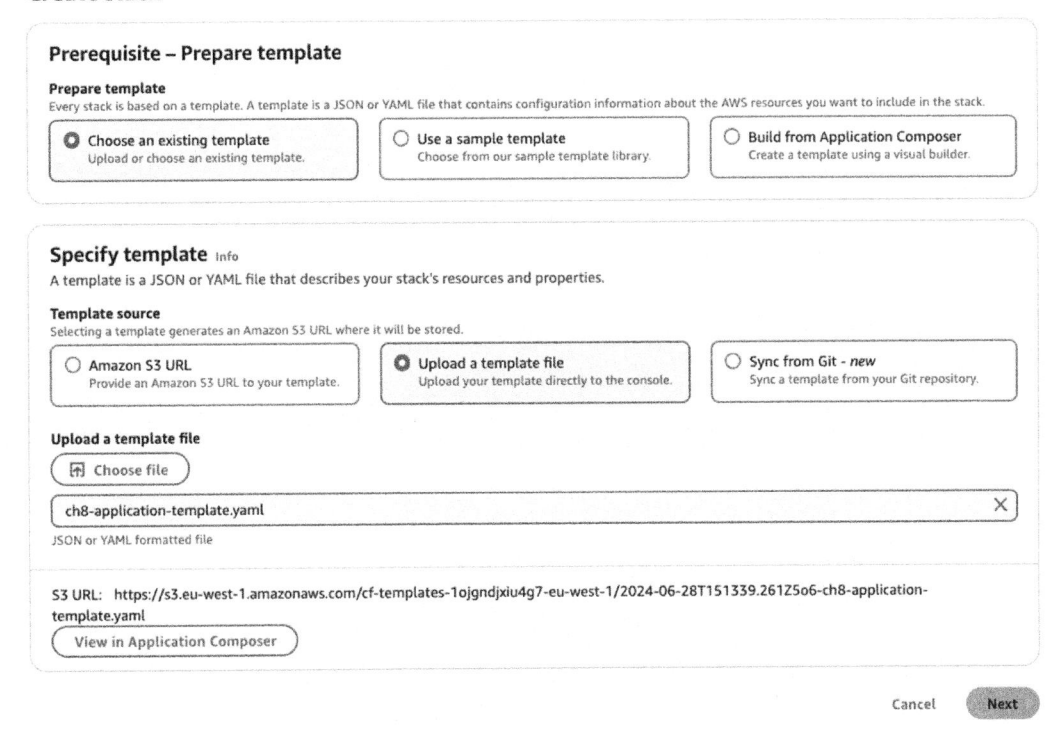

Figure 8.4 – The CloudFormation stack creation screen

Next, you will be asked to configure the parameters in your CloudFormation stack. In *Table 8.2*, you can find a detailed explanation of each parameter.

Parameter	Description
`GitRepoURL`	The Git repository you want to use. By default, you will have the repository associated with this book, but in case you forked it to your own Git account, you can change it accordingly.
`InstanceType`	The type of instance you want to choose for the EC2 instance. You can leave it as is or choose between the four options available.
`LatestAmiId`	The Amazon Machine Image you want to use for your EC2 instance. You can leave it as is.

Table 8.2 – The CloudFormation template parameters

You can proceed until the last page, where you will be asked to acknowledge the creation of IAM roles before proceeding. This notification appears because the template will attempt to create two IAM roles:

- An IAM role associated with the AWS Glue job, to grant the necessary permissions to read and write files to S3
- An IAM role attached to the EC2 instance where the scripts will be executed, to provide enough permissions to copy specific files to your S3 bucket

Click **Submit** and wait until the stack status changes to **CREATE_COMPLETE**, as depicted in *Figure 8.5*.

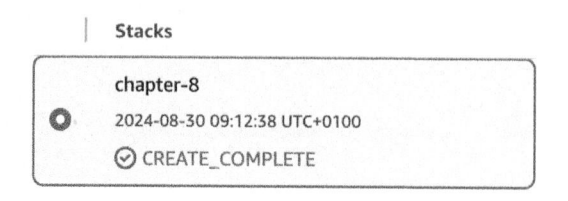

Figure 8.5 – The CloudFormation stack created status

This means that all the resources are provisioned, and you can now proceed.

Section 3 – Clickstream event generator

As with any business intelligence application, the first ingredient needed for further processing is data. In your case, you do not yet have data to be processed; so, in the first part, we created an event generator that you can use to generate clickstream events on demand. To execute the event generator, follow these steps:

1. Go to the CloudShell console at `https://console.aws.amazon.com/cloudshell`.
2. This should open a new terminal window where you can execute scripts. In case you don't have any environment ready, click on **Open [AWS-Region] environment**, as shown in *Figure 8.6*:

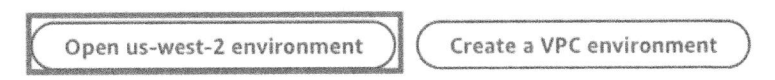

Figure 8.6 – CloudShell terminal creation

By the end, you should be seeing a brand-new terminal window, as depicted in *Figure 8.7*:

Figure 8.7 – The CloudShell terminal window

This new terminal will be used to run commands that will generate events and send them to your recently created S3 bucket.

As part of the deployment process, we generated a file with all the commands that need to be run inside your terminal. To access it, follow these steps:

1. Go to the S3 console at `https://console.aws.amazon.com/s3`.
2. Select your recently created S3 bucket. It should be called `chapter-8-clickstream-XXXXXXXX`.
3. Click on the `aux` folder.
4. Select the `instructions.txt` file.

5. Click on **Download**, as shown in *Figure 8.8*.

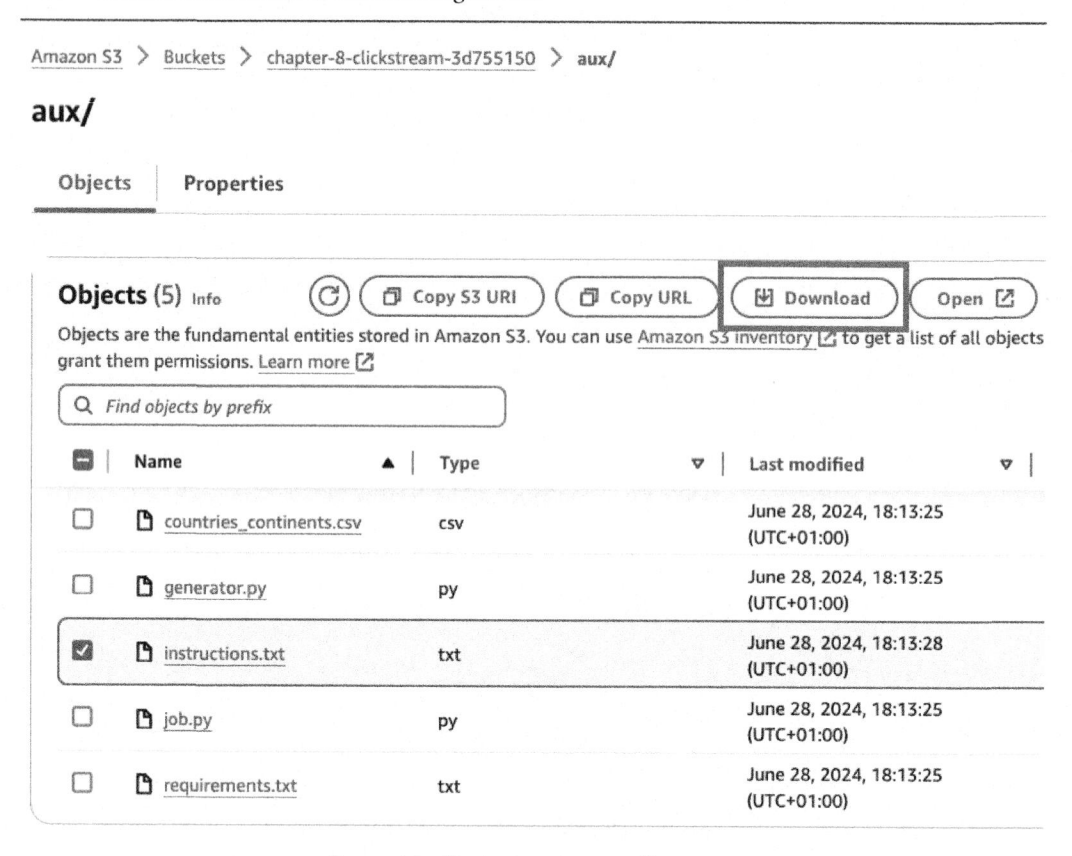

Figure 8.8 – The instructions.txt file access

6. Open the file. Inside the file, you should have three commands:

   ```
   git clone GIT_URL_DEFINED_IN_THE_CLOUDFORMATION_PARAMETER
   cd GIT_NAME/chapter8/code/aux
   pip install -r requirements.txt
   ```

   These three commands will clone the Git repository locally in your CloudShell environment.

7. Next, navigate to the /aux folder where your event simulator file (generator.py) is located, and finally install all the libraries needed with pip.

8. Copy the commands from the instructions.txt file and paste them into the CloudShell terminal.

9. Run the following command:

   ```
   $ python3 generator.py
   ```

This command will start generating a total of 20 events simulating clickstream data and send it to your recently created S3 bucket in the /raw folder. Moreover, the script will create one event per second and print it in the console so you can follow along:

```
...
{'event_type': 'search', 'user_id': 'lyttebmihe', 'user_action':
'home_page', 'product_category': None, 'location': '36', 'user_
age': 30, 'timestamp': 1714680649}
Event uploaded to S3: search_lyttebmihe_1714680649.json

{'event_type': 'click', 'user_id': 'oencotfldn', 'user_action':
'cart_page', 'product_category': 'books', 'location': '1',
'user_age': 42, 'timestamp': 1717732343}
Event uploaded to S3: click_oencotfldn_1717732343.json

Timeout occurred. Exiting script after creating 20 events.
```

As described before, this script will generate the events and store them in your S3 bucket.

To confirm the persistence of the file in your S3 bucket, follow these steps:

1. Go to the S3 console at `https://console.aws.amazon.com/s3`.
2. Select your recently created S3 bucket. It should be called `chapter-8-clickstream-XXXXXXXX`.
3. Click on the `raw` folder.

   Your /raw folder should look like *Figure 8.9* with a total number of JSON files corresponding to the total number of events generated.

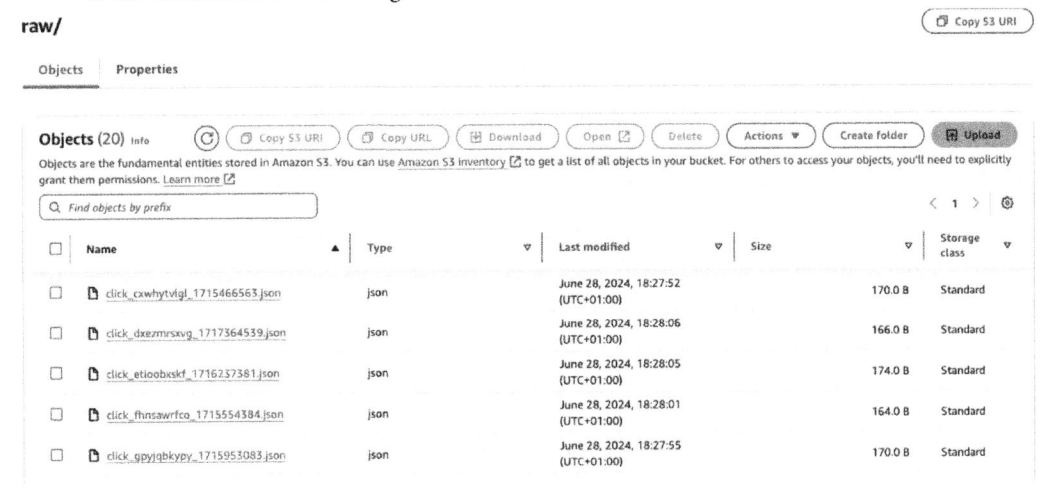

Figure 8.9 – The event data stored in S3

You can run the script as many times as you want, by running the following command:

```
$ python3 generator.py
```

Now that you have your raw data generated and stored, it is time to apply the transformations.

Section 4 – The Glue ETL job

So far, you have a set of files representing the clickstream events you generated, but often these events come with a structure that does not fit analytics purposes. For that reason, now it is time to run your ETL job and apply some changes to your clickstream data to support analytics workloads and information extraction:

1. Go to the Glue console at `https://console.aws.amazon.com/glue`.
2. Click on **Visual ETL** from the left menu.
3. From the **Your jobs** list, select `chapter8-gluejob` and click on **Run job**, as shown in *Figure 8.10*.

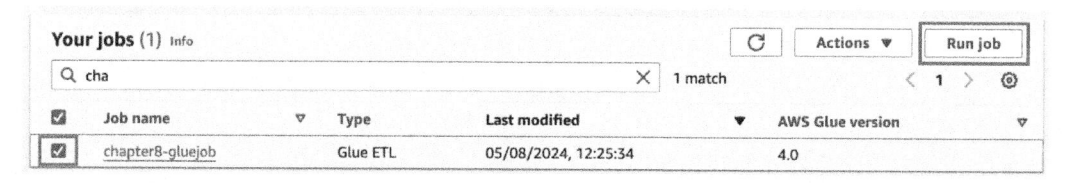

Figure 8.10 – The Glue ETL job running process

While your job is running, it is important to recall the exact actions that are being executed:

I. Read all the event files in your `/raw` folder inside your S3 bucket.
II. Read a reference file with geographic information.
III. Change the schema of each dataset.
IV. Combine both datasets into one.
V. Select a subset of columns.
VI. Creates a single `.csv` file based on the output dataset.
VII. Persist the output `.csv` file in your S3 bucket in the `/results` folder.
VIII. Move all the clickstream events from the `/raw` folder to the `/processed` folder.

4. To explore the code in detail, follow these steps:

    I. Click on the job name (`chapter8-gluejob`).
    II. Select the **Script** tab and review the code.

5. To check your job status, move to the **Runs** tab and wait until **Run status** turns into **Succeeded**, as shown in *Figure 8.11*:

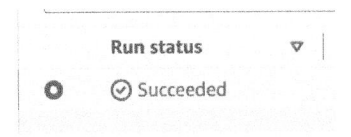

Figure 8.11 – Successful run message

By now, all your data transformation is done, and it is time to explore it.

Section 5 – Data exploration with Athena

So far, you already generated the clickstream data and ran an ETL pipeline that transformed it. Now, it is time to explore your data and extract information from it. As mentioned in the *Requirements* sections, there are two types of profiles interacting with your data, so let us start with the solution for the technical users and try to run SQL queries over your transformed data:

1. Go to the Athena console at https://console.aws.amazon.com/athena.
2. If it is the first time you are accessing the Athena console, you will need to perform the initial configuration. So, click on **Explore the query editor**, as shown in *Figure 8.12*:

Figure 8.12 – The Athena console

3. Go to the **Settings** tab.
4. Click on **Manage**.
5. Select **Browse S3**.
6. Find and click on the S3 bucket you created for this project (the name should start with chapter-8-clickstream-xxxxxxxx).

7. Select the /aux folder.
8. Click on **Choose**, as depicted in *Figure 8.13*.

Choose S3 data set

S3 buckets > chapter-8-clickstream-a0e6b380

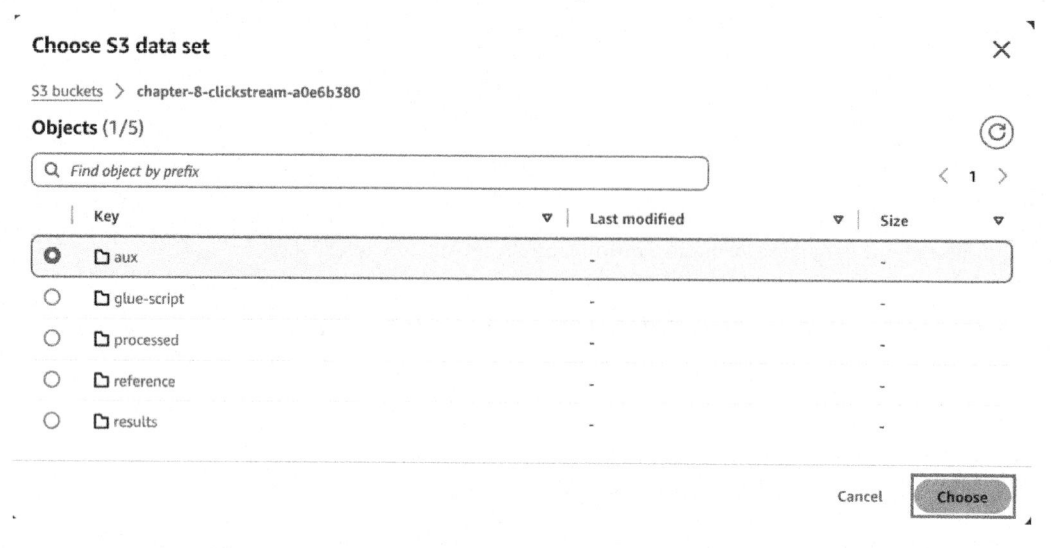

Objects (1/5)

Key	Last modified	Size
● aux	-	-
○ glue-script	-	-
○ processed	-	-
○ reference	-	-
○ results	-	-

Cancel | Choose

Figure 8.13 – Athena configuration

Important note
The bucket you are choosing is the same as the one you are using to store your data. Ideally, you should have a separate bucket for that and take that into consideration whenever you are working on a real project.

After configuring your Athena environment, follow these steps:

1. Switch to the **Editor** tab.
2. Ensure you have selected the following settings:
    - **Data source**: `AwsDataCatalog`
    - **Database**: `clickstream_db`
3. Click on the three dots next to `clickstream_table`.

4. Select **Preview Table**, as shown in *Figure 8.14*.

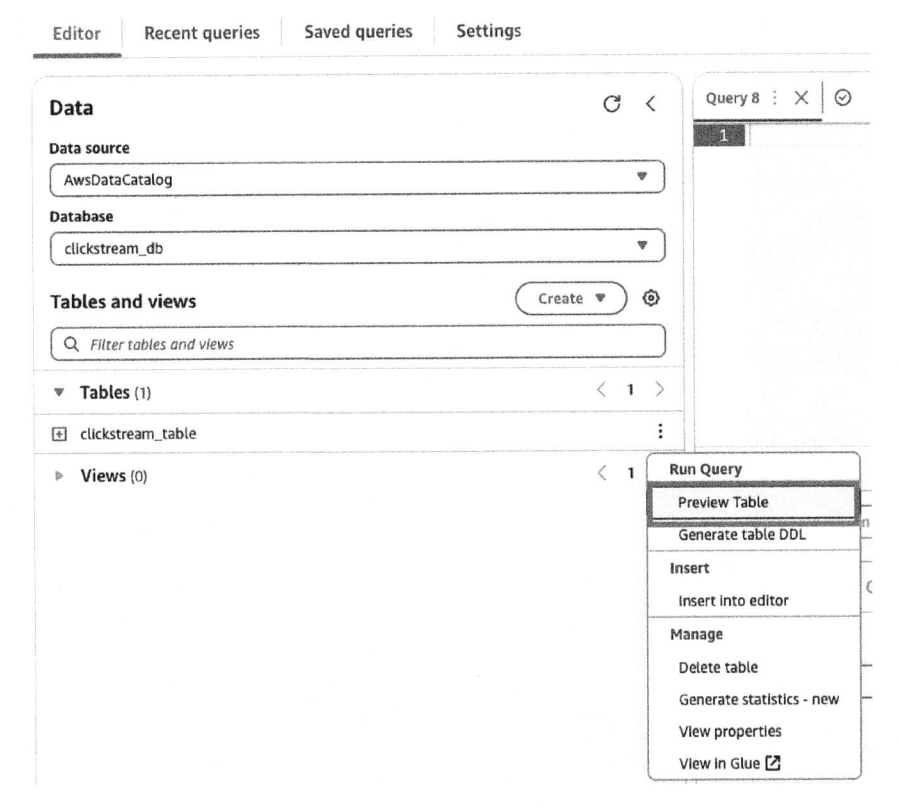

Figure 8.14 – The Athena preview table example

This will open a new tab with an auto-generated query like the following:

```
SELECT * FROM "clickstream_db"."clickstream_table" limit 10;
```

This is an example of how you can explore your results data with pure SQL, and although the auto-generated query is quite simple, you can extend it to answer more complex questions; for example, what is the continent where you are getting more clicks from? Try running the following query to get the answer!

```
SELECT continent, COUNT(*) AS total_records
FROM "clickstream_db"."clickstream_table"
GROUP BY continent
ORDER BY total_records DESC;
```

208   Building a Business Intelligence Application

Now, it is time to explore how non-technical users can interact and extract information from your data without having the technical knowledge or experience with SQL. For that, you will now develop a dashboard in QuickSight to create a visual alternative for exploring your data.

Section 6 – Data visualization with QuickSight

Let's start by setting up your QuickSight. If you are already using QuickSight in your account for other projects, you can skip the initial configuration and select the Region where you've used for this chapter before proceeding with the dataset creation:

1. In the search bar of your AWS console, type `QuickSight`.
2. You will be redirected to the **QuickSight** portal and presented with a form like *Figure 8.15*:

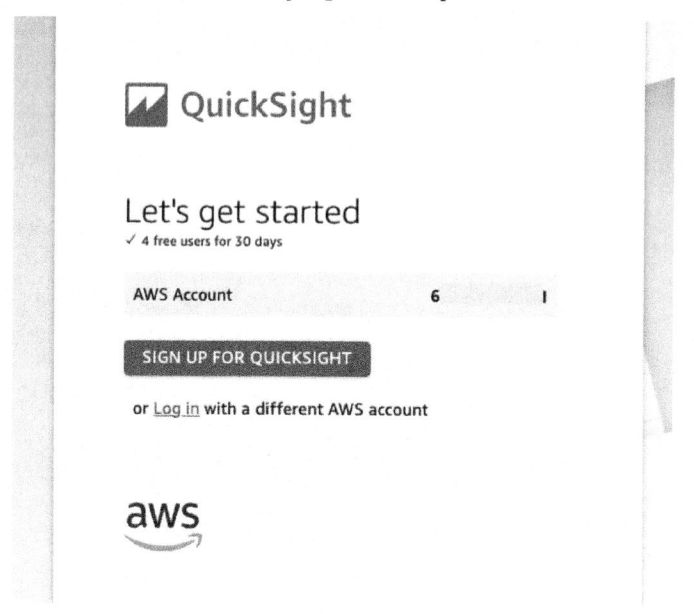

Figure 8.15 – The QuickSight sign-up form

3. Click on **SIGN UP FOR QUICKSIGHT**.
4. Next, you will need to fill out the email for the notifications. You can use your own email or any other of your choice.
5. Go to the QuickSight region selection. From the drop-down menu, choose the same Region you've been using for this chapter's project, as shown in *Figure 8.16*:

Sign up for QuickSight

Contact information

Email for account notifications

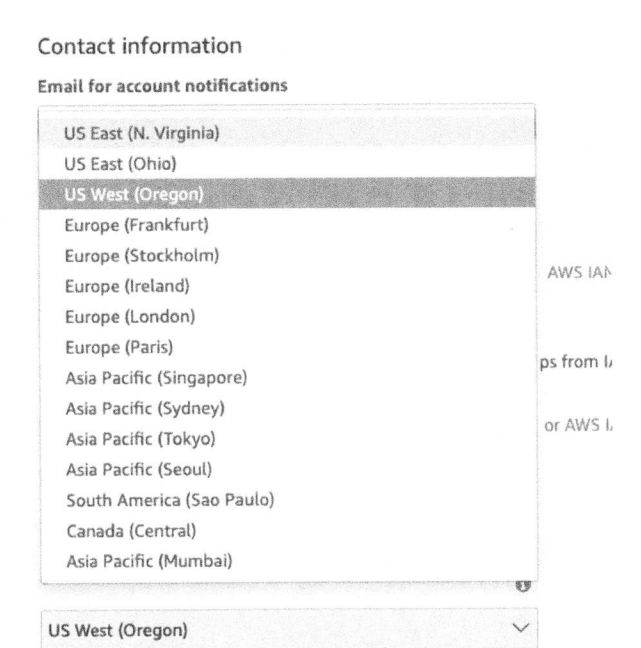

- US East (N. Virginia)
- US East (Ohio)
- **US West (Oregon)**
- Europe (Frankfurt)
- Europe (Stockholm)
- Europe (Ireland)
- Europe (London)
- Europe (Paris)
- Asia Pacific (Singapore)
- Asia Pacific (Sydney)
- Asia Pacific (Tokyo)
- Asia Pacific (Seoul)
- South America (Sao Paulo)
- Canada (Central)
- Asia Pacific (Mumbai)

US West (Oregon)

Figure 8.16 – QuickSight region selection

6. Scroll down and, in the **Allow access and auto discovery for these resources** section, select the S3 bucket you just created (it should start with `chapter8-clickstream-xxx`).

7. Scroll down and, in the **Optional add-on** section, ensure you *untick* the **Add paginated reports** checkbox, as shown in *Figure 8.17*:

Optional add-on

☐ **Add Paginated Reports**   ⓘ Monthly charges begin immediately

$500 /month* **500** unique report units **/month

Create, schedule, and share operational reports and data exports from a single fully-managed business intelligence (BI) cloud solution.
Learn more

Figure 8.17 – QuickSight paginated reports add-on

> **Important note**
> Ensuring that you do not add paginated reports to your subscription is critical to avoid unnecessary costs with features that are not covered in this book.

8. Click on **Finish**.

If everything was set up correctly, on the left menu of the QuickSight portal, you should see a menu with various options, as shown in *Figure 8.18*:

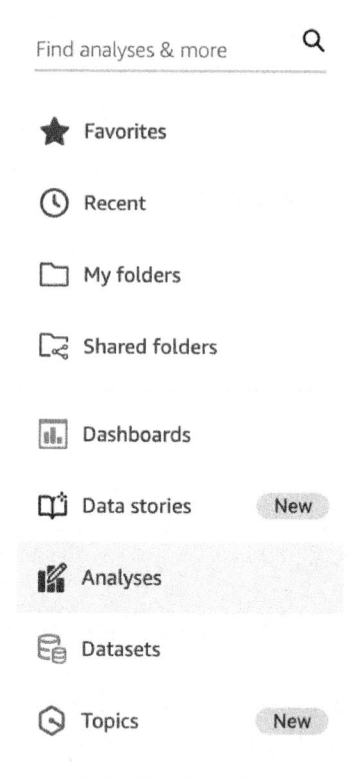

Figure 8.18 – The QuickSight menu

Whenever you start creating any content in QuickSight, the first step is to create a dataset. So, let us start by defining your first one:

1. Click on **Datasets**.
2. In the upper-right corner, click on **New dataset**.
3. Select **Athena**.
4. For the data source name, give it a meaningful name, such as `clickstream`.
5. For the Athena workgroup, ensure **[Primary]** is selected.
6. Click on **Validate connection** to ensure everything is working correctly.
7. Click on **Create data source**.
8. On the next window, select `clickstream_table` from the table list, as shown in *Figure 8.19*:

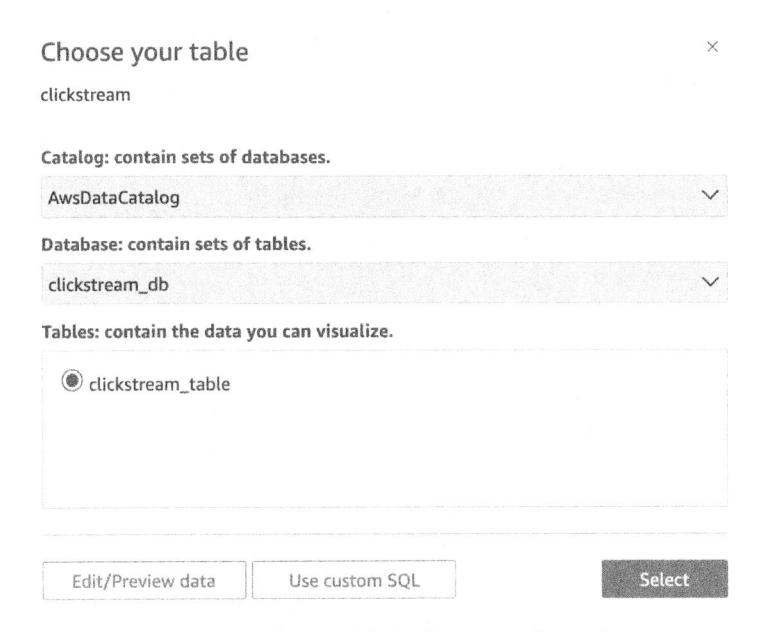

Figure 8.19 – The QuickSight dataset configuration

9. Click on **Select**.
10. Click on **Visualize**.
11. When prompted for the type of report, choose **Interactive Sheet**, as shown in *Figure 8.20*:

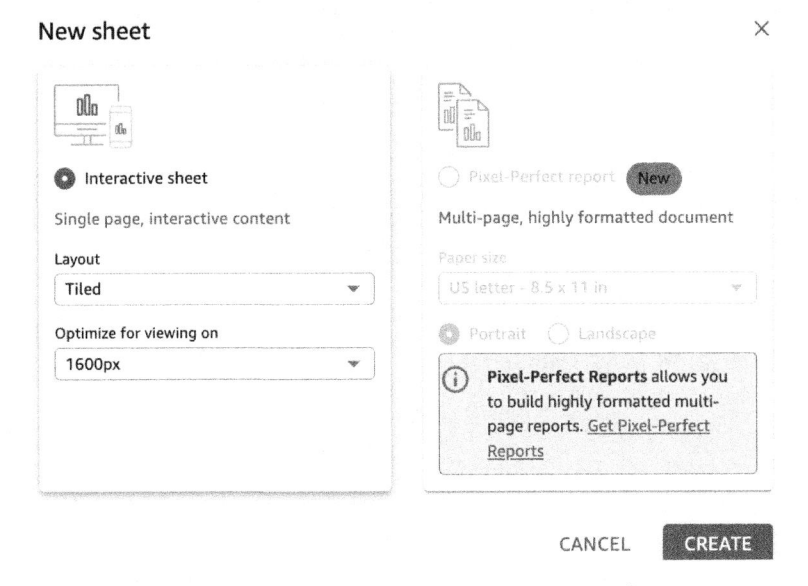

Figure 8.20 – The QuickSight report type creation form

Building a Business Intelligence Application

Now, it is time to start creating the visuals. As this is a learning exercise, you will create a simple dashboard, but you can and should extend it to a more complex and informative one.

Let us start by creating a visual with the geographic distribution of your users based on clicks:

1. From the **Visuals** tab, click on the arrow next to + **ADD**.
2. Select the filled map, as shown in *Figure 8.21*:

Figure 8.21 – The QuickSight Visuals selection

3. From the fields list in the **Data** section, select `country-name`.

By the end, your visual should look like *Figure 8.22*:

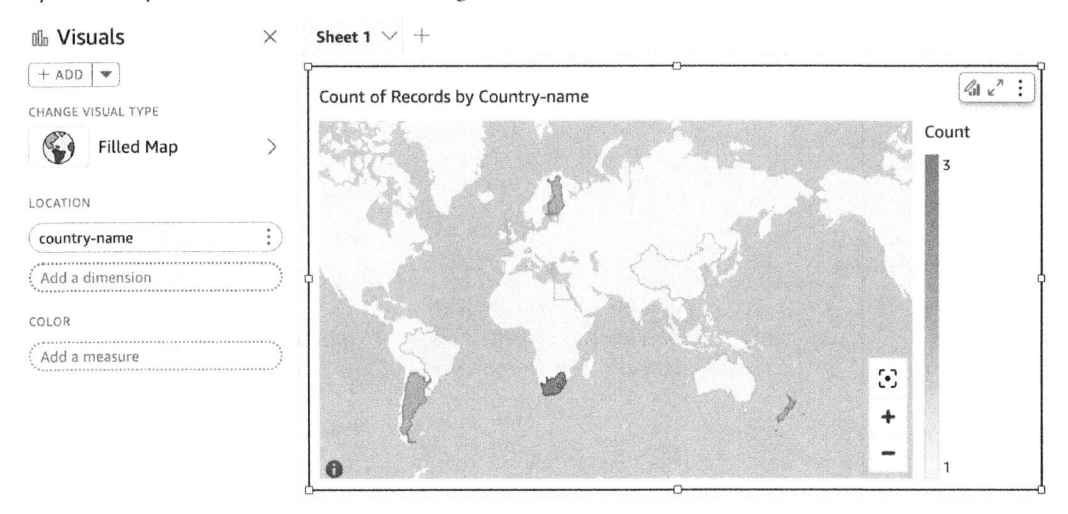

Figure 8.22 – The Filled Map visual creation

Now, let us create a different visual to show the average age of your users based on the click data. For that, you will leverage **Autograph**, a feature in QuickSight that suggests the graph type based on the data you want to visualize:

1. Click outside the map visual.
2. From the **Data** menu, select user_age.

   Note that QuickSight creates a visual with a single number. This is because the aggregation type, by default, is set to **Sum** and thus it is summing the age of all the users.

3. To change it, click on the three dots next to the user_age field, and in the aggregate menu, change it to **Average**, as shown in *Figure 8.23*:

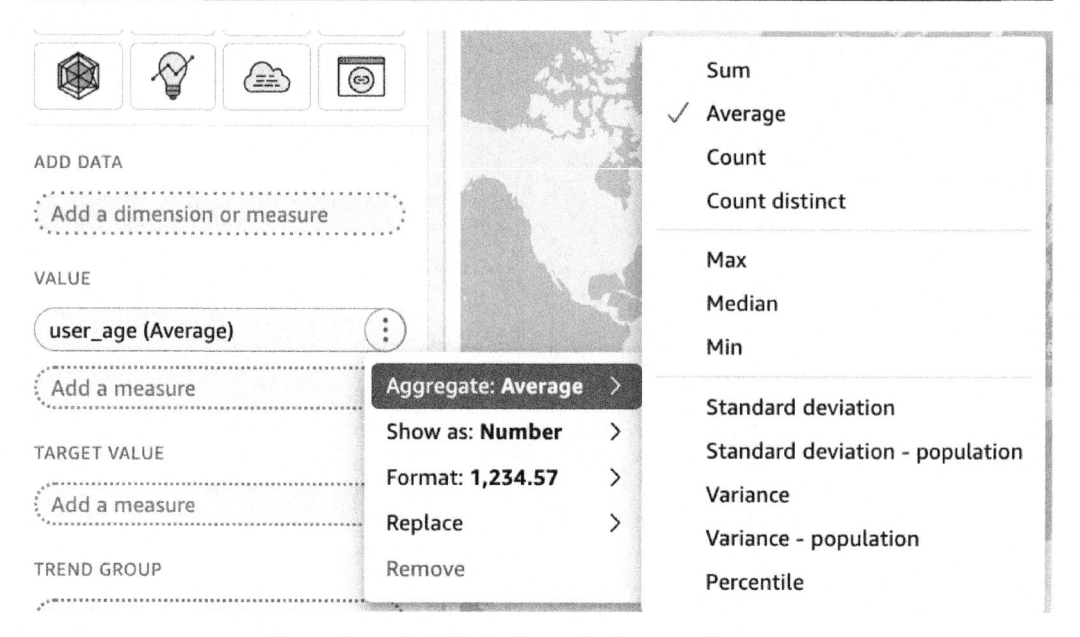

214 Building a Business Intelligence Application

Figure 8.23 – QuickSight data calculation configuration

Your visual should automatically change to show the new calculation.

The last visual you will build is a funnel to show how the number of records evolves by event type. For that, you should follow these steps:

1. Click on **+ ADD** and select **Funnel Chart**.
2. From the data menu, select `event_type`.

    Your dashboard should look like *Figure 8.24*. Feel free to explore additional visual types, rearrange the visuals you already have, and create your own version of the dashboard.

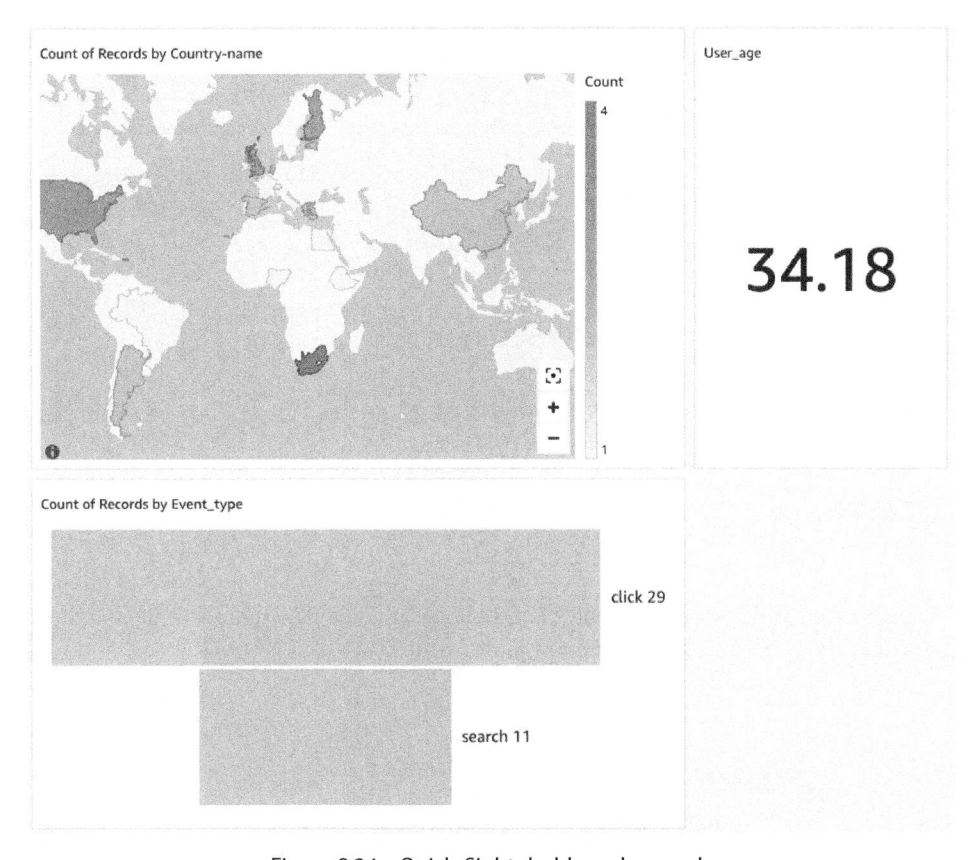

Figure 8.24 – QuicksSight dashboard example

Now, it is time to publish your dashboard so you can share it with other users:

1. In the top-right corner, click on **Publish**.
2. Give it a name to your dashboard.
3. Click on **Publish Dashboard**.

Congratulations, your dashboard is done and ready to be shared! The last thing you will test is the end-to-end workflow to ensure your data gets updated in your dashboard.

To do that, start by generating additional events and running the ETL job as described in *Section 3 – Clickstream event generator* and *Section 4 – The Glue ETL job*, respectively. When your job finishes with a succeeded status, in the QuickSight console, do the following:

1. Click on the QuickSight icon in the upper-left corner.
2. Select **Datasets** from the left menu.
3. Select the dataset you just created.

4. Go to the **Refresh** tab.
5. Click on **REFRESH NOW**, as shown in *Figure 8.25*:

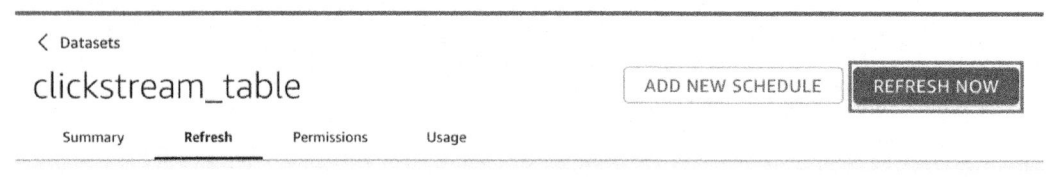

Figure 8.25 – QuicksSight dataset refresh

After completing the refresh process, do the following:

1. Click on the QuickSight icon in the upper-left corner to return to the initial menu.
2. Select **Dashboards** from the left menu.
3. Select the dashboard you just created.

If you compare it with the previous version, your dashboard should have different values in the visuals, which is the result of the data update you just performed.

With all the workflow tested, now, it is time to clean up the resources to avoid unnecessary costs.

Section 7 – Clean up

The first step is to delete your QuickSight subscription while you are still benefiting from the free tier.

> **Important note**
> Deleting your QuickSight subscription will delete all the assets you have in your QuickSight account. If you were already using QuickSight for other projects, you may want to skip this step as it applies only to new subscriptions made for this chapter.

To proceed with the QuickSight subscription termination, perform the following steps:

1. On your QuickSight account, in the upper-right corner, click on the user icon.
2. Select **Manage QuickSight**.
3. On the left, select **Account Settings**.
4. Under **Account termination**, click on **Manage**.
5. Disable account protection by clicking on the toggle button.
6. Type `confirm` in the text box.
7. Click on **Delete account**.

Now, you just need to empty the S3 bucket and delete the CloudFormation template. Let us start with emptying the bucket:

1. Go to the S3 console in your AWS account.
2. Select your frontend S3 bucket (the name of the bucket should start with `chapter-8-clickstream-` followed by a random string).
3. Click on **Empty**. This will delete all the content inside your bucket.

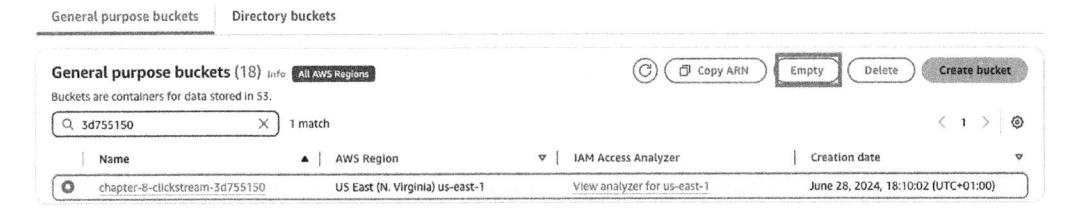

Figure 8.26 – The process of emptying an S3 bucket

With the bucket now empty, you can proceed with the CloudFormation stack deletion:

1. Go to the CloudFormation console in your AWS account.
2. Select the stack you created.
3. Click on **Delete**.

By now, all the resources created in this chapter have been deleted, and it is always important to ensure the clean-up of unused resources to avoid incurring unnecessary costs. In the next section, you will explore the possibilities of improving your application.

Future work

Congratulations, you have successfully built a business intelligence application, including ingesting the data, processing, and exploring both through SQL queries as well as a visual approach. Being the last project for this book, is important to reinforce a message that should always be kept in mind for future projects: technology is constantly evolving, and new features, services, and best practices emerge regularly, so it is important to maintain a mindset of continuous improvement and this project is not an exception. This project can be a starting point for a business intelligence application, but there are specific actions that can make it more robust and production-ready.

Automate the ETL pipeline

One of the key areas for future enhancement lies around automating the ETL pipeline, which currently runs on-demand. A robust business intelligence application should incorporate automation at the orchestration level to ensure timely and reliable data processing. In AWS, AWS Step Functions or even Glue workflows can help you schedule and automate your ETL processes.

Furthermore, implementing a notification system can provide valuable insights into the health and status of your ETL pipeline. Glue already integrates natively with Amazon CloudWatch to deliver new real-time events about the status of the pipelines, which, combined with a notification service, such as Amazon **Simple Notification Service** (**SNS**), can help you intervene whenever something goes wrong in a timely manner.

Data life cycle management

Effective data management and cost optimization are crucial considerations for any business intelligence application, particularly when dealing with large volumes of data, as is the case with clickstream data. S3 offers different storage tiers that can cover all the data access patterns.

For example, you can store frequently accessed clickstream data in the S3 Standard storage class for low-latency access, while archiving older or less frequently accessed data to the S3 Glacier or S3 Glacier Deep Archive storage classes, which offers significant cost savings. This approach not only optimizes storage costs but also ensures that your data is stored in the most appropriate tier based on its life cycle stage, improving overall data management efficiency. Furthermore, by automating the life cycle management process, you can minimize manual intervention and ensure consistent enforcement of your data retention policies, enhancing compliance and reducing the risk of data breaches or accidental deletions.

Summary

In this chapter, you explored the process of building an end-to-end business intelligence application leveraging various AWS services. By combining the power of Amazon Athena for ad hoc querying, Amazon S3 for data storage, and Amazon QuickSight for data visualization and dashboarding, you created a solution that empowers both technical and non-technical users to derive valuable insights from data.

As you continue with future projects, you are now equipped with the knowledge to build an architecture to support the transformation between data and information and empower data-driven decision-making at all levels.

In the next chapter, you will have the opportunity to revisit the architectures of the previous chapters and explore alternative approaches and AWS services while understanding the trade-offs that are behind any architecture choice you make.

9
Exploring Future Work

Congratulations! You have built seven unique applications using multiple AWS services. But learning is a journey that never ends.

In this theory-based chapter, you are going to learn even more about AWS services. Architecture is about trade-offs; knowing what you can use and when will be advantageous in the future. To illustrate this, we will revisit architectures from the previous chapters and redesign them.

Price is a consideration you saw highlighted in the requirements gathering and service selection sections throughout the book. In this chapter, you will learn how to use AWS Pricing Calculator to estimate costs before building out your architectures.

Lastly, you are going to explore multiple different resources AWS has to offer to help you architect and build better applications.

Technical requirements

This is a theory-based chapter, and because of that, there are no technical requirements. If you decide to redesign any of the previous chapters' architectures, based on the learnings of this chapter, you will need your own AWS account.

AWS services overview

AWS currently offers over 200 services, across various categories, including compute, storage, databases, networking, analytics, machine learning, the **Internet of Things (IoT)**, mobile, developer tools, management tools, security, and enterprise applications. The exact number of AWS services will change as new services are introduced. Over the previous eight chapters, you have learned about some of these services and built several applications using them.

The beauty of solutions architecture is that there is no single answer or architecture. It is all about trade-offs. The applications you learned how to build in previous chapters can be built using different approaches and services. In this section, we will study alternative architectures for past chapters' applications using AWS services that you haven't seen yet.

Containers

Containers are lightweight, virtualized computing environments that allow you to package and run applications along with their dependencies in an isolated and portable way. Containers are designed to be lightweight and efficient, as they share the host operating system kernel, unlike traditional **virtual machines (VMs)**, which require a separate guest operating system for each instance. Containers are a computing option, just like VMs.

> **Important note**
> You already used containers in *Chapter 6*; CodePipeline uses a container to run the instructions in each stage.

Because containers are lightweight, the best practice is to isolate different functions in different containers, as shown in *Figure 9.1*, where a single VM became four containers. A single service can be split across more than one container. Notice how **Likes Service** is in two containers, while in the **Virtual Machine** environment, there is just a single one. Containers give you more flexibility.

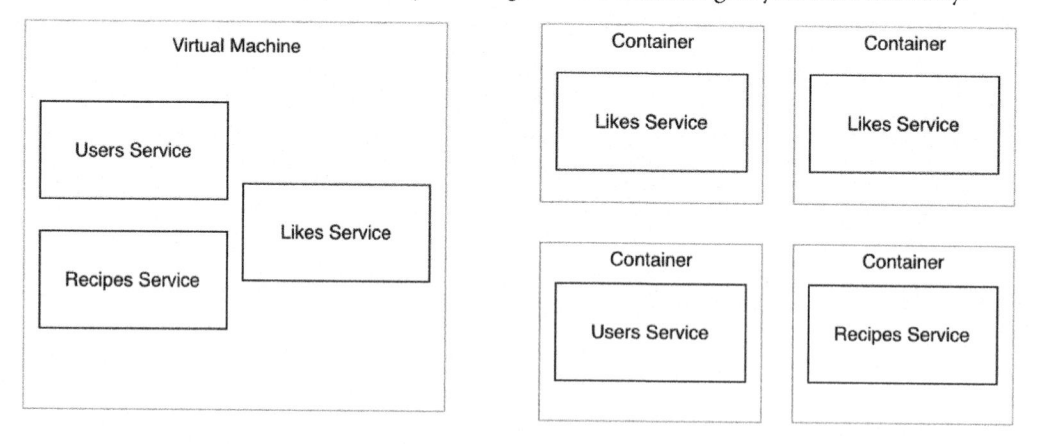

Figure 9.1 – VM versus container decomposition

As applications built with containers become more complex, it requires coordination across multiple containers and hosts; orchestration becomes crucial for efficient management and scaling. Container orchestration platforms provide a centralized control plane and APIs to simplify the deployment, scaling, and management of containerized applications.

In AWS, the most common container orchestration platforms are the following:

- **Amazon Elastic Container Service (ECS)**: A fully managed container orchestration service that helps you deploy, manage, and scale containerized applications across a cluster of EC2 instances or Fargate instances. It supports Docker containers and allows you to run and manage containers at scale.

- **Amazon Elastic Kubernetes Service (EKS)**: A managed Kubernetes service that simplifies the deployment, management, and scaling of containerized applications using Kubernetes on AWS. Kubernetes is an open source container orchestration platform that automates the deployment, scaling, and management of containerized applications.

You can replace any past chapters' computing options with containers. The serverless architecture introduced in *Chapter 4* using containers orchestrated by ECS in an EC2 environment would look as in *Figure 9.2*. You replace the lambda functions such as `put_like` or `get_recipes` for containers that host the same functionality. Your API gateway using a private integration connects to an internal **Application Load Balancer (ALB)** that exposes ECS tasks. You need a private integration because the load balancer and the ECS containers live in a VPC, while the API gateway does not. You can read more about private integrations in the AWS documentation: `https://docs.aws.amazon.com/apigateway/latest/developerguide/getting-started-with-private-integration.html`.

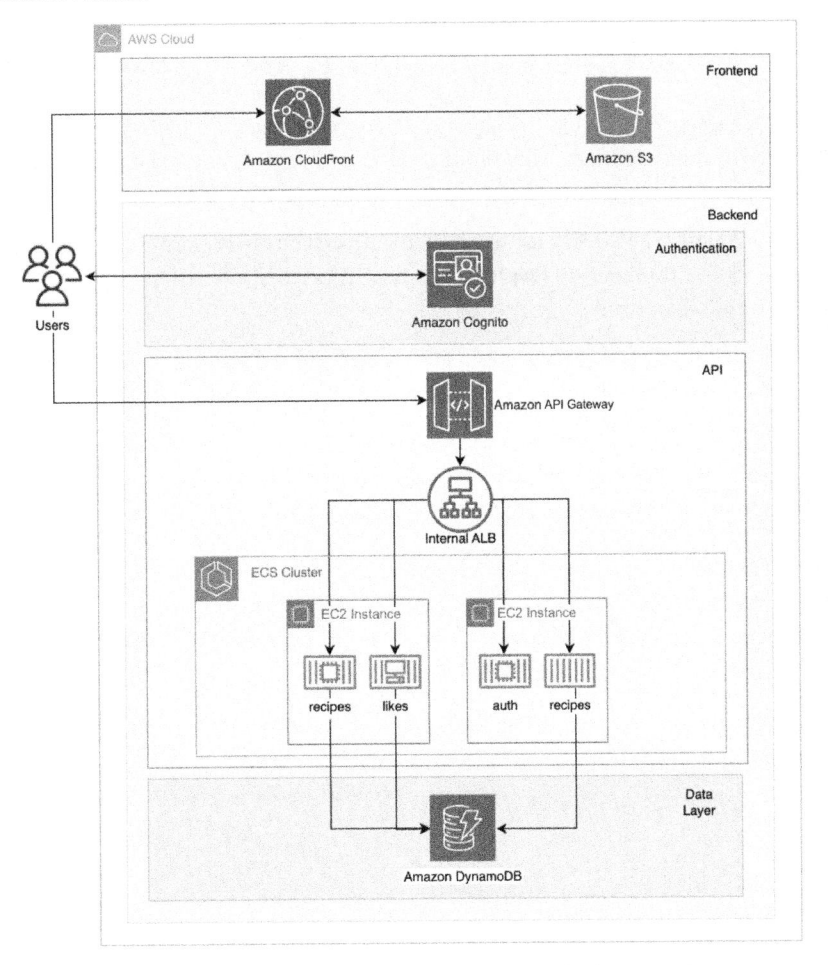

Figure 9.2 – Chapter 4's architecture re-designed using containers

As you can tell by *Figure 9.2*, containers can still run in VMs, in this case, EC2. You can also run containers in a serverless manner using Fargate. Fargate is a serverless compute engine for containers that allows you to run containers without having to manage the underlying EC2 instances. It works seamlessly with both ECS and EKS, eliminating the need to provision and manage servers or clusters.

Other API types

In this book, you only built REST APIs. However, there are other types of APIs that are not RESTful. A very popular example is GraphQL.

GraphQL is a query language and server-side runtime for APIs, originally developed by Facebook in 2012. It provides an efficient, powerful, and flexible approach to building and consuming APIs and has become increasingly popular for use with cloud applications. The reason it has become so popular is that it solves the problems of overfetching, retrieving more data than needed, and underfetching, requiring multiple requests to fetch related data, which are common problems in traditional REST APIs.

There are some important characteristics to have in mind:

- Instead of having multiple endpoints for different resources, GraphQL typically exposes a single endpoint for querying data. This simplifies the API surface and makes it easier to evolve the API over time.

- It uses a strongly typed query language that allows clients to request exactly the data they need from the server. This contrasts with traditional REST APIs where the server often returns more data than the client needs.

- With GraphQL, the client has more control over the data it receives, allowing for better performance and flexibility. It has a client-driven architecture.

- GraphQL APIs are built around a schema that defines the types, queries, mutations, and relationships between different data entities. This schema acts as a contract between the client and server, ensuring data consistency and enabling powerful tooling.

In AWS, AppSync is a managed service that makes it easy to build scalable GraphQL APIs. AppSync simplifies the process of building GraphQL APIs by handling the underlying infrastructure, scaling, and security aspects, allowing developers to focus on building their application logic; this is the same as what an API gateway does for REST APIs.

Chapter 5's architecture re-designed using AWS AppSync is similar, as shown in *Figure 9.3*. You replace the API gateway with AppSync and use Lambda resolvers.

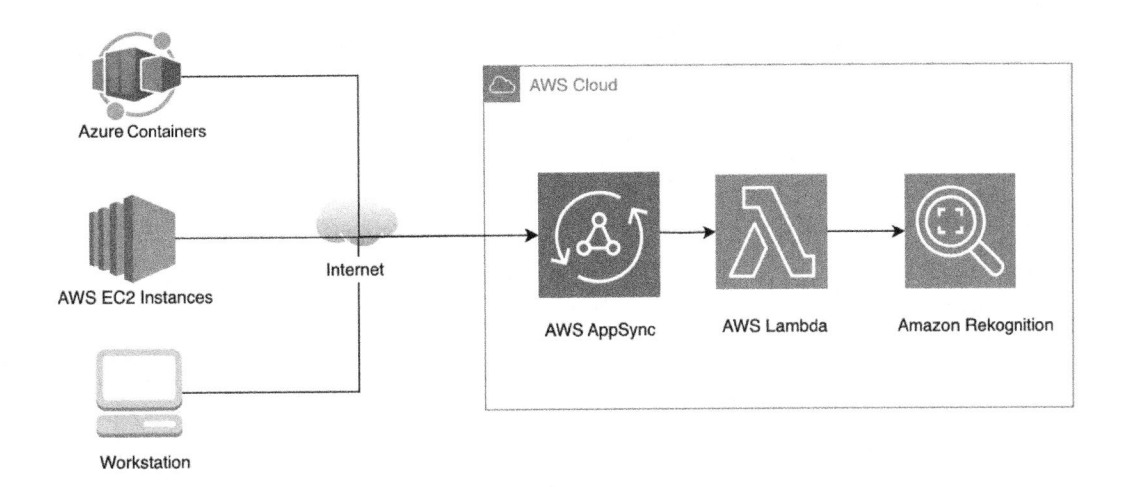

Figure 9.3 – Chapter 5's architecture re-designed using AWS AppSync

The way your clients interact with this application is different. You can still use curl or Postman but you need to send the query in the payload. This is well documented in the AWS documentation: https://docs.aws.amazon.com/appsync/latest/devguide/retrieve-data-with-graphql-query.html.

Generative AI

You have seen different AI-powered applications throughout this book: image analysis in *Chapter 5*, content translation in *Chapter 6*, and Q&A in *Chapter 7*. But there is another type of AI that is taking the world by storm: generative AI.

Generative AI refers to a class of AI models and techniques capable of generating new data, such as text, images, audio, or other multimedia, based on the training data they have been exposed to. Unlike traditional AI models that primarily focus on analyzing or classifying existing data, generative AI models learn the underlying patterns and characteristics of the training data and use this knowledge to create new, original content.

Foundation models (**FMs**) are a powerful type of generative AI model that can be used for a wide range of tasks. Different companies have built their own models, such as OpenAI GPT, Anthropic Claude, and Meta Llama.

You do not need to know how to build these models from scratch, but you should know how to get the most out of them.

Exploring Future Work

In AWS, you can make use of FMs in a serverless manner using Amazon Bedrock. Amazon Bedrock is a fully managed service that offers a choice of high-performing FMs from leading AI companies such as AI21 Labs, Anthropic, Cohere, Meta, Mistral AI, Stability AI, and Amazon via a single API, along with a broad set of capabilities you need to build generative AI applications.

All you must do is invoke a single API, as you would with any other type of AWS service. *Chapter 5's* architecture could be altered to use Bedrock with Claude 3 Sonnet, instead of Rekognition, as shown in *Figure 9.4*.

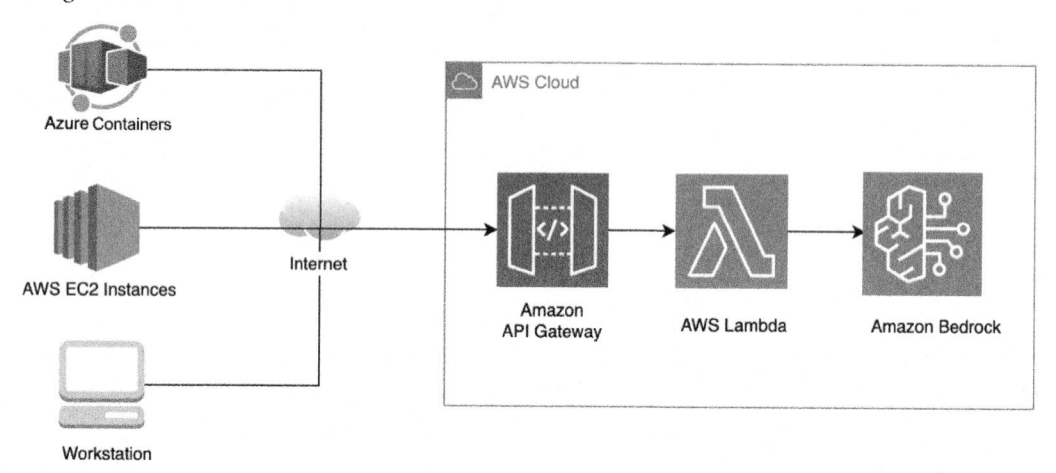

Figure 9.4 – Chapter 5's architecture re-designed using Amazon Bedrock

With this approach, you send the image and ask the model your question in natural language. For example, you might ask, "Is this person smiling?" or "Does this photo look professional?". You send that information along with the image and prompt the model to evaluate. The following is an example interaction between the author of this book and Claude 3 Sonnet. The first line, prefixed with [author], shows the prompt, which consists of a question with an attached image. In this case, the image used is the same one referenced in Chapter 5's code: goodphoto.jpeg

```
[author] is this a professional looking image - attached
goodphoto.jpeg

[agent-Claude] Yes, this image also appears to be a professional-
looking headshot or portrait photograph. It depicts a man with a
friendly, smiling expression and neatly groomed facial hair. The
background is slightly blurred but seems to be an outdoor setting
with a gray or cloudy sky behind him. The lighting is relatively soft
and flattering on his face. While a bit more casual with the hooded
jacket attire, the framing, expression, and overall quality suggest
this was taken with care, likely by a professional photographer or
for professional purposes like corporate headshots or a personal
branding photo. The image has a polished, high-quality look fitting
for professional use.
```

Generative AI is being increasingly adopted for multiple use cases, such as Q&A chatbots, summarizing text, and generating marketing content. Keep it in mind when building your next application.

Other communication patterns

The most prevalent communication pattern is synchronous request/response. For example, when you visit a web page (request), your browser fetches and renders the result (response). This process occurs synchronously, meaning you wait for the response after making the request. But in modern distributed architectures, you will sometimes encounter the need for different communication patterns, for example, in long processing tasks, where blocking the client while waiting for a response interferes with the customer experience, or when you need to deliver the exact same content to many different receivers.

Some popular patterns are asynchronous processing, fan-out and broadcasting, and event-driven. Let's start by looking at asynchronous processing.

Asynchronous processing

Imagine you need to build an application, like the one in *Chapter 5*, that receives a photo and processes. However, the processing is not as lightweight as it was in *Chapter 5*. Instead. It takes four hours to complete and is done by EC2 machines. Many things can happen in four hours: processing can fail, the client can timeout, and so on. In this case, a decoupled architecture adds multiple advantages:

- Clients can send requests without waiting for subscribers to process them.
- Subscribers can consume messages at their own pace.
- In the case of a failure on the subscriber side, another subscriber can work on the same request. It will not simply be lost.

One way to accomplish asynchronous processing is using queues. AWS has Amazon **Simple Queue Service** (**SQS**), a fully managed distributed message queuing service.

The architecture from *Chapter 5* can be updated to support asynchronous processing, as shown in *Figure 9.5*. Messages are stored in SQS and the EC2 fleet is subscribed to SQS for message processing. Each message is only processed once.

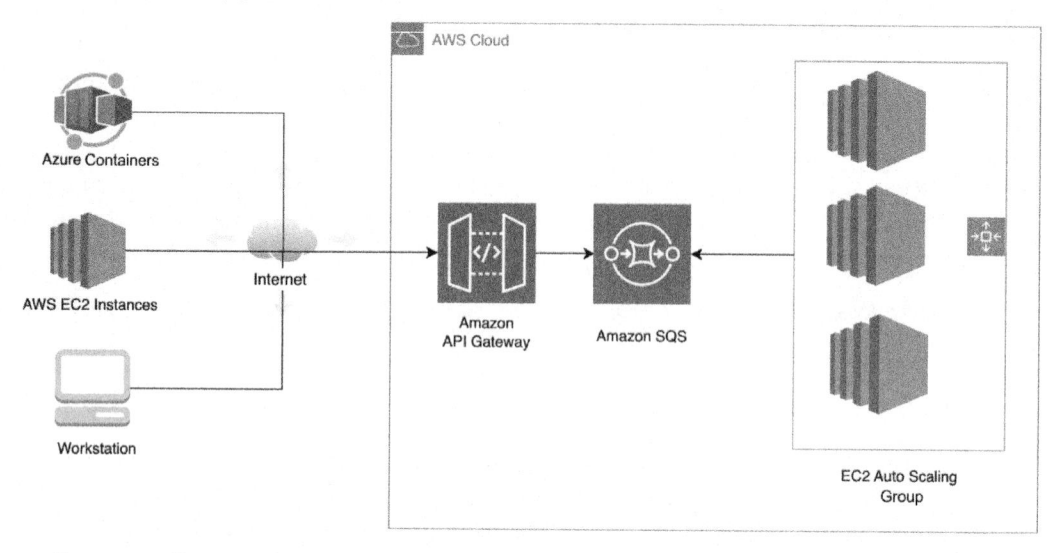

Figure 9.5 – Chapter 5's architecture re-designed using asynchronous processing with SQS and EC2

Note that this architecture does not consider how the client would receive a notification of the task's completion.

Fan-out and broadcasting

Fan-out is used when you need to deliver a single message to multiple endpoints of your choice. Broadcasting applies the same concept but sends the message to all endpoints rather than just the selected ones. Imagine you have a phonebook: fan-out is like messaging every single person individually, while broadcasting is like creating a group chat and sending the message to everyone in the group. This approach is common in notification systems, data replication or synchronization tasks, and event-driven architectures.

In AWS, there is Amazon **Simple Notification Service** (**SNS**). It is a fully managed pub/sub messaging service. Unlike SQS, it allows for a single message to be delivered to multiple consumers. It functions on a push-based mechanism, instead of pull-based like SQS.

Considering the previous asynchronous processing scenario, this time you needed to process the same submitted image twice, and you have two different computing clusters for this. With SQS, messages are only processed once. *Figure 9.6* shows how to accomplish this using SNS and SQS in a fan-out configuration. When SNS is triggered, it replicates the received message and delivers it to both SQS queues. Each of the two compute clusters then polls its respective SQS queue and processes the message.

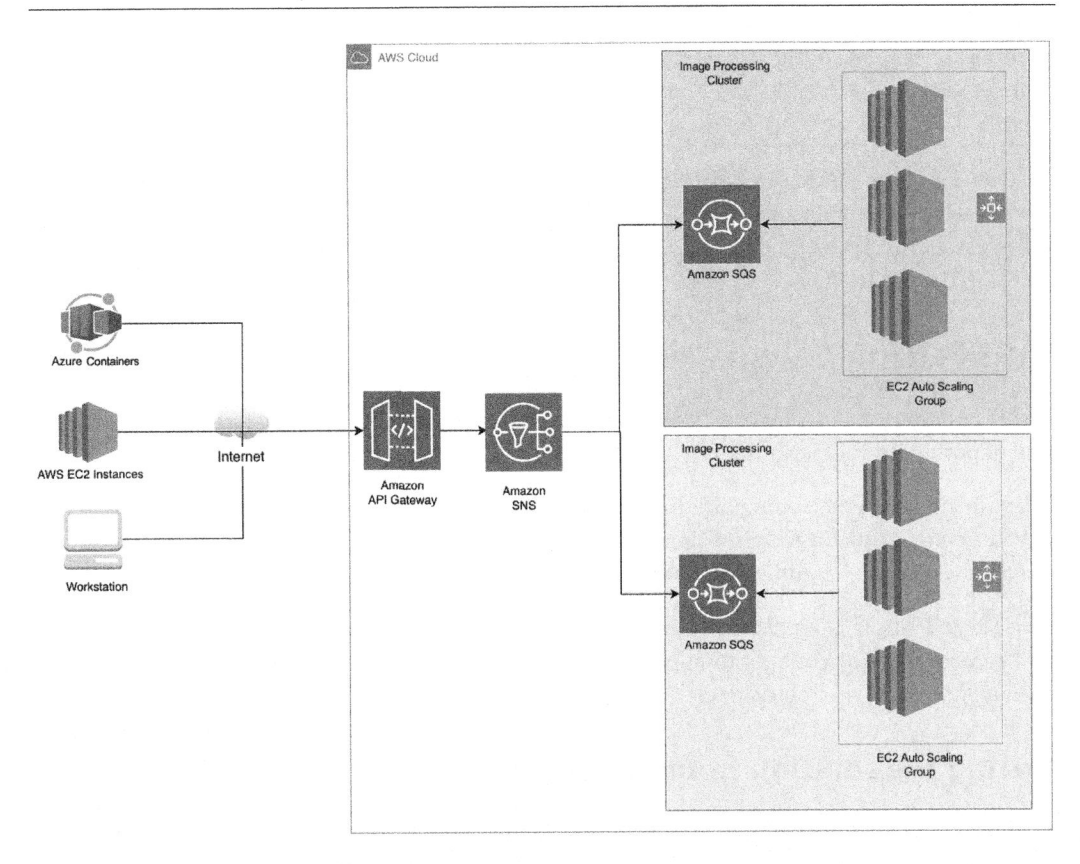

Figure 9.6 – Architecture using the fan-out pattern to distribute the same message to two different compute clusters

Lastly, let us look at the event-driven pattern.

Event-driven

Event-driven refers to a programming paradigm or architectural pattern where the flow of a program is determined by events. In an event-driven system, the program's execution path is triggered by the occurrence of specific events, rather than following a predefined sequential flow of instructions. Events can be generated by various sources, such as user interactions (e.g., clicks or key presses), system notifications (e.g., file changes or network events), hardware interruptions (e.g., timer or sensor data), or messages from other components or systems.

All services in AWS generate events. You can take actions based on them using AWS EventBridge (formerly known as Amazon CloudWatch Events). It is a serverless event bus service.

A common example of the use of event-driven architecture is as follows: a client uploads a file to your S3 bucket, which emits an event. Based on this event, you trigger a processing pipeline for the uploaded file.

All these topics are vast but well documented. Familiarize yourself with them. If you would like to learn more about it, we recommend the AWS whitepaper *Implementing Microservices on AWS*: `https://docs.aws.amazon.com/whitepapers/latest/microservices-on-aws/communication-mechanisms.html`.

AWS Pricing Calculator

Before building your architecture, it is important to know whether it fits your cost requirements. It is also important to compare different service options.

There are many ways to accomplish this, for example, using the AWS services' pricing pages. However, AWS Pricing Calculator is the recommended manner. It allows you to create an estimate for the cost of your use on AWS by adding each service individually to a calculator.

Navigate to `https://calculator.aws/` and create an estimate. Add each service individually and configure it. The configuration parameters differ per service. The result will be an estimate of both monthly and yearly costs.

Pricing the solution from Chapter 2

Revisit *Chapter 2* and recall the architecture depicted in *Figure 2.1*. It used two services: CloudFront and S3. CloudWatch basic monitoring metrics are free. Recreate this architecture in AWS Pricing Calculator.

Add S3 to your estimate. Specify the region you plan to use; pricing can differ per region. To estimate S3 costs, you will need to know how much storage in GB/month you will use, the amount and type of requests, and **data transfer out** (**DTO**) in GB/month.

To store the three website files from Chapter 2 – `index.html`, `index.css`, and `avatar.png`, you need 100 KB. 100 KB is 0.0001 GB. If you have altered the files, check the size of your files.

CloudFront will mostly make GET requests to your S3. Since *Chapter 2*'s project is a website for displaying your CV, you do not expect more than 500 monthly views. Thus, you anticipate 500 GET requests to S3.

Regarding DTO, select CloudFront as the destination. This makes DTO free.

Next, add the second service, CloudFront. In the region where your users will access your site, enter your expected number of requests per month and the amount of DTO. For the number of requests, use the same logic as for S3 requests. Since this is a simple website to display your CV, you estimate 500 monthly requests. For the DTO, calculate 500 times the size of your files. With the website files totaling approximately 100 KB, this amounts to roughly 0.05 GB.

Although both services have a free tier, it is not automatically accounted for by the calculator. For most AWS services, you need to determine what the free tier offers and subtract it from your values before entering them into the calculator. For example, the S3 free tier includes 20,000 GET requests. If you forecasted 40,000 GET requests for your project, you should only enter 20,000 GET requests into the calculator.

For *Chapter 2*, the final calculator output is $0, regardless of whether you subtract the free tier, as shown in *Figure 9.7*. This is because the project's scale is very low.

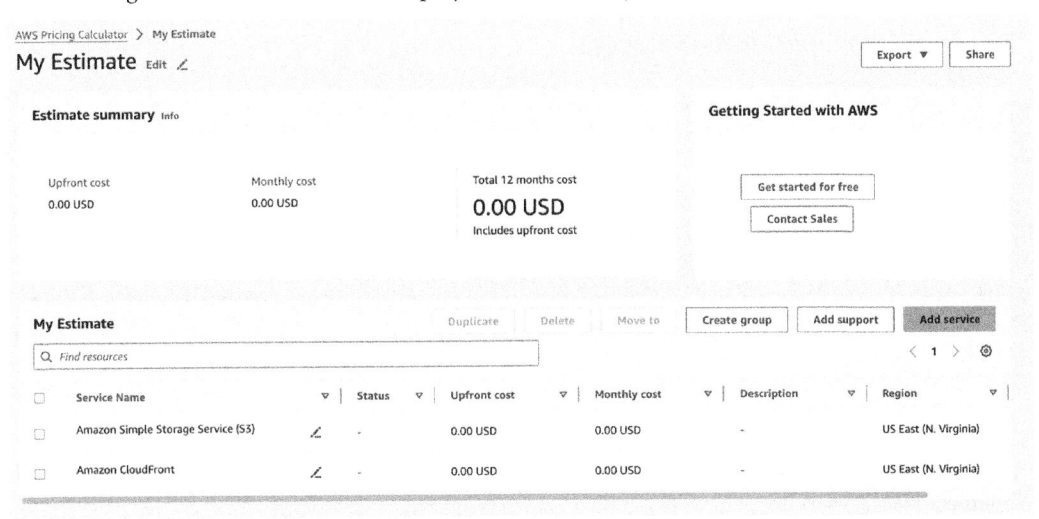

Figure 9.7 – AWS Pricing Calculator for Chapter 2's project

One of the non-functional requirements for this chapter was low-cost. You certainly accomplished that. Play with the calculator to understand how costs rise for a static website with thousands or millions of users.

Pricing the solution from Chapter 6

Revisit *Chapter 6*. Use AWS Pricing Calculator to calculate the pricing for this solution. Start with the static website hosting part of the architecture, which includes the S3 buckets and the CloudFront distribution.

Add S3. The website files from *Chapter 6*, `index.html` and `index.css`, are each less than 10 KB in size. Since these files are stored in two different S3 buckets, the total storage required is 20 KB, or 0.00002 GB. This is an event website, and you expect around 100,000 views per month. In terms of S3, this translates to 100,000 requests.

For CloudFront, it's the same 100,000 requests and it totals 2 GB DTO. However, CloudFront also uses Lambda@Edge. Add Lambda. This service allows to include or exclude the free tier. Add the same 100,000 requests using the minimum memory possible, 128 MB, and assume a 10 ms execution time.

Now, you have completed the static website architecture. Your calculator should output roughly 0.40 USD a month. However, if you drill down to each service cost, you will find that most of the cost comes from CloudFront. The calculator does not include this service's free tier, as it does with Lambda. The CloudFront free tier includes the following:

- 1 TB of DTO to the internet per month
- 10,000,000 HTTP or HTTPS requests per month

Therefore, this architecture at the scale of our solution is almost free. You will be charged less than 0.10 USD a month.

Start another calculator or add in the same calculator the CI/CD components from *Chapter 6*: CodeBuild, CodePipeline, and Amazon Translate.

Add CodeCommit. It will ask for the number of active users. In your case, there is just one active user: you.

Add CodeBuild. In *Chapter 6*, we described the use of 2 GB on-demand Lambdas for compute. Assume you make at least one change a week; that runs for 10 seconds.

Add CodePipeline. You have a single pipeline for this project.

Lastly, add Amazon Translate. Select **Real-Time Document Translation**. The website `index.html` has over 2,400 characters. If you translate it four times a month to a single language, that is almost 10,000 characters translated per month.

Figure 9.8 shows the calculator for the project. S3 and CloudFront costs will be waived by the services' free tiers. Amazon Translate does not have a free tier for real-time document translation, and the AWS Lambda calculator already includes the free tier. The result is 0.22 USD per month, or 2.64 USD per year.

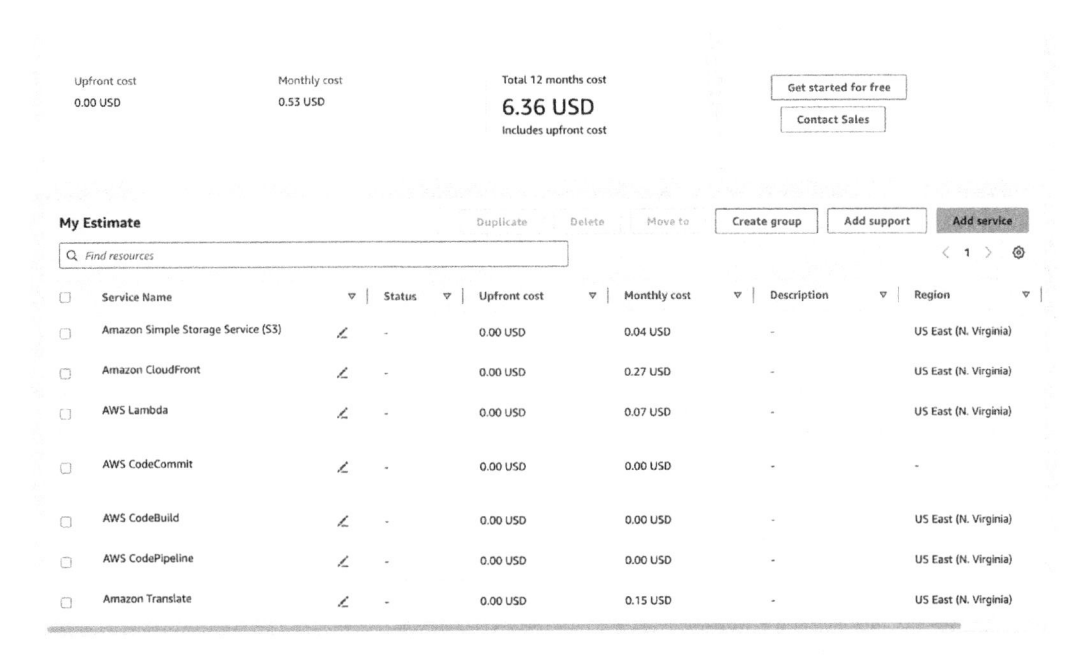

Upfront cost	Monthly cost	Total 12 months cost		Get started for free	
0.00 USD	0.53 USD	**6.36 USD** Includes upfront cost		Contact Sales	

My Estimate

Service Name	Status	Upfront cost	Monthly cost	Description	Region
Amazon Simple Storage Service (S3)	-	0.00 USD	0.04 USD	-	US East (N. Virginia)
Amazon CloudFront	-	0.00 USD	0.27 USD	-	US East (N. Virginia)
AWS Lambda	-	0.00 USD	0.07 USD	-	US East (N. Virginia)
AWS CodeCommit	-	0.00 USD	0.00 USD	-	-
AWS CodeBuild	-	0.00 USD	0.00 USD	-	US East (N. Virginia)
AWS CodePipeline	-	0.00 USD	0.00 USD	-	US East (N. Virginia)
Amazon Translate	-	0.00 USD	0.15 USD	-	US East (N. Virginia)

Figure 9.8 – AWS Pricing Calculator for Chapter 6's project

Change these estimates to represent the project you built. For example, if you are translating your website to multiple languages, you will need to alter Amazon Translate's costs. If you are making changes more often than once a week, you will need to alter the number of CodeBuild executions. If you are using any components not on AWS, for example, GitHub, as in *Chapter 6*, add those costs to the final calculator.

> **Important note**
>
> You can export estimates in JSON, PDF, or CSV format. You can also share a link to your calculator. This is helpful for sharing your architecture with colleagues and customers.

When you are making pricing estimates, you will have to guess capacity and certain characteristics of the project, such as the expected number of requests. Most of the time, you do not need to estimate single- or double-digit units. Use round numbers for easier calculations; for example, instead of 87 KB, use 100 KB. Instead of 1 request per second, that is, 86,000 requests per day, use 100,000 requests per day. This is informally called back-of-the-envelope calculations, and it is widely applied when building architectures.

Practice makes perfect; practice by creating calculators for all the projects in this book.

AWS re:Post

Wouldn't it be great if you could ask other experts questions about errors when you have development or architecture doubts? You can.

AWS re:Post is a repository of official Knowledge Center articles, videos, and other resources created by AWS to help customers better understand and use AWS services. But re:Post also allows you to post your own questions.

Visit `https://repost.aws` and navigate to a topic of your choice. You will see hundreds of questions, many answered by AWS professionals or other users. This is a great resource for getting assistance, collaborating with others, and making your knowledge and work visible in the wider industry.

However, re:Post, as mentioned, is not just a technical forum. AWS re:Post includes the official AWS Knowledge Center, `https://repost.aws/knowledge-center`, which is a repository covering the most frequent questions and requests that AWS receives from customers. In short, questions that are asked often are identified by AWS and become articles. Many, if not all, errors you will face while building your applications will have a prescriptive solution here.

Some useful examples are as follows:

- *How do I create and activate a new AWS account?*: `https://repost.aws/knowledge-center/create-and-activate-aws-account`
- *How do I troubleshoot HTTP 403 errors from API Gateway?*: `https://repost.aws/knowledge-center/api-gateway-troubleshoot-403-forbidden`
- *How do I terminate active resources that I no longer need on my AWS account?*: `https://repost.aws/knowledge-center/terminate-resources-account-closure`

Lastly, people who don't work for AWS can also share prescriptive guidance with others. They can do this through community articles, `https://repost.aws/articles`. As an exercise, write an article about something you have learned while reading this book and share it as a community article on re:Post.

AWS documentation, Solutions Library and Prescriptive Guidance

More important than knowing everything is knowing where to find information about something if you need it.

Throughout this book, you have already visited multiple pages of the AWS documentation, AWS Architecture Center, and others. It is important to know of the various options you have at your disposal. In this section, you will delve into three specific ones: AWS documentation, AWS Solutions Library, and AWS Prescriptive Guidance.

AWS documentation

Every service on AWS has extensive official documentation. On top of that, there is unofficial documentation such as `medium.com`, community articles, this very book, and others.

Throughout this book, you have visited several documentation pages. Nonetheless, it is worth highlighting a couple of documentation pages:

- AWS FAQs: `https://aws.amazon.com/faqs/`
- AWS technical documentation: `https://docs.aws.amazon.com/`
- AWS blog: `https://aws.amazon.com/blogs/`
- What's New with AWS?: `https://aws.amazon.com/new/`
- AWS Skill Builder: `https://explore.skillbuilder.aws/learn`

Familiarize yourself with these resources, so you know where to find them when you need them.

AWS Solutions Library

The AWS Architecture Center was your initial search engine in every chapter after defining your project requirements. This is a one-stop destination that allows you to browse, search for, and even request reference architectures, architecture patterns, best practices, and prescriptive guidance all in one location.

But if you are searching for something pre-built, tested and vetted by others, and accompanied by an IaC template such as CloudFormation, AWS Solutions Library (`https://aws.amazon.com/solutions/`) is the place to go. The library also includes AWS Partner solutions.

Let's add a new requirement to the project from *Chapter 6*. The company requires extensive load testing before deploying the event website to make sure it can handle heavy loads.

If you are not an expert in load testing, search for and navigate to *Distributed Load Testing on AWS* in Solutions Library: `https://aws.amazon.com/solutions/implementations/distributed-load-testing-on-aws/?did=sl_card&trk=sl_card`.

This is a typical Solutions Library documentation. Within it, you will find three components:

- An architecture diagram
- An implementation guide
- A one-click deployment option

This architecture diagram, as shown in *Figure 9.9*, depicts the flow in a step-by-step manner.

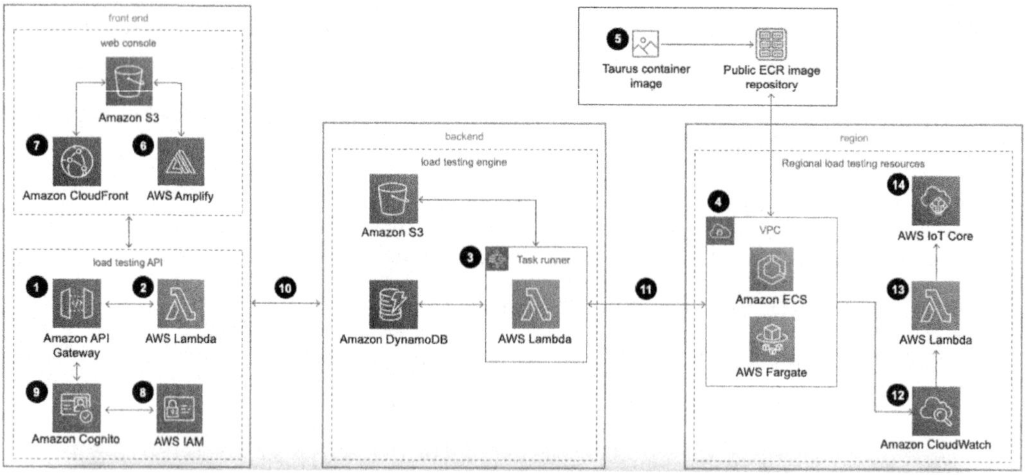

Figure 9.9 – Distributed load testing architecture

The implementation guide, `https://docs.aws.amazon.com/solutions/latest/distributed-load-testing-on-aws/solution-overview.html`, has in-depth documentation of how the solution works, including monitoring and troubleshooting information. Notice also how the implementation guide has a dedicated section for estimated costs.

Lastly, it includes a one-click deployment option, **Launch in the AWS Console**, which allows you to deploy it and immediately test your event website without having to architect another project from scratch.

AWS Prescriptive Guidance

AWS Prescriptive Guidance (APG) (`https://aws.amazon.com/prescriptive-guidance/`) can also be found on the AWS Architecture Center, but it is focused on time-tested strategies, guides, and patterns to help accelerate your cloud migration, modernization, and optimization projects.

Unlike Solutions Library, not all are practical, nor accompanied by architecture diagrams and code.

There are three types of resources:

- **Strategies**: Business perspectives, methodologies, and frameworks for cloud migration and modernization, for CxOs and senior managers.
- **Guides**: Guidance for planning and implementing strategies, with a focus on best practices and tools, for architects, managers, and technical leads.
- **Patterns**: Steps, architectures, tools, and code for implementing common migration, optimization, and modernization scenarios, for builders and other hands-on users.

When you are starting out, patterns are the most useful. They detail popular service configurations.

You have deployed several CloudFront distributions while building the projects in this book. Are they all as secure as they can be? Do you know how to verify this? You can easily automate these types of verifications with the APG pattern *Check an Amazon CloudFront distribution for access logging, HTTPS, and TLS version*: `https://docs.aws.amazon.com/prescriptive-guidance/latest/patterns/check-an-amazon-cloudfront-distribution-for-access-logging-https-and-tls-version.html?did=pg_card&trk=pg_card`. It uses Lambda to check new and modified CloudFront distributions for TLS 1.2, HTTPS, and logging configurations.

Summary

In this chapter, you learned about other AWS services that you could have used to build the different sample projects throughout the book. This has shown how architecture is about trade-offs more than it is about building the perfect solution.

You also learned about AWS Pricing Calculator and how it can help you estimate costs before building your projects. You created pricing estimates for the projects from *Chapters 2* and *6*.

Lastly, you explored many of AWS' learning resources. Some of them may have been new to you, such as AWS re:Posts, while others are part of the now-familiar AWS Architecture Center, the one-stop shop for prescriptive guidance and resources.

There are too many AWS services, architectural patterns, and techniques to cover in a single book. But if you know the fundamentals, that should raise the level of everything you do.

Congratulations on finishing this extensive journey, packed with hands-on projects and cloud knowledge. Although this is the end of the book, it is just the beginning of your AWS cloud journey.

Index

A

Amazon API Gateway 126, 168
  with Lambda 126
Amazon Athena 196
  using, for data exploration 205-208
Amazon CloudFront 28, 93, 168
  characteristics 28
  reference link 28
Amazon CloudWatch metrics
  characteristics 29
  reference link 29
Amazon Cognito 81, 93, 94, 168
Amazon Comprehend 123
Amazon DynamoDB 58, 93, 168
Amazon Elastic Compute Cloud (EC2) instances 56
Amazon Elastic Container Service (ECS) 220
Amazon Elastic Kubernetes Service (EKS) 221
Amazon Kendra 123
Amazon Lambda 94, 168
Amazon Lex 123, 168
  concepts 169
  configuration and build 177, 179

Amazon Machine Image (AMI) 15
Amazon Polly 123
Amazon QuickSight 197
Amazon Rekognition 123
  facial analysis 124, 125
  moderation 124
  object and scene detection 124
  text recognition 124
Amazon SageMaker 137
Amazon Simple Storage Service (S3) 27, 93, 168, 195, 196
  characteristics 27
  limitations 27
  reference link 27
Amazon Transcribe 123
Amazon Translate 123, 144
Amazon Web Services (AWS) 3
  architecting on 4
API Gateway 94
Application Load Balancer (ALB) 57, 221
  health checking 57
  SSL termination 57
architecting, on AWS
  architecture pattern, selecting 5, 6
  diagramming 7, 8
  requirements gathering 4

Index

service, selecting 6, 7
Well-Architected Framework
   (WAR), exploring 9
Artificial Intelligence (AI) 161
asynchronous processing 225, 226
Autograph 213
automatic speech recognition (ASR) 123
Auto Scaling groups (ASGs) 80
AWS Architecture Center
   reference link 5, 193
   URL 25
AWS Certificate Manager (ACM) 39
AWS CLI 13
   exploring 16, 17
   using 14-16
AWS CloudFormation 93
AWS CodeBuild 145, 146
AWS CodePipeline 145, 146
AWS Console
   using 9-13
AWS documentation 233
AWS Glue 196
AWS Lambda 126
AWS Prescriptive Guidance (APG) 234, 235
   types, of resources 234
AWS Pricing Calculator 228-231
AWS re:Post 232
AWS SDK 17
AWS services 26, 56, 93
   Amazon API Gateway 168
   Amazon CloudFront 56, 93, 168
   Amazon Cognito 93, 94, 168
   Amazon DynamoDB 57, 93, 168
   Amazon EC2 57
   Amazon Lambda 94, 168
   Amazon Lex 168, 169
   Amazon S3 56
   Amazon Simple Storage Service (S3) 93, 168
   Amazon VPC 56
   API Gateway 94
   Application Load Balancer (ALB) 57
   AWS CloudFormation 58, 93
   communication patterns 225
   containers 220-222
   generative AI 223-225
   other API types 222, 223
   overview 219
AWS services, communication patterns
   asynchronous processing 225, 226
   event-driven 227
   fan-out and broadcasting 227
AWS Shield 39, 40
   Advanced 40
   reference link 41
   Standard 40
AWS Solutions Library 233, 234
**AWS WAF, to protect REST
   APIs in API gateway**
   reference link 135
AWS Web Application Firewall (WAF) 39, 40
   reference link 40

B

Book Meetings 169
business intelligence application
   architecture design phase 193-195
   architecture patterns 193
   clean up 216, 217
   clickstream event generator 201-203
   data exploration, with Athena 205-208
   data life cycle management 218
   data visualization, with QuickSight 208-216
   ETL pipeline, automating 217
   functional requirements 192
   Glue ETL job 204, 205

non-functional requirements 193
project, cloning 197
scenario 192
solution deployment 198-200
business intelligence application, AWS services
Amazon Athena 196
Amazon QuickSight 197
Amazon Simple Storage
   Service (S3) 195, 196
AWS Glue 196
AWS services 195

C

Chatbots & Virtual Assistants
layers 194
reference link 166
chatbot, with machine learning
actions performed, extending by 189
Amazon Lex configuration
   and build 177, 179
architecture 166-168
architecture patterns 166
AWS services 168, 169
cleaning up 187, 188
data requirements 165
frontend configuration and
   deployment 174-176
functional requirements 163
multilingual support 189
non-functional requirements 165
project, cloning 170
scenario 162
solution deployment 170-173
testing and exploring 179-187
user profiles, maintaining for
   different sessions 190

CI/CD, for infrastructure code
adopting 157
benefits 157
Clickstream Analytics on AWS
reference link 193
clickstream data 191, 192
clickstream event generator 201-203
Cloud Development Kit (CDK) 18
CloudFormation 58
requirements 96
using 19
CloudFront distribution
deleting 37
Command Line Interface (CLI) 3
containers 220-222
orchestration platforms 220
Content Delivery Network (CDN) 26
content translation pipeline
application functionality, expanding 157
architecture 141-143
architecture patterns 141
AWS services 143
CI/CD, adopting for infrastructure code 157
CI/CD pipeline, building 150-154
cleaning up 156
custom names, implementing 157
requirements 140, 141
scenario 140
solution, testing 155, 156
web application, building 146-50
content translation pipeline, AWS services
Amazon Translate 144
AWS CodeBuild 145, 146
AWS CodePipeline 145, 146
Lambda@Edge 144
Continuous Delivery/Deployment (CD) 145

Index

Continuous Integration and Continuous Delivery (CI/CD) 18, 81, 139, 145
  process, components 145
Continuous Integration (CI) 145
cross-site scripting (XSS) 57
custom domain name, for REST APIs in API Gateway
  reference link 136

D

data life cycle management 218
data transfer out (DTO) 228
DetectFaces API
  reference link 131
Distributed Denial-of-Service (DDoS) attacks 39
dynamic websites 25
DynamoDB Accelerator (DAX) 82

E

EC2 pricing models
  reference link 57
ETL pipeline
  automating 217
event-driven pattern 227
extract, transform, and load (ETL) 196

F

fan-out and broadcasting 227
foundation models (FMs) 223
frontend configuration and deployment 99
  aws-exports.ts 100
  configs.tsx 100-104

future work, web application
  authentication 81
  caching 82-84
  infrastructure auto-scaling 80
  logging 81, 82
  managed hosting and CI/CD 81
  monitoring 81, 82
  secure protocols, using 80

G

generative AI 223-225
Glue Data Catalog 196
Glue ETL job 204, 205
Graphical User Interface (GUI) 9

H

HashiCorp Configuration Language (HCL) 20
HTTP APIs 94

I

image classification solutions, on AWS
  reference link 121
inappropriate images detection
  reference link 136
Infrastructure as Code (IaC) 3, 17, 18, 93
  benefits 18
  CloudFormation, using 19
  Terraform, using 20-22
Infrastructure as Code (IaC) service 58
Internet of Things (IoT) 219

L

Lambda@Edge
  events, types 144

M

machine learning (ML) 119

N

Natural Language Processing (NLP) 123, 161

P

personal website
  architecture patterns 25
  custom DNS, implementing 38
  editing 30-33
  final architecture 42
  functional requirements 24
  monitoring 36, 37
  non-functional requirements 24
  observability 41
  publishing 33-36
  requirements 24
  scenario 24
  security 39
photo classification architecture 121-123
photo quality analyzer
  application, testing 132-134
  architecture patterns 121
  authentication, implementing 135
  authorization, implementing 135
  code 131, 132
  custom names, implementing 135
  data requirements 121

functional requirements 120
image analysis algorithm, improving 136
infrastructure, building 127-131
ML model, hosting 136, 137
non-functional requirements 120
requirements 120
scenario 120
security posture, improving 135
technical requirements 121
private REST APIs, in API Gateway
  reference link 135
proof of concept 140

Q

QuickSight
  using, for data visualization 208-216

R

recipe sharing applications
  architecture 54-56
  architecture patterns 53
  business requirements 49
  data requirements 52, 53
  functional requirements 49-51
  non-functional requirements 51
  requirements 48
  scenario 48
  technical requirements 52
REST APIs 94
Route 53 38
rulesets 40

Index

S

S3 bucket
  deleting 38
Serverless Land
  reference link 90
serverless recipe-sharing application
  Admin page 106-108
  architecture 91, 92
  architecture patterns 90
  business requirements 87
  cleaning up 113, 114
  data requirements 90
  enriching, with media content 115
  exploring 104, 105, 109-113
  frontend configuration and deployment 99
  functional requirements 87, 88
  non-functional requirements 89
  project, cloning 95
  requirements 87
  solution, coding 94
  solution deployment 95-99
  technical requirements 89
  testing 104, 105, 109-113
  User page 109
  user profile 115, 116
Simple Notification Service (SNS) 218, 226
Simple Queue Service (SQS) 225
single-page application (SPA) 53
Software as a Service (SaaS) 127
Software Development Kits (SDKs) 3
solution coding, web application 58
  additional configurations 69
  certificate issuing 62-64
  DNS configuration and certificate issuing 60
  DNS configuration, in Route 53 61, 62
  frontend configuration and deployment 70-73
  project, cloning 59, 60
  solution deployment 65-69
static website
  architecture 25, 26

T

tags, w3school website
  reference link 31
Terraform 18
  using 20-22

V

virtual machines (VMs) 220

W

web application 47
  backend, exploring 74
  backend testing 74
  certificate, cleaning up 78, 79
  cleaning up 77
  DNS management configuration, cleaning up 78, 79
  DynamoDB table, exploring 76
  DynamoDB table, testing 76
  exploring 73
  frontend, exploring 74
  frontend testing 74
  future work 80
  HTTP communication, enabling in browser 75, 76
  testing 73
Well-Architected Framework (WAR)
  exploring 9

<packt>

packtpub.com

Subscribe to our online digital library for full access to over 7,000 books and videos, as well as industry leading tools to help you plan your personal development and advance your career. For more information, please visit our website.

Why subscribe?

- Spend less time learning and more time coding with practical eBooks and Videos from over 4,000 industry professionals
- Improve your learning with Skill Plans built especially for you
- Get a free eBook or video every month
- Fully searchable for easy access to vital information
- Copy and paste, print, and bookmark content

Did you know that Packt offers eBook versions of every book published, with PDF and ePub files available? You can upgrade to the eBook version at packtpub.com and as a print book customer, you are entitled to a discount on the eBook copy. Get in touch with us at customercare@packtpub.com for more details.

At www.packtpub.com, you can also read a collection of free technical articles, sign up for a range of free newsletters, and receive exclusive discounts and offers on Packt books and eBooks.

Other Books You May Enjoy

If you enjoyed this book, you may be interested in these other books by Packt:

Mastering Elastic Kubernetes Service on AWS

Malcolm Orr, Yang-Xin Cao (Eason)

ISBN: 978-1-80323-121-1

- Understand Amazon EKS architecture and how every component works
- Effectively manage Kubernetes cluster on AWS with Amazon EKS
- Build a Docker image and push it to AWS ECR
- Efficiently scale and provision resources leveraging Amazon EKS
- Dive deep into security and networking with Amazon EKS
- Understand Fargate serverless and apply it to the workload

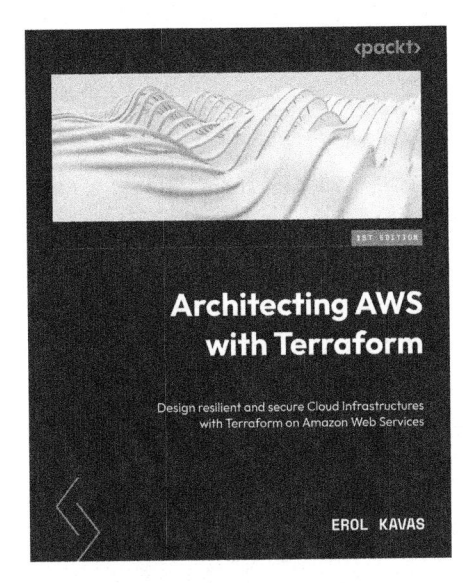

Architecting AWS with Terraform

Erol Kavas

ISBN: 978-1-80324-856-1

- Get to grips with Terraform frameworks and best practices
- Use Terraform providers and modules
- Develop your first AWS resource in Terraform
- Build an infrastructure project with Terraform
- Govern an infrastructure project in Terraform
- Deploy Terraform projects to AWS with CI/CD

Packt is searching for authors like you

If you're interested in becoming an author for Packt, please visit `authors.packtpub.com` and apply today. We have worked with thousands of developers and tech professionals, just like you, to help them share their insight with the global tech community. You can make a general application, apply for a specific hot topic that we are recruiting an author for, or submit your own idea.

Share Your Thoughts

Now you've finished *AWS Cloud Projects*, we'd love to hear your thoughts! Scan the QR code below to go straight to the Amazon review page for this book and share your feedback or leave a review on the site that you purchased it from.

`https://packt.link/r/1835889298`

Your review is important to us and the tech community and will help us make sure we're delivering excellent quality content.

Download a free PDF copy of this book

Thanks for purchasing this book!

Do you like to read on the go but are unable to carry your print books everywhere?

Is your eBook purchase not compatible with the device of your choice?

Don't worry, now with every Packt book you get a DRM-free PDF version of that book at no cost.

Read anywhere, any place, on any device. Search, copy, and paste code from your favorite technical books directly into your application.

The perks don't stop there, you can get exclusive access to discounts, newsletters, and great free content in your inbox daily

Follow these simple steps to get the benefits:

1. Scan the QR code or visit the link below

   `https://packt.link/free-ebook/9781835889282`

2. Submit your proof of purchase
3. That's it! We'll send your free PDF and other benefits to your email directly

Printed in Dunstable, United Kingdom